KILLING RAGE

Previous books by bell hooks

Outlaw Culture: Resisting Representation (1994)

Teaching to Transgress:
Education as the Practice of Freedom (1994)

Sisters of the Yam:
Black Women and Self-Recovery (1993)

A Woman's Mourning Song (poems) (1993)

Black Looks: Race and Representation (1992)

Yearning: Race, Gender, and Cultural Politics (1990)

Talking Back: Thinking Feminist, Thinking Black (1989)

Feminist Theory: From Margin to Center (1984)

Ain't I a Woman: Black Women and Feminism (1981)

bell hooks

KILLING RAGE

ENDING RACISM

A HOLT PAPERBACK

HENRY HOLT AND COMPANY | NEW YORK

Holt Paperbacks
Henry Holt and Company, LLC
Publishers since 1866
175 Fifth Avenue
New York, New York 10010
www.henryholt.com

Earlier versions of some of the chapters in this book appeared in the following
publications: "Black Beauty and the Black Power: Internalized Racism" and "Marketing
Blackness: Class and Commodification" reprinted from *Outlaw Culture: Resisting
Representation*, by bell hooks (New York: Routledge, 1994); "Representations of
Whiteness in the Black Imagination" and "Loving Blackness as Political Resistance"
from *Black Looks*, by bell hooks (Boston: South End Press, 1992); "Overcoming White
Supremacy: A Comment" from *Talking Back: Thinking Feminist, Thinking Black*,
by bell hooks (Boston: South End Press, 1989); and "Keeping a Legacy
of Shared Struggle" from *Z Magazine*, September 1992.

Library of Congress Cataloging-in-Publication Data
hooks, bell.
Killing rage: ending racism / bell hooks.—1st ed.
p. cm.
ISBN-13: 978-0-8050-5027-1
ISBN-10: 0-8050-5027-2
1. Racism—United States. 2. United States—Race relations.
3. Feminism—United States. 4. Afro-American women. I. Title.
E185.615.H645 1995 95-6395
305.8'00973—dc20 CIP

Originally published in hardcover in 1995
by Henry Holt and Company

First Holt Paperbacks Edition 1996

Designed by Victoria Hartman

Printed in the United States of America
15

CONTENTS

Introduction: Race Talk   1

Killing Rage: Militant Resistance   8

Beyond Black Rage: Ending Racism   21

Representations of Whiteness in the
Black Imagination   31

Refusing to Be a Victim: Accountability
and Responsibility   51

Challenging Sexism in Black Life   62

The Integrity of Black Womanhood   77

Feminism: It's a Black Thing   86

Revolutionary Feminism: An Anti-Racist
Agenda   98

Teaching Resistance: The Racial Politics
of Mass Media   108

Black Beauty and Black Power:
Internalized Racism   119

Healing Our Wounds: Liberatory Mental
Health Care   133

Loving Blackness as Political Resistance   146

Black on Black Pain: Class Cruelty   163

Marketing Blackness: Class and
Commodification   172

Overcoming White Supremacy: A Comment   184

Beyond Black Only: Bonding Beyond Race   196

Keeping a Legacy of Shared Struggle   204

Where Is the Love: Political Bonding
Between Black and White Women   215

Black Intellectuals: Choosing Sides   226

Black Identity: Liberating Subjectivity   240

Moving from Pain to Power: Black
Self-Determination   251

Beloved Community: A World Without Racism   263

Selected Bibliography   273

i keep the letters that i write to you
in a folder with a postcard attached.
it is a reproduction of the image of a black
man and woman in south africa in 1949
walking down a road side by side—
the caption reads "seek what is true"—
it is that seeking that brings us together
again and again, that will lead us home.

INTRODUCTION

RACE TALK

When race and racism are the topic in public discourse the voices that speak are male. There is no large body of social and political critique by women on the topics of race and racism. When women write about race we usually situate our discussion within a framework where the focus is not centrally on race. We write and speak about race and gender, race and representation, etc. Cultural refusal to listen to and legitimize the power of women speaking about the politics of race and racism in America is a direct reflection of a long tradition of sexist and racist thinking which has always represented race and racism as male turf, as hard politics, a playing field where women do not really belong. Traditionally seen as a discourse between men just as feminism has been seen as the discourse of women, it presumes that there is only one gender when it comes to blackness so black women's voices do not count—how can they if our very existence is not acknowledged. It presumes that the business of race is down and dirty stuff, and therefore like all male locker rooms, spaces no real woman would want to enter. Since white women's bodies embody the sexist racist fantasy of real womanness, they must not sully themselves by claiming a political voice within public discourse about race. When race politics are the issue, it is one of the rare moments when white men prick up their ears to hear what black men have to say. No one wants to interrupt those moments of interracial homo-social patriarchal bonding to hear women speak. Given these institutionalized exclusions, it is not surprising that so few women choose to publicly "talk race."

In the past year, I have been on many panels with black men discussing race. Time and time again, I find the men talking to one another as though nothing I or any other woman has to say on the topic could be a meaningful insightful addition to the discussion. And if I or any other black woman chooses to speak about race from a standpoint that includes feminism, we are seen as derailing the more important political discussion, not adding a necessary dimension. When this sexist silencing occurs, it usually happens with the tacit complicity of audiences who have over time learned to think always of race within blackness as a male thing and to assume that the real political leaders emerging from such public debates will always and only be male. Not listening to the voices of progressive black women means that black political discourse on race always suffers from critical gaps in theoretical vision and concrete strategy. Despite backlash and/or the appropriation of a public rhetoric that denounces sexism, most black male leaders are not committed to challenging and changing sexism in daily life. That means that there is a major gap between what they say and how they deal with women on the street, in the workplace, at home, and between the sheets. Concurrently, many black women are self-censoring and -silencing for fear that talking race desexualizes, makes one less feminine. Or that to enter these discussions places one in direct competition with black males who feel this is their turf. Facing this resistance and daring to "talk race," to be as political as we wanna be, is the contemporary challenge to all black women, especially progressive black females on the Left.

Certainly fear of male disapproval or silencing has not been a factor curtailing my entering a political discussion of race. I find myself reluctant to "talk race" because it hurts. It is painful to think long and hard about race and racism in the United States. Confronting the great resurgence of white supremacist organizations and seeing the rhetoric and beliefs of these groups surface as part of accepted discourse in every aspect of daily life in the United States startles, frightens, and is enough to throw one back into silence. No one in the dominant culture seems to consider the impact it has on African Americans and people of color in general to turn on radios and televisions, look at magazines and books which tell us information like that reported in Andrew Hacker's book *Two Nations*. Many white folks believe that "Africans— and Americans who trace their origins to that continent— are seen as languishing at a lower evolutionary level than members of other races." By the time we reach this passage in Hacker's book, we have already heard it—at some cocktail party, in the grocery store, on the subway, or in a fancy museum where folks are dismissing and de-intellectualizing the art by black artists hanging on the wall. These days white racism can let it all hang out, hold nothing back. The anti- black backlash is so fierce it astounds. It comes to us via what Nobel Prize–winning writer Toni Morrison calls "race talk, the explicit insertion into everyday life of racial signs and symbols that have no meaning other than pressing African Americans to the lowest level of the racial hierarchy." For this to happen, Morrison adds, "popular culture, shaped by film, theater, advertising, the press, television and literature, is heavily engaged in race talk." In many ways race talk surfaces as the vernacular discourse of white supremacy. It repeatedly tells us that blacks are inferior to whites, more likely to commit crimes, come from broken homes, are all on welfare, and if we are not we are still whining and beggin ole massa and kindly miss ann for a handout. Even when we win literary prizes it lets the world know that up in the big house folks are not really sure that judging was fair, or the writin that good. And if we put on airs and act like we fancy intellectuals there is always some pure soul ready to let the world know we ain't as we seem. Meanwhile back at the plantation, in an entire book that painstakingly documents the harsh reality of white supremacy and anti-black sentiment, Hacker can undermine his own research with statements like: "Something called racism obviously exists." Even though he continues and states: "But racism is real, an incubus that has haunted this country since Europeans first set foot on the continent. It goes beyond prejudice and discrimination and even transcends bigotry, largely because it arises from outlooks and assumptions of which we are largely unaware." The "we" of unaware does not include black people. We do not have the luxury to be unaware and when we act unaware it is just that, an act—psychologists have a name for it—"denial." Yet come to think of it can it not be that white folks are into "denial" bigtime themselves—that denial keeps us all as unaware as we wanna be. Denial is in fact a cornerstone of white European culture, and it has been called out by the major critical voices who speak to, for, and from the location of whiteness (Marx, Freud, Foucault). After all if we all pretend racism does not exist, that we do not know what it is or how to change it—it never has to go away.

Overt racist discrimination is not as fashionable as it once was and that is why everyone can pretend racism does not exist, so we need to talk about the vernacular discourse of neo-colonial white supremacy—similar to racism but not the same thing. Everyone in this society, women and men, boys and girls, who want to see an end to racism, an end to white supremacy, must begin to engage in a counter hegemonic "race talk" that is fiercely and passionately calling for change.

For some of us talking race means moving past the pain to speak, not getting caught, trapped, silenced by the sadness and sorrow. I was not born into a world where anyone wanted me to talk about race. I was born into a world where folks talked about crackers, coons, and spooks with hushed voices and contorted facial expressions. I came into that world with no clue of the pain hidden behind the laughter, the performance art that took racism and made it into a little show, "how they see us versus how we see ourselves." These shows made us laugh as children. Even though we lived in the midst of life-threatening racial apartheid we had not yet seen racism clearly. It had not stared us down. It had no face. We were ourselves before it came. They wanted us to be that way—to not see racism—old black folks. They wanted us to have a childhood—full of fun and innocence and sweet things—a childhood without racial pain. In those days we did not realize that the pain would never be acknowledged, not even by the folks who loved us, that acknowledging it would alienate and estrange us from the world we knew most intimately.

Nowadays, it has become fashionable for white and black folks alike to act like they do not have the slightest clue as to why black folks might want to separate, to be together in some corner, or neighborhood, or even at some dining table in a world where we are surrounded by whiteness. It is not a mystery. Those of us who remember living in the midst of racial apartheid know that the separate spaces, the times apart from whiteness, were for sanctuary, for reimagining and re-membering ourselves. In the past separate space meant down time, time for recovery and renewal. It was the time to dream resistance, time to theorize, plan, create strategies and go forward. The time to go forward is still upon us and we have long surrendered segregated spaces of radical opposition. Our separation now is usually mere escape—a sanctuary for hiding and forgetting. The time to remember is now. The time to speak a counter hegemonic race talk that is filled with the passion of remembrance and resistance is now. All our words are needed. To move past the pain, to feel the power of change, transformation, revolution, we have to speak now—acknowledge our pain now, claim each other and our voices now.

Reading much of the popular contemporary literature on race and racism written by men in this society, I discovered repeated insistence that racism will never end. The bleak future prophesied in these works stands in sharp contrast to the more hopeful vision offered in progressive feminist writing on the issue of race and racism. This writing is fundamentally optimistic even as it is courageously and fiercely critical precisely because it emerges from concrete struggles on the part of diverse groups of women to work together for a common cause, forging a politics of solidarity. The positive revolutionary vision in this work is the outcome of a willingness to examine race and racism from a standpoint that considers the interrelatedness of race, class, and gender. Yet it is not this insightful writing that receives the attention of the mainstream mass media. As we search as a nation for constructive ways to challenge racism and white supremacy, it is absolutely essential that progressive female voices gain a hearing.

The essays in this collection are my speaking. They talk race in myriad ways—look at it in terms of white supremacy, black and white relations, the interdependency and coalition politics between people of color. They observe it from a feminist standpoint, talk class and interrelated systems of domination. They critique, challenge, and call for change— sharing the vision of a beloved community where we can affirm race difference without pain, where racism is no more. Covering a span of twenty years, these essays reflect the vision of revolutionary hope that has always been present in the work of politicized feminist writers who think deeply about race relations in our society. A few of the essays are taken from earlier books and included because readers felt that they provoked thought on the issues and were a mean- ingful catalyst for change. Combined with recent writing on the issue of race, they bear witness to the passion for racial justice that remains a powerful legacy handed down to this generation from freedom fighters of all races who dared to create an anti-racist discourse, who dared to create and sus- tain an anti-racist social movement. In counter hegemonic race talk I testify in this writing—bear witness to the reality that our many cultures can be remade, that this nation can be transformed, that we can resist racism and in the act of resistance recover ourselves and be renewed.

KILLING RAGE

MILITANT RESISTANCE

I am writing this essay sitting beside an anonymous white male that I long to murder. We have just been involved in an incident on an airplane where K, my friend and traveling companion, has been called to the front of the plane and publicly attacked by white female stewardesses who accuse her of trying to occupy a seat in first class that is not assigned to her. Although she had been assigned the seat, she was not given the appropriate boarding pass. When she tries to explain they ignore her. They keep explaining to her in loud voices as though she is a child, as though she is a foreigner who does not speak airline English, that she must take another seat. They do not want to know that the airline has made a mistake. They want only to ensure that the white male who has the appropriate boarding card will have a seat in first class. Realizing our powerlessness to alter the moment we take our seats. K moves to coach. And I take my seat next to the anonymous white man who quickly apologizes to K as she moves her bag from the seat he has comfortably settled in. I stare him down with rage, tell him that I do not want to hear his liberal apologies, his repeated insistence that "it was not his fault." I am shouting at him that it is not a question of blame, that the mistake was understandable, but that the way K was treated was completely unacceptable, that it reflected both racism and sexism.

He let me know in no uncertain terms that he felt his apology was enough, that I should leave him be to sit back and enjoy his flight. In no uncertain terms I let him know that he had an opportunity to not be complicit with the racism and sexism that is so all-pervasive in this society (that he knew no white man would have been called on the loud-·speaker to come to the front of the plane while another white male took his seat—a fact that he never disputed). Yelling at him I said, "It was not a question of your giving up the seat, it was an occasion for you to intervene in the harassment of a black woman and you chose your own comfort and tried to deflect away from your complicity in that choice by offering an insincere, face-saving apology."

From the moment K and I had hailed a cab on the New York City street that afternoon we were confronting racism. The cabbie wanted us to leave his taxi and take another; he did not want to drive to the airport. When I said that I would willingly leave but also report him, he agreed to take us. K suggested we just get another cab. We faced similar hostility when we stood in the first-class line at the airport. Ready with our coupon upgrades, we were greeted by two young white airline employees who continued their personal conversation and acted as though it were a great interruption to serve us. When I tried to explain that we had upgrade coupons, I was told by the white male that "he was not talking to me." It was not clear why they were so hostile. When I suggested to K that I never see white males receiving such treatment in the first-class line, the white female insisted that "race" had nothing to do with it, that she was just trying to serve us as quickly as possible. I noted that as a line of white men stood behind us they were indeed eager to complete our transaction even if it meant showing no courtesy. Even when I requested to speak with a supervisor, shutting down that inner voice which urged me not to make a fuss, not to complain and possibly make life more difficult for the other black folks who would have to seek service from these two, the white attendants discussed together whether they would honor that request. Finally, the white male called a supervisor. He listened, apologized, stood quietly by as the white female gave us the appropriate service. When she handed me the tickets, I took a cursory look at them to see if all was in order. Everything seemed fine. Yet she looked at me with a gleam of hatred in her eye that startled, it was so intense. After we reached our gate, I shared with K that I should look at the tickets again because I kept seeing that gleam of hatred. Indeed, they had not been done properly.

I went back to the counter and asked a helpful black sky-cap to find the supervisor. Even though he was black, I did not suggest that we had been the victims of racial harassment. I asked him instead if he could think of any reason why these two young white folks were so hostile.

Though I have always been concerned about class elitism and hesitate to make complaints about individuals who work long hours at often unrewarding jobs that require them to serve the public, I felt our complaint was justified. It was a case of racial harassment. And I was compelled to complain because I feel that the vast majority of black folks who are subjected daily to forms of racial harassment have accepted this as one of the social conditions of our life in white supremacist patriarchy that we cannot change. This acceptance is a form of complicity. I left the counter feeling better, not feeling that I had possibly made it worse for the black folks who might come after me, but that maybe these young white folks would have to rethink their behaviors if enough folks complained.

We were reminded of this incident when we boarded the plane and a black woman passenger arrived to take her seat in coach, only the white man sitting there refused to move. He did not have the correct boarding pass; she did. Yet he was not called to the front. No one compelled him to move as was done a few minutes later with my friend K. The very embarrassed black woman passenger kept repeating in a soft voice, "I am willing to sit anywhere." She sat elsewhere.

It was these sequences of racialized incidents involving black women that intensified my rage against the white man sitting next to me. I felt a "killing rage." I wanted to stab him softly, to shoot him with the gun I wished I had in my purse. And as I watched his pain, I would say to him tenderly "racism hurts." With no outlet, my rage turned to overwhelming grief and I began to weep, covering my face with my hands. All around me everyone acted as though they could not see me, as though I were invisible, with one exception. The white man seated next to me watched suspiciously whenever I reached for my purse. As though I were the black nightmare that haunted his dreams, he seemed to be waiting for me to strike, to be the fulfillment of his racist imagination. I leaned towards him with my legal pad and made sure he saw the title written in bold print: "Killing Rage."

In the course on black women novelists that I have been teaching this semester at City University, we have focused again and again on the question of black rage. We began the semester reading Harriet Jacobs's autobiography, *Incidents in the Life of a Slave Girl*, asking ourselves "where is the rage?" In the graduate seminar I teach on Toni Morrison we pondered whether black folks and white folks can ever be subjects together if white people remain unable to hear black rage, if it is the sound of that rage which must always remain repressed, contained, trapped in the realm of the unspeakable. In Morrison's first novel, *The Bluest Eye*, her narrator says of the dehumanized colonized little black girl Pecola that there would be hope for her if only she could express her rage, telling readers "anger is better, there is a presence in anger." Perhaps then it is that "presence," the assertion of subjectivity colonizers do not want to see, that surfaces when the colonized express rage.

In these times most folks associate black rage with the *underclass*, with desperate and despairing black youth who in their hopelessness feel no need to silence unwanted passions. Those of us black folks who have "made it" have for the most part become skilled at repressing our rage. We do what Ann Petry's heroine tells us we must in that prophetic forties novel about black female rage *The Street*. It is Lutie Johnson who exposes the rage underneath the calm persona. She declares: "Everyday we are choking down that rage." In the nineties it is not just white folks who let black folks know they do not want to hear our rage, it is also the voices of cautious upper-class black academic gatekeepers who assure us that our rage has no place. Even though black psychiatrists William Grier and Price Cobbs could write an entire book called *Black Rage*, they used their Freudian standpoint to convince readers that rage was merely a sign of powerlessness. They named it pathological, explained it away. They did not urge the larger culture to see black rage as something other than sickness, to see it as a potentially healthy, potentially healing response to oppression and exploitation.

In his most recent collection of essays, *Race Matters*, Cornel West includes the chapter "Malcolm X and Black Rage" where he makes rage synonymous with "great love for black people." West acknowledges that Malcolm X "articulated black rage in a manner unprecedented in American history," yet he does not link that rage to a passion for justice that may not emerge from the context of great love. By collapsing Malcolm's rage and his love, West attempts to explain that rage away, to temper it. Overall, contemporary reassessments of Malcolm X's political career tend to deflect away from "killing rage." Yet it seems that Malcolm X's passionate ethical commitment to justice served as the catalyst for his rage. That rage was not altered by shifts in his thinking about white folks, racial integration, etc. It is the clear defiant articulation of that rage that continues to set Malcolm X apart from contemporary black thinkers and leaders who feel that "rage" has no place in anti-racist struggle. These leaders are often more concerned about their dialogues with white folks. Their repression of rage (if and when they feel it) and their silencing of the rage of other black people are the sacrificial offering they make to gain the ear of white listeners. Indeed, black folks who do not feel rage at racial injustice because their own lives are comfortable may feel as fearful of black rage as their white counterparts. Today degrees and intensities of black rage seem to be overdetermined by the politics of location—by class privilege.

I grew up in the apartheid South. We learned when we were very little that black people could die from feeling rage and expressing it to the wrong white folks. We learned to choke down our rage. This process of repression was aided by the existence of our separate neighborhoods. In all black schools, churches, juke joints, etc., we granted ourselves the luxury of forgetfulness. Within the comfort of those black spaces we did not constantly think about white supremacy and its impact on our social status. We lived a large part of our lives not thinking about white folks. We lived in denial. And in living that way we were able to mute our rage. If black folks did strange, weird, or even brutally cruel acts now and then in our neighborhoods (cut someone to pieces over a card game, shoot somebody for looking at them the wrong way), we did not link this event to the myriad abuses and humiliations black folks suffered daily when we crossed the tracks and did what we had to do with and for whites to make a living. To express rage in that context was suicidal. Every black person knew it. Rage was reserved for life at home—for one another.

To perpetuate and maintain white supremacy, white folks have colonized black Americans, and a part of that colonizing process has been teaching us to repress our rage, to never make them the targets of any anger we feel about racism. Most black people internalize this message well. And though many of us were taught that the repression of our rage was necessary to stay alive in the days before racial integration, we now know that one can be exiled forever from the promise of economic well-being if that rage is not permanently silenced. Lecturing on race and racism all around this country, I am always amazed when I hear white folks speak about their fear of black people, of being the victims of black violence. They may never have spoken to a black person, and certainly never been hurt by a black person, but they are convinced that their response to blackness must first and foremost be fear and dread. They too live in denial. They claim to fear that black people will hurt them even though there is no evidence which suggests that black people routinely hurt white people in this or any other culture. Despite the fact that many reported crimes are committed by black offenders, this does not happen so frequently as to suggest that all white people must fear any black person.

Now, black people are routinely assaulted and harassed by white people in white supremacist culture. This violence is condoned by the state. It is necessary for the maintenance of racial difference. Indeed, if black people have not learned our place as second-class citizens through educational institutions, we learn it by the daily assaults perpetuated by white offenders on our bodies and beings that we feel but rarely publicly protest or name. Though we do not live in the same fierce conditions of racial apartheid that only recently ceased being our collective social reality, most black folks believe that if they do not conform to white-determined standards of acceptable behavior they will not survive. We live in a society where we hear about white folks killing black people to express their rage. We can identify specific incidents throughout our history in this country whether it be Emmett Till, Bensonhurst, Howard Beach, etc. We can identify rare incidents where individual black folks have randomly responded to their fear of white assault by killing. White rage is acceptable, can be both expressed and condoned, but black rage has no place and everyone knows it.

When I first left the apartheid South, to attend a predominantly white institution of higher education, I was not in touch with my rage. I had been raised to dream only of racial uplift, of a day when white and black would live together as one. I had been raised to turn the other cheek. However, the fresh air of white liberalism encountered when I went to the West Coast to attend college in the early seventies invited me to let go some of the terror and mistrust of white people that living in apartheid had bred in me. That terror keeps all rage at bay. I remember my first feelings of political rage against racism. They surfaced within me after I had read Fanon, Memmi, Freire. They came as I was reading Malcolm X's autobiography. As Cornel West suggests in his essay, I felt that Malcolm X dared black folks to claim our emotional subjectivity and that we could do this only by claiming our rage.

Like all profound repression, my rage unleashed made me afraid. It forced me to turn my back on forgetfulness, called me out of my denial. It changed my relationship with home— with the South—made it so I could not return there. Inwardly, I felt as though I were a marked woman. A black person unashamed of her rage, using it as a catalyst to develop critical consciousness, to come to full decolonized self-actualization, had no real place in the existing social structure. I felt like an exile. Friends and professors wondered what had come over me. They shared their fear that this new militancy might consume me. When I journeyed home to see my family I felt estranged from them. They were suspicious of the new me. The "good" southern white folks who had always given me a helping hand began to worry that college was ruining me. I seemed alone in understanding that I was undergoing a process of radical politicization and self-recovery.

Confronting my rage, witnessing the way it moved me to grow and change, I understood intimately that it had the potential not only to destroy but also to construct. Then and now I understand rage to be a necessary aspect of resistance struggle. Rage can act as a catalyst inspiring courageous action. By demanding that black people repress and annihilate our rage to assimilate, to reap the benefits of material privilege in white supremacist capitalist patriarchal culture, white folks urge us to remain complicit with their efforts to colonize, oppress, and exploit. Those of us black people who have the opportunity to further our economic status willingly surrender our rage. Many of us have no rage. As individual black people increase their class power, live in comfort, with money mediating the viciousness of racist assault, we can come to see both the society and white people differently.

We experience the world as infinitely less hostile to blackness than it actually is. This shift happens particularly as we buy into liberal individualism and see our individual fate as black people in no way linked to the collective fate. It is that link that sustains full awareness of the daily impact of racism on black people, particularly its hostile and brutal assaults.

Black people who sustain that link often find that as we "move on up" our rage intensifies. During that time of my life when racial apartheid forbid possibilities of intimacy and closeness with whites, I was most able to forget about the pain of racism. The intimacy I share with white people now seldom intervenes in the racism and is the cultural setting that provokes rage. Close to white folks, I am forced to witness firsthand their willful ignorance about the impact of race and racism. The harsh absolutism of their denial. Their refusal to acknowledge accountability for racist conditions past and present. Those who doubt these perceptions can read a white male documenting their accuracy in Andrew Hacker's work *Two Nations: Black and White, Separate, Hostile, Unequal.* His work, like that of the many black scholars and thinkers whose ideas he draws upon, highlights the anti-black feelings white people cultivate and maintain in white supremacist capitalist patriarchy. Racial hatred is real. And it is humanizing to be able to resist it with militant rage.

Forgetfulness and denial enable masses of privileged black people to live the "good life" without ever coming to terms with black rage. Addictions of all sorts, cutting across class, enable black folks to forget, take the pain and the rage away, replacing it with dangerous apathy and hard-heartedness. Addictions promote passive acceptance of victimization. In recent times conservative black thinkers have insisted that many black folks are wedded to a sense of victimization. That is only a partial truth. To tell the whole truth they would have to speak about the way mainstream white culture offers the mantle of victimization as a substitute for transformation of society. White folks promote black victimization, encourage passivity by rewarding those black folks who whine, grovel, beg, and obey. Perhaps this is what Toni Morrison's character Joe Trace is talking about when he shares in *Jazz* the knowledge his play-father Mr. Frank taught him, "the secret of kindness from white people—they had to pity a thing before they could like it." The presence of black victimization is welcomed. It comforts many whites precisely because it is the antithesis of activism. Internalization of victimization renders black folks powerless, unable to assert agency on our behalf. When we embrace victimization, we surrender our rage.

My rage intensifies because I am not a victim. It burns in my psyche with an intensity that creates clarity. It is a constructive healing rage. Vietnamese Buddhist monk Thich Nhat Hanh teaches that self-recovery is ultimately about learning to see clearly. The political process of decolonization is also a way for us to learn to see clearly. It is the way to freedom for both colonized and colonizer. The mutuality of a subject-to-subject encounter between those individuals who have decolonized their minds makes it possible for black rage to be heard, to be used constructively.

Currently, we are daily bombarded with mass media images of black rage, usually personified by angry young black males wreaking havoc upon the "innocent," that teach everyone in the culture to see this rage as useless, without meaning, destructive. This one-dimensional misrepresentation of the power of rage helps maintain the status quo. Censoring militant response to race and racism, it ensures that there will be no revolutionary effort to gather that rage and use it for constructive social change. Significantly, contemporary reinterpretations and critiques of Malcolm X seek to redefine him in a manner that strips him of rage as though this were his greatest flaw. Yet his "rage" for justice clearly pushed him towards greater and greater awareness. It pushed him to change. He is an example of how we can use rage to empower. It is tragic to see his image recouped to condone mindless anger and violence in black life.

As long as black rage continues to be represented as always and only evil and destructive, we lack a vision of militancy that is necessary for transformative revolutionary action. I did not kill the white man on the plane even though I remain awed by the intensity of that desire. I did listen to my rage, allow it to motivate me to take pen in hand and write in the heat of that moment. At the end of the day, as I considered why it had been so full of racial incidents, of racist harassment, I thought that they served as harsh reminders compelling me to take a stand, speak out, choose whether I will be complicit or resist. All our silences in the face of racist assault are acts of complicity. What does our rage at injustice mean if it can be silenced, erased by individual material comfort? If aware black folks gladly trade in their critical political consciousness for opportunistic personal advancement then there is no place for rage and no hope that we can ever live to see the end of white supremacy.

Rage can be consuming. It must be tempered by an engagement with a full range of emotional responses to black struggle for self-determination. In midlife, I see in myself that same rage at injustice which surfaced in me more than twenty years ago as I read the *Autobiography of Malcolm X* and experienced the world around me anew. Many of my peers seem to feel no rage or believe it has no place. They see themselves as estranged from angry black youth. Sharing rage connects those of us who are older and more experienced with younger black and non-black folks who are seeking ways to be self-actualized, self-determined, who are eager to participate in anti-racist struggle. Renewed, organized black liberation struggle cannot happen if we remain unable to tap collective black rage. Progressive black activists must show how we take that rage and move it beyond fruitless scapegoating of any group, linking it instead to a passion for freedom and justice that illuminates, heals, and makes redemptive struggle possible.

BEYOND BLACK RAGE

ENDING RACISM

Before *Newsweek* published its cover story "The Hidden Rage of Successful Blacks," before a disturbed black man shot white commuters on a New York train, I wrote an essay about killing rage, about the anger that was surfacing in me in response to racism in this society. In that essay I emphasized that it is a mark of the way black Americans cope with white supremacy that there are few reported incidents of black rage against racism leading us to target white folks. Shortly after this essay was written a black man randomly shot people on a New York train. They were not all white even though mass media made it appear that was the case. However, the motive behind the random killings was depicted as anger at racism. In notes he carried on his person he expressed anger at "racism By Caucasians and Uncle Tom Negroes." Even though the gunman carried in his pocket a list containing the names of black male leaders, the white-dominated mass media turned his pathological expression of anger towards blacks and whites alike into a rage against white people. Despite being psychologically disturbed, the suspect never made racism synonymous with white people. He held accountable all the groups who help perpetuate and maintain institutionalized racism, including black folks. That the media chose to reduce his complex understanding of the nature of neo-colonial racism to rage against whites set the stage for white folks to further demonize and dehumanize all black folks while representing themselves as a group that is never carried away by killing rage. In newspaper articles reporting the incident there was no mention of enraged white folks killing blacks. Indeed the wife of one of the white victims shared her feeling that lots of whites "hate blacks, but they don't go around shooting them." Of course in saying this, she revealed her ignorance of a long, well-documented history of racist aggression towards blacks wherein enraged whites have done just that. Contrary to her uninformed assertion, the annals of history document the slaughter of black folks by enraged white Americans. Just days before the train incident, the newspaper *USA Today* carried a brief statement reporting that Ku Klux Klan informant Henry Alexander, dying of cancer, confessed to his wife that in 1957 he and three white male associates abducted a black man "and forced him to jump from a bridge into a river" in Alabama. The man was killed by the fall.

Despite all the documented cases of shootings, lynchings, and various slaughters of black folks by hostile white racists we will never really know the exact numbers. And that is not really even important. It is important that everyone in the United States understand that white supremacy promotes, encourages, and condones all manner of violence against black people. Institutionalized racism allows this violence to remain unseen and/or renders it insignificant by suggesting it is justifiable punishment for some offense. Mass media do not see it as newsworthy. Yet when a black man carrying notes about racism randomly kills folks on a train, that is deemed newsworthy. Reported everywhere in the world, this incident was used not to highlight white supremacy and its potential "maddening impact." It became just another way to stereotype black males as irrational, angry predators.

White-dominated mass media used this incident to continue a long line of what Toni Morrison, in her editorial "On the Backs of Blacks," calls "race talk": "the explicit insertion into everyday life of racial signs and symbols that have no meaning other than pressing African Americans to the lowest level of the racial hierarchy." She reminds us that "popular culture, shaped by film, theater, advertising, the press, television and literature, is heavily engaged in race talk. It participates freely in this most enduring and efficient rite of passage into American culture: negative appraisals of the native-born black population." Even though the black man on the New York train was not native born, his actions were presented as though they revealed secrets about the nature of all black people in this society. The secrets have to do with what *Newsweek* magazine had already informed the public about: the "hidden rage of successful blacks." Significantly, when white-dominated mass media call attention to that rage, the point is to suggest that it is misguided, misplaced, an inappropriate response since these are the black people one white man told me who "have been allowed to make it." He does not hear the racial paternalism in his use of the word "allow." Or understand that the rage expressed in this article was about the failure of success to mediate and break down racist barriers. That despite their success, the individuals who had made it still encountered racial discrimination.

The persistence of racial discrimination was one of the social realities that consistently disturbed the peace of mind of the black man on the train. Newspapers all around the

United States suggested that it was overreactive concern about racism that led to the random killings. Professors at the university where the black suspect had been a student testified that "race was an obsession with him." White folks responded to the incident by expressing their weariness of hearing about racism, especially from affluent black folks, or individuals like the man on the train who, though from a privileged background, had not attained desired success. Clearly, he attributed his lack of success to institutionalized racism. Ironically, even though he is a Jamaican immigrant from an upper-class family, class was not perceived as an issue in this incident. Newspaper and magazine articles did not discuss whether there are differences in the rage of successful blacks and that of the underclass. Instead this incident became an occasion for white-dominated mass media to send a very clear message to all African Americans that there is no place in this society for the speaking of black rage, or for acting it out.

Indeed, this incident became the catalyst for a public discourse wherein black rage could be mocked and trivialized, talked about as though there are no social conditions that should invoke such an extreme, potentially insane response. That public discussion intensified during the time that the white lawyers representing the defendant used "black rage" as an explanation for this crime. A recent editorial in *New York* magazine, "Capitalizing on a Killer" by Eric Pooley, is an example of this trend; it carried the subtitle "A Spurious 'Black Rage' Defense." Pooley asserts: "Over and over in the past decade, activists have used black rage as the largely unspoken justification for all kinds of despicable behavior— the outrageous lies of Al Sharpton during the Tawana Brawley caper, the gang rape by teenagers in the Central Park jogger case, the black boycott of a Korean grocery, the reign of terror in Crown Heights. . . . The black rage theory insults

African-Americans because it allows any behavior by blacks to be excused—even celebrated—as a response to oppression." One wonders how it can be that Pooley knows that black folks attempt to justify corruption on the basis of black rage if until recently it was never overtly cited as the reason for aberrant behavior. Pooley can accept black anger but he is unable to make a distinction between the rage many black people feel and the way mainstream mass media represent that rage or the black response to it. He does not tell readers how the vast majority of black folks responded to the shooting on the train. Most black folks felt that the assailant was psychologically "crazy" even though they also added that the conditions of racism can "drive one mad." Unlike mass media, most black folks can recognize that it is ethically and morally wrong to kill folks even as we can also sympathize with mental illness that is either engendered or exacerbated by life in white supremacist capitalist patriarchy.

A complex understanding of black rage will not emerge with this case since as spectacle, it is already being designed to invalidate the reality of black response to racism. That invalidation is happening both by racist whites who want to see the suspect murdered by the state and the liberal white lawyers Kunstler and Kuby who began by launching a defense of blaming white racism for black rage. They insist: "We are not saying he is justified. We're not saying that people should name their children after him or follow in his footsteps. We're just saying that he was not responsible for his own conduct. We're saying white racism is to blame."

Already a carnivalesque aura surrounds public debate about black rage. Overall, that atmosphere undermines the possibility that there will be any serious understanding of the way in which living in a white supremacist context, suffering racist discrimination and/or exploitation and oppression, can create and/or exacerbate mental illness. By deploying a defense that seeks to pathologize "black rage" as though all rage is inherently pathological, Kunstler and Kuby invalidate the idea that rage against racism does not signal insanity or pathology. By concocting a defense that relies on biased Eurocentric one-dimensional explanations for black rage, they perpetuate racist stereotypes.

Many African Americans feel uncontrollable rage when we encounter white supremacist aggression. That rage is not pathological. It is an appropriate response to injustice. However, if not processed constructively, it can lead to pathological behavior—but so can any rage, irrespective of the cause that serves as a catalyst. In my own case, the anger I felt about white supremacy that surfaced so intensely as to be murderous shocked me. I had never felt such uncontrollable "killing rage." Had I killed the white man whose behavior evoked that rage, I feel that it would not have been caused by "white racism" but by the madness engendered by a pathological context. Until this culture can acknowledge the pathology of white supremacy, we will never create a cultural context wherein the madness of white racist hatred of blacks or the uncontrollable rage that surfaces as a response to that madness can be investigated, critically studied, and understood. Denying that rage is at times a useful and constructive response to exploitation, oppression, and continued injustice, but it creates a cultural climate where the psychological impact of racism can be ignored, and where race and racism become topics that are depoliticized. Racism can then be represented as an issue for blacks only, a mere figment of our perverse paranoid imaginations, while all whites continue to be brainwashed to deny the existence of an institutionalized racist structure that they work to perpetuate and maintain. Rage about racism in this society intensifies among blacks and

our allies in struggle as white denial reaches epidemic pathological proportions. The danger of that denial cannot be understood, nor the rage it evokes, as long as the public refuses to
acknowledge that this is a white supremacist culture and that
white supremacy is rooted in pathological responses to difference. Concurrently, without a more sophisticated understanding of those particularly extreme expressions of rage which
indicate serious mental disorder, we will not be able to address
the complexity and multidimensional nature of black rage. We
will not be able to understand the psychological displacement
of grief and pain into rage. And without that understanding the
deeper dimensions of black rage cannot be acknowledged, nor
the psychological wounds it masks attended to.

None of the successful black people quoted in the *Newsweek* article spoke about feeling "killing rage." Yet in the
aftermath of the train incident, I heard many well-off black
people express their identification with the killer. They described incident after incident in which they found themselves suppressing the longing to violently respond to verbal
racist statements and/or assault. Even though I experienced
killing rage, I was appalled by the intensity of those feelings.
They did not lead me to feel any covert, passive-aggressive
"pleasure" about the train incident even though I heard
many wealthy and privileged black folks express pleasure.
These revelations surprised me since so many of these folks
spend their working and intimate lives in the company of
white colleagues, friends, and loved ones. Listening to them
it was clear that they felt no militant rage about the way
white supremacy exploits and oppresses black people, but
collectively they were enraged by the reality that they are
not exempt from racist assault. Their rage erupts because
they have spent so much time acquiescing to white power to
achieve—assimilating, changing themselves, suppressing true

feelings. Their rage surfaces because they make these changes believing that doing so will mean they will be accepted as equals. When they are not treated as equals by the whites they have admired, subordinated their integrity to, they are shocked. Again, it must be stated that their rage is not a militant rage at the way white supremacy exploits and/or oppresses black people collectively. It is a narcissistic rage rooted in the ideology of hierarchical privilege that says "they," not all black people, should be treated better. They see themselves as more deserving. Unlike underclass and underprivileged black people, they have a sense of entitlement. And it is the sense that they will be selected out and treated better, bred into them at birth by their class values, that erupts into rage when white folks arbitrarily choose to make no distinction between a black person from an "elite" class and someone from the underclass. And even though some whites may respond to the rage of successful blacks by dismissing it as "whining," plenty of other white people respond by rewarding them for wearing the mantle of victimhood. Pimping white guilt in competitive workplaces is seen by some individual successful blacks as a useful networking strategy not unlike those used by white folks who pimp shared white genealogy, background, schooling, etc. When ass kissing, sucking face, and brown nosing do not work to counter racist barriers, it is no wonder that these individuals who have compromised to "make it" harbor repressed pathological rage that may be more intense than any rage felt by an underclass black person who has never trusted white people or endeavored to please them to receive rewards.

All the public attention that the rage of successful blacks is receiving (and the train incident represents a perversion of this rage since the suspect suggested in his notes that he was angry because he had done all the right things to succeed and should have had no problems) strategically trivializes both the actual concrete brutal oppressive manifestations of racism in this society as well as resistance to that racism. Mass media's trivialization of black rage reinforces white denial that white supremacy exists, that it is institutionalized, perpetuated by a system that condones the dehumanization of black people, by encouraging everyone to dismiss rage against racism as in no way a response to concrete reality since the black folks they see complaining are affluent. Concurrently, affluent blacks are rarely linking their rage to any progressive challenge and critique of white supremacy rooted in solidarity with the black masses. Made to feel ashamed that they or anyone else dare to even speak about rage at racial discrimination, often privileged-class black people are the group most eager to silence discussions of militant rage because they are not interested in fundamentally challenging and changing white supremacist capitalist patriarchy. They simply want equal access to privilege within the existing structure. However, when they speak their narcissistic rage, public trivialization of it leads to the mocking of all black rage, to censorship and repression. The black rage that white power wants to suppress is not the narcissistic whine of the black privileged classes, it is the rage of the downtrodden and oppressed that could be mobilized to mount militant resistance to white supremacy.

It is useful for white supremacist capitalist patriarchy to make all black rage appear pathological rather than identify the structure wherein that rage surfaces. At times black rage may express itself pathologically. However, it also can express itself in ways that lead to constructive empowerment. Black rage against injustice, against systems of domination, particularly as it is expressed in black youth culture, is mirrored in the rebellion against the white supremacist bourgeois sensibility expressed by white youth. Calling attention to this connection in a recent interview in *Artforum*, radical gay filmmaker John Waters comments: "One thing that I find fascinating, now that my generation has kids and those kids are rebelling, is that if they're white the only way they can rebel is to be black. My generation marched for Martin Luther King Jr., but they didn't want their kids to be blacks. That's the difference between my generation and their kids." This is a generation of kids who are tired of racism and white supremacy, who are less willing to engage in denial, a generation that may be willing to launch organized collective resistance. White and black conservatives alike fear them and want to wipe out both their sense of connectedness and any possibility that they might join together to engage in processes of radical politicization that would transform this nation. Racist white adults want their children to fear blackness so that they will not cross race boundaries and unite in political solidarity. They want them to see black rage as always and only pathological rather than as a just response to an unjust situation. These bourgeois whites, like many of their black counterparts, do not want rage against the status quo to assume the form of strategic resistance. Hence their mutual investment in mocking and trivializing black rage.

The rage of the oppressed is never the same as the rage of the privileged. One group can change their lot only by changing the system; the other hopes to be rewarded within the system. Public focus on black rage, the attempt to trivialize and dismiss it, must be subverted by public discourse about the pathology of white supremacy, the madness it creates. We need to talk seriously about ending racism if we want to see an end to rage. White supremacy is frightening. It promotes mental illness and various dysfunctional behaviors on the part of whites and non-whites. It is the real and present danger—not black rage.

REPRESENTATIONS OF WHITENESS IN THE BLACK IMAGINATION

Although there has never been any official body of black people in the United States who have gathered as anthropologists and/or ethnographers to study whiteness, black folks have, from slavery on, shared in conversations with one another "special" knowledge of whiteness gleaned from close scrutiny of white people. Deemed special because it was not a way of knowing that has been recorded fully in written material, its purpose was to help black folks cope and survive in a white supremacist society. For years, black domestic servants working in white homes, acting as informants, brought knowledge back to segregated communities—details, facts, observations, and psychoanalytic readings of the white Other.

Sharing the fascination with difference that white people have collectively expressed openly (and at times vulgarly) as they have traveled around the world in pursuit of the Other and Otherness, black people, especially those living during the historical period of racial apartheid and legal segregation, have similarly maintained steadfast and ongoing curiosity about the "ghosts," "the barbarians," these strange apparitions they were forced to serve. In the chapter on "Wildness" in *Shamanism, Colonialism, and the Wild Man*, Michael Taussig urges a stretching of our imagination and understanding of the Other to include inscriptions "on the edge of official history." Naming his critical project, identifying the passion he brings to the quest to know more deeply *you who are not ourselves,* Taussig explains:

> I am trying to reproduce a mode of perception—a way of seeing through a way of talking—figuring the world through dialogue that comes alive with sudden transformative force in the crannies of everyday life's pauses and juxtapositions, as in the kitchens of the Putumayo or in the streets around the church in the Niña Maria. It is always a way of representing the world in the roundabout "speech" of the collage of things. . . . It is a mode of perception that catches on the debris of history. . . .

I, too, am in search of the debris of history. I am wiping the dust off past conversations to remember some of what was shared in the old days when black folks had little intimate contact with whites, when we were much more open about the way we connected whiteness with the mysterious, the strange, and the terrible. Of course, everything has changed. Now many black people live in the "bush of ghosts" and do not know themselves separate from whiteness. They do not know this thing we call "difference." Systems of domination, imperialism, colonialism, and racism actively coerce black folks to internalize negative perceptions of blackness, to be self-hating. Many of us succumb to this. Yet blacks who imitate whites (adopting their values, speech, habits of being, etc.) continue to regard whiteness with suspicion, fear, and even hatred. This contradictory longing to possess the reality of the Other, even though that reality is one that wounds and negates, is expressive of the desire to understand the mystery, to know intimately through imitation, as though such knowing worn like an amulet, a mask, will ward away the evil, the terror.

Searching the critical work of post-colonial critics, I found much writing that bespeaks the continued fascination with the way white minds, particularly the colonial imperialist traveler, perceive blackness, and very little expressed interest in representations of whiteness in the black imagination. Black cultural and social critics allude to such representations in their writing, yet only a few have dared to make explicit those perceptions of whiteness that they think will discomfort or antagonize readers. James Baldwin's collection of essays *Notes of a Native Son* explores these issues with a clarity and frankness that is no longer fashionable in a world where evocations of pluralism and diversity act to obscure differences arbitrarily imposed and maintained by white racist domination. Addressing the way in which whiteness exists without knowledge of blackness even as it collectively asserts control, Baldwin links issues of recognition to the practice of imperialist racial domination. Writing about being the first black person to visit a Swiss village with only white inhabitants in his essay "Stranger in the Village," Baldwin notes his response to the village's yearly ritual of painting individuals black who were then positioned as slaves and bought so that the villagers could celebrate their concern with converting the souls of the "natives":

> I thought of white men arriving for the first time in an
> African village, strangers there, as I am a stranger here,
> and tried to imagine the astounded populace touching

their hair and marveling at the color of their skin. But there is a great difference between being the first white man to be seen by Africans and being the first black man to be seen by whites. The white man takes the astonishment as tribute, for he arrives to conquer and to convert the natives, whose inferiority in relation to himself is not even to be questioned, whereas I, without a thought of conquest, find myself among a people whose culture controls me, has even, in a sense, created me, people who have cost me more in anguish and rage than they will ever know, who yet do not even know of my existence. The astonishment with which I might have greeted them, should they have stumbled into my African village a few hundred years ago, might have rejoiced their hearts. But the astonishment with which they greet me today can only poison mine.

My thinking about representations of whiteness in the black imagination has been stimulated by classroom discussions about the way in which the absence of recognition is a strategy that facilitates making a group the Other. In these classrooms there have been heated debates among students when white students respond with disbelief, shock, and rage as they listen to black students talk about whiteness, when they are compelled to hear observations, stereotypes, etc., that are offered as "data" gleaned from close scrutiny and study. Usually, white students respond with naive amazement that black people critically assess white people from a standpoint where "whiteness" is the privileged signifier. Their amazement that black people watch white people with a critical "ethnographic" gaze is itself an expression of racism. Often their rage erupts because they believe that all ways of looking that highlight difference subvert the liberal belief in a universal subjectivity (we are all just people) that they think will make racism disappear. They have a deep emotional investment in the myth of "sameness," even as their actions reflect the primacy of whiteness as a sign informing who they are and how they think. Many of them are shocked that black people think critically about whiteness because racist thinking perpetuates the fantasy that the Other who is subjugated, who is subhuman, lacks the ability to comprehend, to understand, to see the working of the powerful. Even though the majority of these students politically consider themselves liberals and anti-racist, they too unwittingly invest in the sense of whiteness as mystery.

In white supremacist society, white people can "safely" imagine that they are invisible to black people since the power they have historically asserted, and even now collectively assert over black people, accorded them the right to control the black gaze. As fantastic as it may seem, racist white people find it easy to imagine that black people cannot see them if within their desire they do not want to be seen by the dark Other. One mark of oppression was that black folks were compelled to assume the mantle of invisibility, to erase all traces of their subjectivity during slavery and the long years of racial apartheid, so that they could be better, less threatening servants. An effective strategy of white supremacist terror and dehumanization during slavery centered around white control of the black gaze. Black slaves, and later manumitted servants, could be brutally punished for looking, for appearing to observe the whites they were serving, as only a subject can observe, or see. To be fully an object then was to lack the capacity to see or recognize reality. These looking relations were reinforced as whites cultivated the practice of denying the subjectivity of blacks (the better to dehumanize and oppress), of relegating them to the realm of the invisible. Growing up in a Kentucky household where black servants lived in the same dwelling with the white family who employed them, newspaper heiress Sallie Bingham recalls, in her autobiography *Passion and Prejudice*, "Blacks, I realized, were simply invisible to most white people, except as a pair of hands offering a drink on a silver tray." Reduced to the machinery of bodily physical labor, black people learned to appear before whites as though they were zombies, cultivating the habit of casting the gaze downward so as not to appear uppity. To look directly was an assertion of subjectivity, equality. Safety resided in the pretense of invisibility.

Even though legal racial apartheid no longer is a norm in the United States, the habits that uphold and maintain institutionalized white supremacy linger. Since most white people do not have to "see" black people (constantly appearing on billboards, television, movies, in magazines, etc.) and they do not need to be ever on guard nor to observe black people to be safe, they can live as though black people are invisible, and they can imagine that they are also invisible to blacks. Some white people may even imagine there is no representation of whiteness in the black imagination, especially one that is based on concrete observation or mythic conjecture. They think they are seen by black folks only as they want to appear. Ideologically, the rhetoric of white supremacy supplies a fantasy of whiteness. Described in Richard Dyer's essay "White," this fantasy makes whiteness synonymous with goodness:

> Power in contemporary society habitually passes itself off as embodied in the normal as opposed to the superior. This is common to all forms of power, but it works in a peculiarly seductive way with whiteness, because of the way it seems rooted, in common-sense thought,

in things other than ethnic difference. . . . Thus it is said (even in liberal textbooks) that there are inevitable associations of white with light and therefore safety, and black with dark and therefore danger, and that this explains racism (whereas one might well argue about the safety of the cover of darkness, and the danger of exposure to the light); again, and with more justice, people point to the Jewish and Christian use of white and black to symbolize good and evil, as carried still in such expressions as "a black mark," "white magic," "to blacken the character" and so on. Socialized to believe the fantasy, that whiteness represents goodness and all that is benign and non-threatening, many white people assume this is the way black people conceptualize whiteness. They do not imagine that the way whiteness makes its presence felt in black life, most often as terrorizing imposition, a power that wounds, hurts, tortures, is a reality that disrupts the fantasy of whiteness as representing goodness.

Collectively black people remain rather silent about representations of whiteness in the black imagination. As in the old days of racial segregation where black folks learned to "wear the mask," many of us pretend to be comfortable in the face of whiteness only to turn our backs and give expression to intense levels of discomfort. Especially talked about is the representation of whiteness as terrorizing. Without evoking a simplistic essentialist "us and them" dichotomy that suggests black folks merely invert stereotypical racist interpretations so that black becomes synonymous with goodness and white with evil, I want to focus on that representation of whiteness that is not formed in reaction to stereotypes but emerges as a response to the traumatic pain and anguish that remains a consequence of white racist domination, a psychic state that informs and shapes the way black folks "see" whiteness. Stereotypes black folks maintain about white folks are not the only representations of whiteness in the black imagination. They emerge primarily as responses to white stereotypes of blackness. Lorraine Hansberry argues that black stereotypes of whites emerge as a trickle-down process of white stereotypes of blackness, where there is the projection onto an Other all that we deny about ourselves. In *Young, Gifted, and Black*, she identifies particular stereotypes about white people that are commonly cited in black communities and urges us not to "celebrate this madness in any direction":

> Is it not "known" in the ghetto that white people, as an entity, are "dirty" (especially white women—who never seem to do their own cleaning); inherently "cruel" (the cold, fierce roots of Europe; who else could put all those people into ovens *scientifically*); "smart" (you really have to hand it to the m.f.'s), and anything *but* cold and passionless (because look who has had to live with little else than their passions in the guise of love and hatred all these centuries)? And so on.

Stereotypes, however inaccurate, are one form of representation. Like fictions, they are created to serve as substitutions, standing in for what is real. They are there not to tell it like it is but to invite and encourage pretense. They are a fantasy, a projection onto the Other that makes them less threatening. Stereotypes abound when there is distance. They are an invention, a pretense that one knows when the steps that would make real knowing possible cannot be taken or are not allowed.

Looking past stereotypes to consider various representations of whiteness in the black imagination, I appeal to memory, to my earliest recollections of ways these issues were raised in black life. Returning to memories of growing up in the social circumstances created by racial apartheid, to all black spaces on the edges of town, I reinhabit a location where black folks associated whiteness with the terrible, the terrifying, the terrorizing. White people were regarded as terrorists, especially those who dared to enter that segregated space of blackness. As a child, I did not know any white people. They were strangers, rarely seen in our neighborhoods. The "official" white men who came across the tracks were there to sell products, Bibles, and insurance. They terrorized by economic exploitation. What did I see in the gazes of those white men who crossed our thresholds that made me afraid, that made black children unable to speak? Did they understand at all how strange their whiteness appeared in our living rooms, how threatening? Did they journey across the tracks with the same "adventurous" spirit that other white men carried to Africa, Asia, to those mysterious places they would one day call the "third world"? Did they come to our houses to meet the Other face-to-face and enact the colonizer role, dominating us on our own turf?

Their presence terrified me. Whatever their mission, they looked too much like the unofficial white men who came to enact rituals of terror and torture. As a child, I did not know how to tell them apart, how to ask the "real white people to please stand up." The terror that I felt is one black people have shared. Whites learn about it secondhand. Confessing in *Soul Sister* that she too began to feel this terror after changing her skin to appear "black" and going to live in the South, Grace Halsell described her altered sense of whiteness:

> Caught in this climate of hate, I am totally terror-
> stricken, and I search my mind to know why I am fearful
> of my own people. Yet they no longer seem my people,
> but rather the "enemy" arrayed in large numbers against
> me in some hostile territory. . . . My wild heartbeat is a
> secondhand kind of terror. I know that I cannot possibly
> experience what *they*, the black people, experience. . . .

Black folks raised in the North do not escape this sense of
terror. In her autobiography, *Every Good-bye Ain't Gone*, Itabari
Njeri begins the narrative of her northern childhood with a memory of southern roots. Traveling south as an adult to investigate the
murder of her grandfather by white youth who were drag racing
and ran him down in the streets, Njeri recalls that for many
years "the distant and accidental violence that took my grandfather's life could not compete with the psychological terror that
had begun to engulf my own." Ultimately, she begins to link
that terror with the history of black people in the United States,
seeing it as an imprint carried from the past to the present:

> As I grew older, my grandfather assumed mythic propor-
> tions in my imagination. Even in absence, he filled my
> room like music and watched over me when I was fear-
> ful. His fantasized presence diverted thoughts of my
> father's drunken rages. With age, my fantasizing ceased,
> the image of my grandfather faded. What lingered was
> the memory of his caress, the pain of something missing
> in my life, wrenched away by reckless white youths. I
> had a growing sense—the beginning of an inevitable
> comprehension—that this society deals blacks a dispro-
> portionate share of pain and denial.

Njeri's journey takes her through the pain and terror of the
past, only the memories do not fade. They linger as does the

pain and bitterness: "Against a backdrop of personal loss, against the evidence of history that fills me with a knowledge of the hateful behavior of whites toward blacks, I see the people of Bainbridge. And I cannot trust them. I cannot absolve them." If it is possible to conquer terror through ritual reenactment, that is what Njeri does. She goes back to the scene of the crime, dares to face the enemy. It is this confrontation that forces the terror of history to loosen its grip.

To name that whiteness in the black imagination is often a representation of terror. One must face written histories that erase and deny, that reinvent the past to make the present vision of racial harmony and pluralism more plausible. To bear the burden of memory one must willingly journey to places long uninhabited, searching the debris of history for traces of the unforgettable, all knowledge of which has been suppressed. Njeri laments that "nobody really knows us." She writes, "So institutionalized is the ignorance of our history, our culture, our everyday existence that, often, we do not even know ourselves." Theorizing black experience, we seek to uncover, restore, as well as to deconstruct, so that new paths, different journeys, are possible. Indeed, Edward Said, in his essay "Traveling Theory," argues that theory can "threaten reification, as well as the entire bourgeois system on which reification depends, with destruction." The call to theorize black experience is constantly challenged and subverted by conservative voices reluctant to move from fixed locations. Said reminds us:

> Theory . . . is won as the result of a process that begins when consciousness first experiences its own terrible ossification in the general reification of all things under capitalism; then when consciousness generalizes (or classes)

itself as something opposed to other objects, and feels itself as contradiction to (or crisis within) objectification, there emerges a consciousness of change in the *status quo*; finally, moving toward freedom and fulfillment, consciousness looks ahead to complete self-realization, which is of course the revolutionary process stretching forward in time, perceivable now only as theory or projection.

Traveling, moving into the past, Njeri pieces together fragments. Who does she see staring into the face of a southern white man who was said to be the murderer? Does the terror in his face mirror the look of the unsuspecting black man whose death history does not name or record? Baldwin wrote that "people are trapped in history and history is trapped in them." There is then only the fantasy of escape, or the promise that what is lost will be found, rediscovered, and returned. For black folks, reconstructing an archaeology of memory makes return possible, the journey to a place we can never call home even as we reinhabit it to make sense of present locations. Such journeying cannot be fully encompassed by conventional notions of travel.

Spinning off from Said's essay, James Clifford, in "Notes on Travel and Theory," celebrates the idea of journeying, asserting:

> This sense of worldly, "mapped" movement is also why it may be worth holding on to the term "travel," despite its connotations of middle class "literary" or recreational journeying, spatial practices long associated with male experiences and virtues. "Travel" suggests, at least, profane activity, following public routes and beaten tracks. How do different populations, classes and genders

travel? What kinds of knowledges, stories, and theories
do they produce? A crucial research agenda opens up.

Reading this piece and listening to Clifford talk about theory
and travel, I appreciated his efforts to expand the travel/
theoretical frontier so that it might be more inclusive, even
as I considered that to answer the questions he poses is to
propose a deconstruction of the conventional sense of travel,
and put alongside it, or in its place, a theory of the journey
that would expose the extent to which holding on to the
concept of "travel" as we know it is also a way to hold on
to imperialism.

For some individuals, clinging to the conventional sense
of travel allows them to remain fascinated with imperialism,
to write about it, seductively evoking what Renato Rosaldo
aptly calls, in *Culture and Truth*, "imperialist nostalgia." Significantly, he reminds readers that "even politically progressive North American audiences have enjoyed the elegance of
manners governing relations of dominance and subordination
between the 'races.' " Theories of travel produced outside
conventional borders might want the Journey to become the
rubric within which travel, as a starting point for discourse,
is associated with different headings—rites of passage, immigration, enforced migration, relocation, enslavement, and
homelessness. "Travel" is not a word that can be easily
evoked to talk about the Middle Passage, the Trail of Tears,
the landing of Chinese immigrants, the forced relocation of
Japanese Americans, or the plight of the homeless. Theorizing diverse journeying is crucial to our understanding of any
politics of location. As Clifford asserts at the end of his essay:

> Theory is always written from some "where," and that
> "where" is less a place than itineraries: different, con-

crete histories of dwelling, immigration, exile, migration. These include the migration of third world intellectuals into the metropolitan universities, to pass through or to remain, changed by their travel but marked by places of origin, by peculiar allegiances and alienations.

Listening to Clifford "playfully" evoke a sense of travel, I felt such an evocation would always make it difficult for there to be recognition of an experience of travel that is not about play but is an encounter with terrorism. And it is crucial that we recognize that the hegemony of one experience of travel can make it impossible to articulate another experience or for it to be heard. From certain standpoints, to travel is to encounter the terrorizing force of white supremacy. To tell my "travel" stories, I must name the movement from racially segregated southern community, from rural black Baptist origin, to prestigious white university settings. I must be able to speak about what it is like to be leaving Italy after I have given a talk on racism and feminism, hosted by the parliament, only to stand for hours while I am interrogated by white officials who do not have to respond when I inquire as to why the questions they ask me are different from those asked the white people in line before me. Thinking only that I must endure this public questioning, the stares of those around me, because my skin is black, I am startled when I am asked if I speak Arabic, when I am told that women like me receive presents from men without knowing what those presents are. Reminded of another time when I was strip-searched by French officials, who were stopping black people to make sure we were not illegal immigrants and/or terrorists, I think that one fantasy of whiteness is that the threatening Other is always a terrorist. This projection enables many white people to imagine there is no representation of whiteness as terror, as terrorizing. Yet it is this representation of whiteness in the black imagination, first learned in the narrow confines of poor black rural community, that is sustained by my travels to many different locations.

To travel, I must always move through fear, confront terror. It helps to be able to link this individual experience to the collective journeying of black people, to the Middle Passage, to the mass migration of southern black folks to northern cities in the early part of the twentieth century. Michel Foucault posits memory as a site of resistance. As Jonathan Arac puts it in his introduction to *Postmodernism and Politics*, the process of remembering can be a practice which "transforms history from a judgement on the past in the name of a present truth to a 'counter-memory' that combats our current modes of truth and justice, helping us to understand and change the present by placing it in a new relation to the past." It is useful, when theorizing black experience, to examine the way the concept of "terror" is linked to representations of whiteness.

In the absence of the reality of whiteness, I learned as a child that to be "safe" it was important to recognize the power of whiteness, even to fear it, and to avoid encounter. There was nothing terrifying about the sharing of this knowledge as survival strategy; the terror was made real only when I journeyed from the black side of town to a predominantly white area near my grandmother's house. I had to pass through this area to reach her place. Describing these journeys "across town" in the essay "Homeplace: A Site of Resistance," I remembered:

> It was a movement away from the segregated blackness of our community into a poor white neighborhood. I remember the fear, being scared to walk to Baba's, our

grandmother's house, because we would have to pass that terrifying whiteness—those white faces on the porches staring us down with hate. Even when empty or vacant those porches seemed to say *danger*, you do not belong here, you are not safe.

Oh! that feeling of safety, of arrival, of homecoming when we finally reached the edges of her yard, when we could see the soot black face of our grandfather, Daddy Gus, sitting in his chair on the porch, smell his cigar, and rest on his lap. Such a contrast, that feeling of arrival, of homecoming—this sweetness and the bitterness of that journey, that constant reminder of white power and control. Even though it was a long time ago that I made this journey, associations of whiteness with terror and the terrorizing remain. Even though I live and move in spaces where I am surrounded by whiteness, there is no comfort that makes the terrorism disappear. All black people in the United States, irrespective of their class status or politics, live with the possibility that they will be terrorized by whiteness.

This terror is most vividly described by black authors in fiction writing, particularly Toni Morrison's novel *Beloved*. Baby Suggs, the black prophet, who is most vocal about representations of whiteness, dies because she suffers an absence of color. Surrounded by a lack, an empty space, taken over by whiteness, she remembers: "Those white things have taken all I had or dreamed and broke my heartstrings too. There is no bad luck in the world but white folks." If the mask of whiteness, the pretense, represents it as always benign, benevolent, then what this representation obscures is the representation of danger, the sense of threat. During the period of racial apartheid, still known by many folks as Jim Crow, it was more difficult for black people to internalize this pretense, hard for us not to know that the shapes under white sheets had a mission to threaten, to terrorize. That representation of whiteness, and its association with innocence, which engulfed and murdered Emmett Till, was a sign; it was meant to torture with the reminder of possible future terror. In Morrison's *Beloved*, the memory of terror is so deeply inscribed on the body of Sethe and in her consciousness, and the association of terror with whiteness is so intense, that she kills her young so that they will never know the terror. Explaining her actions to Paul D., she tells him that it is her job "to keep them away from what I know is terrible." Of course Sethe's attempt to end the historical anguish of black people only reproduces it in a different form. She conquers the terror through perverse reenactment, through resistance, using violence as a means of fleeing from a history that is a burden too great to bear.

It is the telling of our history that enables political self-recovery. In contemporary society, white and black people alike believe that racism no longer exists. This erasure, however mythic, diffuses the representation of whiteness as terror in the black imagination. It allows for assimilation and forgetfulness. The eagerness with which contemporary society does away with racism, replacing this recognition with evocations of pluralism and diversity that further mask reality, is a response to the terror. It has also become a way to perpetuate the terror by providing a cover, a hiding place. Black people still feel the terror, still associate it with whiteness, but are rarely able to articulate the varied ways we are terrorized because it is easy to silence by accusations of reverse racism or by suggesting that black folks who talk about the ways we are terrorized by whites are merely evoking victimization to demand special treatment.

When I attended a recent conference on cultural studies,

I was reminded of the way in which the discourse of race is increasingly divorced from any recognition of the politics of racism. Attending the conference because I was confident that I would be in the company of like-minded, "aware," progressive intellectuals, I was disturbed when the usual arrangements of white supremacist hierarchy were mirrored both in terms of who was speaking, of how bodies were arranged on the stage, of who was in the audience. All of this revealed the underlying assumptions of what voices were deemed worthy to speak and be heard. As the conference progressed, I began to feel afraid. If these progressive people, most of whom were white, could so blindly reproduce a version of the status quo and not "see" it, the thought of how racial politics would be played out "outside" this arena was horrifying. That feeling of terror that I had known so intimately in my childhood surfaced. Without even considering whether the audience was able to shift from the prevailing standpoint and hear another perspective, I talked openly about that sense of terror. Later, I heard stories of white women joking about how ludicrous it was for me (in their eyes I suppose I represent the "bad" tough black woman) to say I felt terrorized. Their inability to conceive that my terror, like that of Sethe's, is a response to the legacy of white domination and the contemporary expressions of white supremacy is an indication of how little this culture really understands the profound psychological impact of white racist domination.

At this same conference, I bonded with a progressive black woman and her companion, a white man. Like me, they were troubled by the extent to which folks chose to ignore the way white supremacy was informing the structure of the conference. Talking with the black woman, I asked her: "What do you do, when you are tired of confronting white racism, tired of the day-to-day incidental acts of racial terrorism? I mean, how do you deal with coming home to a white person?" Laughing she said, "Oh, you mean when I am suffering from White People Fatigue Syndrome? He gets that more than I do." After we finish our laughter, we talk about the way white people who shift locations, as her companion has done, begin to see the world differently. Understanding how racism works, he can see the way in which whiteness acts to terrorize without seeing himself as bad, or all white people as bad, and all black people as good. Repudiating us-and-them dichotomies does not mean that we should never speak of the ways observing the world from the standpoint of "whiteness" may indeed distort perception, impede understanding of the way racism works both in the larger world as well as in the world of our intimate interactions.

In *The Post-Colonial Critic*, Gayatri Spivak calls for a shift in locations, clarifying the radical possibilities that surface when positionality is problematized. She explains that "what we are asking for is that the hegemonic discourses, and the holders of hegemonic discourse, should dehegemonize their position and themselves learn how to occupy the subject position of the other." Generally, this process of repositioning has the power to deconstruct practices of racism and make possible the disassociation of whiteness with terror in the black imagination. As critical intervention it allows for the recognition that progressive white people who are anti-racist might be able to understand the way in which their cultural practice reinscribes white supremacy without promoting paralyzing guilt or denial. Without the capacity to inspire terror, whiteness no longer signifies the right to dominate. It truly becomes a benevolent absence. Baldwin ends his essay "Stranger in the Village" with the declaration: "This world is white no longer, and it will never be white again." Critically examining the association of whiteness as terror in the black imagination, deconstructing it, we both name racism's impact and help to break its hold. We decolonize our minds and our imaginations.

REFUSING TO BE A VICTIM

ACCOUNTABILITY AND RESPONSIBILITY

When *Feminist Theory: From Margin to Center* was published in 1984, I urged women engaged in feminist movement to beware of embracing a mantle of victimization in our quest to draw public attention to the need to end sexism and sexist exploitation and oppression. Critiquing a vision of sisterhood rooted in "shared victimization" I encouraged women to bond on the basis of political solidarity. It seemed ironic to me that white women who talked the most about being victims as I wrote then "were more privileged and powerful than the vast majority of women in our society." And if shared victimhood was the reason to be feminist then women who were empowered, who were not victims, would not embrace feminism. My repudiation of the victim identity emerged out of my awareness of the way in which thinking of oneself as a victim could be disempowering and disenabling.

Coming to womanhood in the segregated South, I had never heard black women talk about themselves as victims. Facing hardship, the ravages of economic lack and deprivation, the cruel injustice of racial apartheid, I lived in a world where women gained strength by sharing knowledge and resources, not by bonding on the basis of being victims. Despite the incredible pain of living in racial apartheid, southern black people did not speak about ourselves as victims even when we were downtrodden. We identified ourselves more by the experience of resistance and triumph than by the nature of our victimization. It was a given that life was hard, that there was suffering. It was by facing that suffering with grace and dignity that one experienced transformation. During civil rights struggle, when we joined hands to sing "we shall overcome," we were empowered by a vision of fulfillment, of victory. Much of the awareness that I brought to feminist struggle about the danger of identifying with victimhood was knowledge that came from the oppositional life practices of black folks in the segregated South. When I cautioned women involved in feminist movement to beware of embracing a victim identity, I was confident that black people active in liberation struggle already possessed this awareness. And yet by the end of the eighties black folks were more and more talking about victimhood, claiming a victim identity. Suddenly, individual black critics were raising a public voice cautioning black folks about the danger of embracing victimhood. One such thinker was Shelby Steele. His essays *The Content of Our Character* were published with a cover heading that stated he was presenting "a new vision of race in America." This vision was simple. It called for a repudiation of the rhetoric of victimhood.

Most black Americans were in agreement with Steele's assertion that to claim victimhood in an absolutist way was dangerously disempowering. However, his demand that we repudiate a victim identity was undermined by his insistence that racist aggression was no longer a threat to the well-being of black folks. This line of argument seemed to be opportunistically directed at white readers; it was such an utterly unsubstantiated claim. Practically all African Americans experience some degree of racist harassment in this society, however relative, on a daily basis. Steele's will to deny this reality was linked to his refusal to call attention to the ways white Americans are responsible for perpetuating and maintaining white supremacy. By not calling attention to white accountability, he implied that black folks must assume sole responsibility for the task of ending racism, of repudiating the victim identity. This seemed ironic given the reality that it was precisely the collective white repudiation of militant black resistance to racism that lay the groundwork for an emphasis on victimhood.

The word "victim" does not appear in the vast majority of resistance writing from the civil rights era. Yet as early as 1965 Martin Luther King Jr. was sharing the insight that the demand for a "realization of equality" was not being heard by whites. In *Where Do We Go from Here* King identified a growing feeling of disempowerment signaled by white backlash against the gains of the civil rights movement:

> The Negroes of America had taken the president, the press and the pulpit at their word when they spoke in broad terms of freedom and justice. But the absence of brutality and unregenerate evil is not the presence of justice. To stay murder is not the same thing as to ordain brotherhood. The word was broken, and the free-running expectations of the Negro crashed into the stone walls of white resistance. The result was havoc. Negroes felt cheated, especially in the North, while many whites felt that the Negroes had gained so much it was virtually impudent and greedy to ask for more so soon.

Militant resistance to white supremacy frightened white Americans, even those liberals and radicals who were committed to the struggle to end racial discrimination. There was a great difference between a civil rights struggle that worked primarily to end discrimination and radical commitment to black self-determination. Ironically, many whites who had struggled side by side with black folks responded positively to images of black victimization. Many whites testified that they looked upon the suffering of black people in the segregated South and were moved to work for change. The image of blacks as victims had an accepted place in the consciousness of every white person; it was the image of black folks as equals, as self-determining that had no place—that could evoke no sympathetic response. In complicity with the nation-state, all white Americans responded to black militancy by passively accepting the disruption of militant black organizations and the slaughter of black leaders.

In the wake of militant calls for black self-determination, privileged-class white women, many of whom had been active in civil rights struggle, began to organize women's liberation movement. Drawing on the rhetoric of black freedom struggle, these groups of women (not all of whom were white and privileged) found that it was useful to embrace a victim identity. Without witnessing the assassination of any of the leaders of feminist movement, without any police brutality, without a mass movement for social justice, white women were able to collectively redress wrongs enacted by a system of gender discrimination. The rhetoric of victimhood worked for white women. In the wake of feminist movement white women were suddenly receiving gains in the workforce. They were primary recipients of rewards from affirmative action. By the eighties white women had made greater gains in the short space of ten years than black women *and* men had made over decades of struggle. Those black males who were convinced that patriarchy should have allowed them to gain greater rights than white women were the most angered by the way the struggle for women's liberation was actually most successful when the focus was on gaining greater access to mainstream, traditionally white male–dominated spheres of power. This rage did not keep black males from deploying a similar rhetoric in the competition for favors and reparations from the white male power structure. White women active in contemporary feminist movement often behaved as did their nineteenth-century counterparts who when struggling for the vote were quite willing to evoke white supremacy as that structure of bonding that should lead white men to give them rights and privileges before extending them to black males.

When the rare white woman feminist of the early seventies wrote about racial hierarchy she usually did so to draw attention to her closeness to the white male power structure, to show the way she had been wronged. In 1970 Shulamith Firestone published *The Dialectic of Sex: The Case for Feminist Revolution* in which she argued that "racism is sexism extended"—that "racism is a sexual phenomenon." Drawing on Freudian paradigms, Firestone, like other white women during this time, saw race relations solely in terms of hierarchical relations within the white nuclear family. Firestone unabashedly wrote:

> The white man is father, the woman wife-and-mother, her status dependent on his; the blacks, like children, are his property, their physical differentiation branding them the subservient class, in the same way that children form so easily a distinguishable, servile class vis-à-vis adults. This power hierarchy created the psychology of racism, just as, in the nuclear family, it creates the psychology of sexism.

The flaw in Firestone's analysis was her refusal to see the way in which patriarchal thinking mediates racism to disrupt the model she outlines. Since at the time of her writing, black folks were indeed no longer property of white men but rather dependents, it would have been more accurate to see white women and black men as siblings engaged in a rivalry for the attention of the father, to consider the absence of the "mother" in patriarchal formations of power hierarchy. Certainly, black male and white female responses to the early stages of contemporary feminism made it clear that they saw themselves as rivals, competing to be included within the white male power structure. Black women were indeed outside the loop.

Just when black women active in feminist movement, like myself, were demanding that there be a re-visioning of feminist theory and practice that would repudiate the centrality of a focus on victimization, black males were appropriating the rhetoric of victimization to turn the spotlight back on themselves. Careful reading of the literature of black civil rights and black power struggle makes it clear that the emphasis in those movements was solidly on the gaining of rights and privileges for men—just as the early literature of feminist movement focused exclusively on calling attention to the needs of white women. To some extent the white-dominated women's movement shifted the public gaze away from black men and focused it on individual white women who wanted equality with men of their class. Jockeying for white male attention, black male leaders emphasized victimization, particularly the pain they suffered as a result of white racist aggression. Like their white female counterparts, they deployed a rhetoric of victimization because it was less threatening to white males. To name white males as all-powerful victimizers was to pay homage to their power, to see them as possessing the cure for all that ails.

As the rhetoric of victimization became more common-place, it appeared to be an accurate description of the state of black America after the powerful forces of white suprem-acy had suppressed militant resistance. Despair and feelings of hopelessness are central to the formation of a psychology of victimization. The assassination of revolutionary black male political leaders naturally created a climate of loss and chaos that was ripe for the growth of feelings of disempowerment. Suddenly a spirit of resistance that had been grounded in an oppositional belief that white power was limited, that it could be challenged and transformed, had dissipated. In its place was a rhetoric that represented that structure as all-powerful, unchanging.

The black church has always been a place in the United States where African Americans have learned oppositional ways of thinking that enhance our capacity to survive and flourish. Black liberation theology always intervened in any tendency to elevate humans to the status of all-powerful be-ings. This insistence on the limitations of humans was crucial for black people suffering at the hands of white oppressors and/or exploiters. The assumption that their power was lim-ited, subject to forces beyond control, even a belief in the miraculous, was an empowering worldview running counter to the teachings of white colonizing forces. As religion be-comes less central to the lives of contemporary African Americans, particularly to youth, those forms of oppositional thinking are not taught. Without alternative belief systems black folks embrace the values of the existing system, which daily reinforce learned helplessness. Mass media continually bombard us with images of African Americans which spread the message that we are hopeless, trapped, unable to change our circumstances in meaningful ways. No wonder then that a generation of black folks who learn much of their knowl-edge of race and struggles to end racism from movies and television see themselves as victims. Or that they see the only way out of being a victim is to assume the role of victimizer. While Shelby Steele chastised black folks for accepting the equation of blackness as victimization—"to be black is to be a victim; therefore, not to be a victim is not to be black"—he does not examine white investment in this equation. Yet those black folks who embrace victim identity do so because they find it mediates relations with whites, that it is easier to make appeals that call for sympathy rather than redress and reparations. As long as white Americans are more willing to extend concern and care to black folks who have a "victim-focused black identity," a shift in paradigms will not take place.

In order not to identify as victims, black folks must create ways to highlight issues of accountability that accurately address both the nature of our victimization within white supremacist capitalist patriarchy and the nature of our complicity. When individual black people project a victim identity because it brings their concerns into greater visibility, they are acting in complicity with an assaultive structure of racist domination in which they invest in the absence of agency. To name oneself a victim is to deny agency. As long as white Americans have difficulty coping with the assertion of agency and self-determination by individual or collective groups of black folks, victimization will continue to be the location of visibility.

All marginal groups in this society who suffer grave injustices, who are victimized by institutionalized systems of domination (race, class, gender, etc.), are faced with the peculiar dilemma of developing strategies that draw attention to one's plight in such a way that will merit regard and consideration without reinscribing a paradigm of victimization. When African Americans locate our concerns about racism and white supremacy within a discourse that centers around victimization, we may gain the attention of whites while surrendering a focus on self-determination. It is no accident that the voice that speaks loudest against the evocation of a framework of victimization is most often the one that focuses on the need for racial separatism, for black folks to assume total responsibility for improving our lot. Both discourses are totalizing. A renewed organized struggle for black self-determination is needed to shift the focus from a framework of victimization to one of accountability. For it is that discourse that allows African Americans to recognize our complicity, our need for an ongoing process of decolonization and radical politicization, while remaining steadfastly clear about the primary role the vast majority of white Americans play in perpetuating and maintaining white supremacy. Indeed, the very white folks who see black folks as scamming to get something for nothing via a public discourse of victimhood tend to resist divesting of that racist socialization that makes them more comfortable with black folks who are wounded. White folks who want all black Americans to repudiate a victim-focused identity must be prepared to engage in a subject-to-subject encounter with black folks who are self-determining. To embrace this shift would be to open up to the very vision of full racial equality which King found so many white Americans could not imagine. Those white Americans who are eager to live in a society that promotes and rewards racial equality must be willing to surrender outmoded perceptions of black neediness that socialize them to feel comfortable with us only when they are in a superior, caretaking role. Until masses of white Americans confront their obsessive need for a black victim who lacks the agency to call for an accounting that would really demand a shift in the structure of this society, the rhetoric of victimization will continue to flourish.

Black Americans who exploit the rhetoric of victimization

do so not only because it grants them moral authority but because it provides a platform from which demands can be made that are not mutual. If only white folks need to change then black folks are not required to undergo processes of radical politicization. Ironically, many African Americans feel more victimized (even though our ancestors certainly suffered harsher repression and injustice) because there has been an increased level of expectation. Those black folks raised in the segregated South who were taught to expect only exploitation at the hands of whites were not disappointed or psychologically crushed by forms of social exclusion and discrimination that were deemed minor. Nowadays, most black folks are taught by the rhetoric of liberal democracy, coming to us all from mass media, that they can expect to be treated equally. When this does not happen a disenabling sense of powerlessness and helplessness surfaces. That sense of victimization is linked to higher levels of expectation. Recently, I was giving a talk at Harvard University about black rage at white supremacy. I was saddened by the number of black female graduate students in the audience who spoke at great length about the terrible hardships they faced. Acutely aware of the myriad ways racial victimization articulates itself, they expressed a victim-focused identity. Yet their sense of victimization seemed to be totally out of proportion to a larger reality. They saw themselves as victims because they had imagined they would be treated as equals and when this did not happen they lacked the inner resources to confront and cope effectively. Contrary to Shelby Steele's assertion that black folks "claim more racial victimization than we have actually endured," the specific incidences they named documented actual victimization. However, their inability to respond to racist aggression with militant resistance seemed to intensify the feeling of victimization. One student described being in a class on feminist theory where my work was read. She found in that work a space of recognition and support. Yet the day it was discussed in class the white woman professor declared that no one was really moved by my work, that I was too negative. Unwilling to assert her agency, her engagement with the text, this young black woman felt both silenced and victimized. She felt like dropping out of graduate school. Had she resisted in this classroom setting, she would not have felt victimized. Instead she felt her blackness devalued even as she surrendered her personal agency and with it a sense of personal integrity. While militant response might not have gained her rewards, it would have preserved her sense of self. Teaching in privileged white institutions, I constantly encounter black students who feel victimized, who do not contextualize racist aggression so that they distinguish between the pain of being not invited to a party or left out of a discussion from severe economic deprivation, lack of access to basic skills and resources, etc.

To counter the fixation on a rhetoric of victimhood, black folks must engage in a discourse of self-determination. That discourse need not be rooted in separatist movement but can be part of an inclusive struggle to end racist domination. Progressive struggle to end white supremacy recognizes the political importance of accountability and does not embrace the rhetoric of victimhood even as it vigilantly calls attention to actual victimization.

CHALLENGING SEXISM
IN BLACK LIFE

Contemporary feminist movement has had little positive impact on black life in the United States. There has not been any mass-based effort to do education for critical consciousness in black communities so that black folks would engage the politics of feminism—its meaning for our lives. Ironically, more black women are just beginning to embrace narrow notions of feminism (i.e., the idea of woman as victim, man as oppressor/enemy) long after those ideas have been challenged by revolutionary feminist thinking, which is much more concerned with understanding how sexism and sexist oppression are perpetuated and maintained by all of us, not just men. While male domination continues to be a serious problem, it can never be the sole focus of feminist movement.

Individual black women have galvanized energy to critique black male sexism in the wake of the Thomas hearings and the case against Mike Tyson. More than any feminist writings these events were catalysts, allowing public acknowledgment that sexism is a problem in black life. Among academic black women, taking on issues of gender is often an opportunistic move to advance careers. Like many professional women they may be concerned with challenging gender inequality primarily when it impedes their progress. Rarely do they link that concern to revolutionary feminism that seeks to transform society, that includes a radical critique of racism, capitalism, and imperialism as well as sexism. These individuals then do little to actively share feminist thinking and practice with other black people. They come to voice publicly in moments of crisis, like the Thomas hearings, to champion the cause of woman wronged and by doing so they advance the notion that feminism really is simply about responding to the actions of men. Rather than creating spaces within black life where feminism might gain consideration, black females who are recent converts to crude liberal reformist feminism usually further antagonisms between black women and men.

Revolutionary feminism is not anti-male. Indeed, it embraces a critique of patriarchy that includes an understanding of the way in which the lives of black men are threatened by their uncritical absorption and participation in patriarchy. Unfortunately, there are too few black critical thinkers engaged in creating feminist theory. Our collective understanding of the various ways sexism and sexist oppression operate as systems of domination in black life continues to be limited, confined primarily to a discussion about black male abuse of black females. Regrettably, I find myself continually restating in essays about feminism and blackness that one of the major barriers impeding our capacity as black people to collectively challenge sexism and sexist oppression is the continued equation of black liberation with the development of black patriarchy. In this essay, I want to extend this critique to suggest that our efforts to create renewed black liberation struggle are seriously impeded by the fact that in diverse black settings the assumption prevails that we need only listen to patriarchal men, that our very capacity to move forward as a people depends on strong black male leadership. It not only leads to the complete dismissal of black female feminist voices and visions which could offer necessary guidance and direction, it also promotes and encourages folks to uncritically accept that black males who act like "powerful patriarchs" are the only bringers of necessary knowledge. This holds true for black social relations among whites as well. White people are often far more willing to listen to black males who assert themselves in a patriarchal manner than those who do not. Concurrently, they are often (and this is especially true of white women) not as disturbed by black male sexism since they seem (like many black folks) to equate black manhood with the assertion of sexist values and sexist thinking.

The major writings of black male critical thinkers and writers from the nineteenth century to the present who sought to influence and shape the nature of black life are supportive of patriarchy. Their work documents the extent to which they believed that the development of black patriarchy was essential to the advancement of the race. Whether we are reading Delaney, Du Bois, Douglass, Garvey, Cleaver, George Jackson, King, or Malcolm X, often they suggest that the wounds of white supremacy will be healed as black men assert themselves not as decolonized free subjects in struggle but as "men." While more recent black male academics and intellectuals give lip service to a critique of sexism in their work (often, like their bourgeois female counterparts, to advance their careers—any black male who speaks on behalf of ending sexism appears unique, special), rarely do they change their habits in professional and private life in ways that testify to a repudiation of patriarchy or sexist habits of thinking and being. The exception to this has been primarily in the lives and works of black gay men—for example, Joseph Beam and Essex Hemphill.

A distinction must be made between the nineteenth-century masculinist vision of black patriarchy that was rooted in the notion that black men should lead the struggle for racial uplift, educate themselves, and provide for families as heads of households and a more contemporary understanding of black manhood as making itself known first and foremost via the domination of women. This shift from a concern with benevolent patriarchy to a concern with the assertion of brute domination represents a crucial difference between the radical thinking of nineteenth-century black male leaders and their twentieth-century counterparts. Discussing the politics of race and gender in *The Black Atlantic*, black British cultural critic Paul Gilroy suggests that in our times "gender is the modality in which race is lived." I understand this comment to be a restating of black feminist critiques that call attention to the way in which the equation of black liberation with black manhood promotes and condones black male sexism. Within the context of white supremacist capitalist patriarchy one can assert manhood simply by demonstrating that one has the power to control and dominate women. Given these conditions, black men are not required to become providers and protectors to be "men." Instead as Gilroy contends, "an amplified and exaggerated masculinity has become the boastful centerpiece of a culture of compensation that self-consciously salves the misery of the disempowered and subordinated." In my first book, *Ain't I a Woman: Black Women and Feminism*, I stated this more plainly, suggesting that racial integration created a social context where black people were eager to throw off oppositional ways of thinking and being that were seen to be needed for civil rights work.

Once that struggle was perceived as won (i.e., that black people had gained equal rights) then one assertion of our new freedom was to make mainstream socialization about gender roles the norm in black life. In the age of integration, black men asserted masculinist subjectivity not by vigilantly challenging white supremacy but by first insisting on the subordination of women, particularly black women. Suddenly, black men who would never have access to jobs within this capitalist framework that would allow them to provide for families could still feel themselves to be "men." Manhood had been redefined. Manhood was not providing and protecting; it was proved by one's capacity to coerce, control, dominate.

This contemporary shift, more than any other, created a crisis in black life that remains unresolved. Unprecedented tension and hostility surfaced between black women and men. Many black women believe that this crisis would be resolved if black males would assume the role of benevolent patriarchs—protectors and providers. Socialized by democratic fantasies that there is work for all, they do not see mass black male unemployment or underemployment as necessary for the maintenance of our current economic system, and do not see that there will never be a day when all black men who want to can work and provide for families. Many black males and even some black females believe the crisis would be resolved if black women would simply accept a subordinate status irrespective of whether black males worked or not. This was certainly the message of Shahrazad Ali's successful book *The Blackman's Guide to Understanding the Blackwoman*: "When the Blackwoman accepts her rightful place as queen of the universe and mother of civilization the Blackman will regenerate his powers that have been lost to him for over 400 years directly." The assumption that black patriarchy would redeem the race, solve all our problems, is pure fantasy. We have only to examine critically the lives and works of black males who have attained the status of respected patriarch to find evidence that their gaining the right to exercise patriarchal power in the home and workplace did not and does not lead to rejuvenation of the race, or even to a better life for black men, women, and children.

Gilroy affirms concerns expressed in most of my feminist writing, particularly my essay "Reconstructing Black Masculinity," from my book *Black Looks*, when he points to the dangers that arise when "the integrity of the race" becomes "interchangeable with the integrity of black masculinity." He suggests: "This results in a situation where the social and economic crises of entire communities become most easily intelligible to those they engulf as a protracted crisis of masculinity. Without wanting to undermine struggles over the meaning of black masculinity and its sometimes destructive and anti-communitarian consequences, it seems important to reckon with the limitations of a perspective which seeks to restore masculinity rather than work carefully towards something like its transcendence." Masculinity need not be equated with sexist notions of manhood. Were black folks to take seriously the feminist critique that suggests we must interrogate patriarchal masculinity to see the ways it has been and is destructive to black males, our focus would be on repudiating this masculinity and redefining masculinity in terms that would be more life affirming. Just as we have needed to reconceptualize blackness so that we throw off the internalized racism that would have us see it solely as a negative sign, we must rethink our understanding of masculinity and manhood.

Richard Majors's book *Cool Pose* is an example of one black male scholar's attempt to question destructive notions of self and identity for black men. Co-authored with a white female scholar, this book is useful even though it does not embrace a feminist standpoint. Similar to Robert Bly's work, Majors's volume offers strategies black men can use to be in touch with their feelings, desires, needs, etc., without challenging patriarchy. Underlying Majors's work is the assumption that benevolent patriarchy is not problematic. While critical of black male violence, he does not relate that violence to attempts to live up to sexist-defined notions of manhood. The glaring absence of references to black feminist work, even when he made similar arguments, suggests Majors's desire to disassociate his work from ours. That is a pity.

Since black men and women are not solving the dilemmas of black life by creating a strong black patriarchy, if many of us could stop clinging to the utopian belief that this is the "answer" to our problems we could collectively begin to think about different models for social change in black life. Even at its best the patriarchal paradigm as a model for social organization undermines the unity of family and community. Reliance on a single male authority figure is dangerous because it creates a climate of autocracy where the politics of coercion (and that includes violence) are used to maintain that authority.

If we start with the premise that black liberation struggle, and all our efforts at self-determination, are strengthened when black males and females participate as equals in daily life and in struggle, it is clear that we cannot create a cultural climate where these conditions exist without first committing ourselves to a feminist agenda that is specific to black life, that concerns itself with ending sexism and sexist oppression in our diverse communities. To advance this agenda we would need to rethink our notions of manhood and womanhood. Rather than continuing to see them as opposites, with different "inherent" characteristics, we would need to recognize biological differences without seeing them as markers of specific character traits. This would mean no longer thinking that it is "natural" for boys to be strong and girls to be weak, for boys to be active and girls passive. Our task in parenting and in education would be to encourage in both females and males the capacity to be wholistic, to be capable of being both strong and weak, active and passive, etc., in response to specific contexts. Rather than defining manhood in relation to sexuality, we would acknowledge it in relation to biology: boys become men, girls women, with the understanding that both categories are synonymous with selfhood.

Usually when black folks urge young black males to be "men" they are really urging them to be responsible, to be accountable for their actions. These are qualities needed for self-actualization. They are needed by both black males and females. When they are equated in the male child's imagination with this mysterious unattainable "manhood" not only do they seem unrealizable but they seem more to be traits that confine and limit rather than liberate. Hence the need to rebel against them. Growing up in a patriarchal household with a strong black male provider and disciplinarian, it was evident that my brother resented the pressure to be a "man" and saw it as a burden. For example: When we were children together we shared a toy—a little red wheelbarrow. My brother was taught that it was his task as the "male" to push me in the wheelbarrow. He associated the pushing with work and getting the ride with pleasure. As soon as we were out of the sight of adults he would dump me. His early sense of what it was to be "the little man" was associated with having no pleasure. How differently we could have seen things if we had both been taught to share mutually the pleasure of riding and the work of pushing. Throughout my brother's growth into manhood, he has resisted efforts to be responsible, seeing them as meaning the absence of pleasure. In this sense he did not want to conform to a patriarchal sexist notion of malehood. Without an alternative that would have given him a sense of self-actualization that would have included pleasure, he fell into shiftless patterns and addictive habits.

Most black females have not been socialized to be "women" in the traditional sexist sense—that is, to be weak and/or subordinate. Had we been socialized this way historically, most black communities and families would not have survived. Other traits were needed so that we could enter the workforce, head families, if need be act as providers and protectors. In an oppositional manner, black females learned these traits while also learning ways to be feminine, to act subordinate (not surprising many of us do not choose to be subordinate), depending on the social context. More than ever before, black females today are concerned with issues of femininity even though most of us cannot lead lives where our primary focus is on how we look, what we will wear, and how well we will submit to male authority.

It would be liberatory both to black males and females for us to rethink whether appropriation of conventional sexist norms has advanced black life. To expect black men to act as "protectors" and "providers" as a way of earning the status of patriarch seems ludicrous given the economy, the shift in gender roles, the inability of many black males to provide either economically or emotionally for themselves, and their inability to protect themselves against life-threatening white supremacist capitalist patriarchal assault, with which they are all too often complicit—for example, black on black homicide. (This homicide is itself an expression of patriarchal masculinity, as it is patriarchy that demands that males prove their manhood.)

Connected to the utopian hope that the establishment of black patriarchy will heal our collective wounds is our persistent clinging to the trope of "family" as the only site of redemption. Usually the vision of a "healthy" black family is equated with patriarchal, father-headed households. Gilroy suggests we should rethink our investment in this unidimensional sense of family: "I want to ask whether the growing centrality of the family trope within black political and academic discourse points to the emergence of a distinctive and emphatically post-national variety of racial essentialism. The appeal to family should be understood as both the symptom and the signature of a neo-nationalist outlook that is best understood as a flexible essentialism." Importantly, Gilroy contrasts the idea of an "ideal, imaginary, and pastoral black family" with the reality of "authoritarian representations of blackness." Unlike Gilroy, I do not have problems with a vision of social change in black life that returns to a trope of family life as a location for redemption. I think it is a crucial and important site for education for critical consciousness, decolonization, etc. The problem lies with the insistence that the redemptive family be patriarchal. It should be more than clear if not from black life then from the experiences of white folks, documented in feminist writings, that the patriarchal family presents no model for liberation.

Contrary to popular belief, black folks have always upheld the primacy of patriarchy if only symbolically. Whether males have been present in black families in the United States or not, many black females in their roles as heads of households assumed an authoritarian, symbolically patriarchal stance. Contrary to racist/sexist stereotypes that would have everyone believe black women were more than willing to assume the "male" role, in their roles as heads of households, most black women validated the superiority of maleness, the importance of the male role, even as they may also have critiqued black men for not assuming that role. Like all other groups in this society, black families in the United States have been just as invested in structuring families so that the ideology of patriarchy and authoritarianism is reproduced even when no males are present. Black males raised by single mothers offer endless testimony of the extent to which they were bombarded with socialization about the importance of "being a man." The absence of men in these homes did not mean that male presence was not overvalued and longed for. All too often folks assume that the black female critique of no-good shiftless black masculinity is a declaration of independence, when in fact it usually masks a deep longing for that benevolent patriarchal male to appear so that she will not have to be responsible for every aspect of life.

Family is a significant site of socialization and politicization precisely because it is there that most of us learn our ideas about race, gender, and class. If we ignore family and act as though we can look to other structures for education for critical consciousness, we ignore the significance of early identity and value formation. To speak about a progressive, nonauthoritarian black family as one site of redemption (as I often do in my work) is important. This is not the same notion of family as mini-nation, sentimentally evoked by fascists and narrow nationalist thinkers, the family Hitler dreamed of when he declared: "If we say the world of the man is the state, the world of the man is his commitment, his struggle on behalf of the community, we could then perhaps say that the world of the woman is a smaller world. For her world is her husband, her family, her children and her home. But where would the big world be if no one wanted to look after the small world. . . . The big world cannot survive if the small world is not secure." It is this vision of family that must be altered in black consciousness if we are to address the serious crisis in black life. Rather than working from a seriously flawed patriarchal model as the "ideal," we need to address the real black family which is diverse and acknowledge the positive possibilities that exist for transformation in all black family structures.

The reality is this. Patriarchal families are not safe, constructive places for the development of identities and kinship ties free of the crippling weight of domination. Patriarchy is about domination. Rather than organize black families around the principle of authoritarian rule of the strong over the weak, we can organize (as some of us do) our understanding of family around anti-patriarchal, anti-authoritarian models that posit love as the central guiding principle. Recognizing love as the effort we make to create a context of growth, emotional, spiritual, and intellectual, families would emphasize mutual cooperation, the value of negotiation, processing, and the sharing of resources. Embracing a feminist standpoint can serve as an inspiration for transforming the family as we now know it. We need to have black scholars look at existing nonpatriarchal black families to document the ways that they work better, to share this knowledge with us. Rather than endlessly attacking single-parent households, particularly those headed by black females, we need to call attention to those households that are nonpatriarchal and show that they are sites for productive self-actualization for black adults and children. Even those black folks who continue to believe that the patriarchal family is the only "healthy" model are willing to acknowledge that homes characterized by male abuse of women and children are not more healthy than single-parent families where love abides. Unfortunately, these folks often refuse to see how widespread male domination and abuse is in the home or that patriarchal values promote the use of aggression and coercion. While offer-

ing no model for change, Nathan McCall emphasizes the
potential for abuse in black family life in *Makes Me Wanna
Holler*: "A two-parent home is no better off than a single-
parent one if the father is fucked up in the head and beaten
down. There's nothing more dangerous and destructive in a
household than a frustrated, oppressed black man." Yet
McCall does not challenge patriarchy as an organizing principle in black family life. We cannot end abuse in black family
life without repudiating the patriarchal model.

This repudiation requires critical examination of the behaviors that are seen as affirming manhood. Within black
life, as well as in mainstream society, males prove they are
"men" by the exhibition of antisocial behavior, lack of consideration for the needs of others, refusal to communicate, un-
willingness to show nurturance and care. Here I am not
speaking about traits adult males cultivate, I am talking about
the traits little boys learn early in life to associate with manhood and act out. These traits are the subject of John Stoltenberg's book *The End of Method: A Book for Men of
Conscience*, which is full of great ideas yet often written in
an inaccessible manner. Stoltenberg offers the powerful insight that males in patriarchy learn to value the assertion of
manhood over all else (and that includes love of justice),
sharing that this manhood is constantly determined by the
dynamics of male interpersonal relationships. He contends:
"When a man has decided to love manhood more than justice, there are predictable consequences in all his relationships with women. When a man remains loyal to other men's
judgment on his manhood, any woman he relates to is set
up to be a potential 'third party' in some truce he may need
to transact with another man, in order to pass in that other
man's eyes as having an adequate manhood act." Certainly,
black males know intimately that aspect of homo-social bond-

ing that is centered on measuring one's self against the standards set by other men. Usually this begins with boys measuring themselves against authoritarian adult males or boys with more status and power.

Since most black men (along with most black women and children) are socialized to equate manhood with justice, the first issue on our agenda has to be individual and collective acknowledgment that justice and the integrity of the race must be defined by the extent to which black males and females have the freedom to be self-determining. Black freedom can never be measured by the extent to which black males gain the right to assert patriarchal power. Once this thinking is unlearned, black folks can begin to create a cultural climate where we can embrace an ethical commitment to freedom and justice that includes us all. When this happens we make it possible for black males to break with patriarchal thinking that would deny "justice" to everyone and we challenge them to open their hearts and minds to receive a redemptive vision of freedom. It is this love of justice that can transform black male consciousness. It can emerge only as black males refuse to play the game—refuse patriarchal definitions of manhood. Stoltenberg shares the insight that "learning to live as a man of conscience is a matter of learning how to recognize those dynamics and deciding to keep the effects of these dynamics out of the way of your life. . . . Learning to live as a man of conscience means deciding that your loyalty to the people whom you love is *always* more important than whatever lingering loyalty you may sometimes feel to other men's judgment on your manhood." Black male repudiation of the equation of patriarchal manhood with freedom would create a profound positive revolution in black life. Tragically, none of our powerful black male leaders (for example, Malcolm X, who before his death had begun to think critically about the need to be disloyal to patriarchy) have offered this liberatory message to black communities even if they have used this way of thinking to transform their lives. Black males are afraid of being seen as "pussywhipped" by women, by other black men, by males or females who advocate feminist politics. Primarily, black straight men who are in recovery movements and/or individual therapy are among those individuals daring both to critique traditionally sexist notions of black masculinity and to change their behaviors, but they do not yet have a public forum. These men must join in solidarity with black female comrades and make their voices heard.

The crisis in black life has been created in part because of the continued support of patriarchy and the misguided paradigms for social change that emerge from a patriarchal mindset. Unless black folks, male and female, along with our allies in struggle can rise to the challenge—dare to critique patriarchy as well as courageously to offer redemptive liberatory models for social change—collectively we will remain at an impasse, stuck, unable to move forward. Until challenging sexism is always on the agenda we will remain unable to create the life-affirming, redemptive, transformational politics that would counter the rampant despair and sense of hopelessness in black life.

THE INTEGRITY OF
BLACK WOMANHOOD

C hallenging and changing the devaluation of black womanhood in this society is central to any effort to end racism. As early as 1887 black woman activist Ida B. Wells wrote an article titled "Our Women" which appeared in the newspaper *New York Freeman*, in which she emphasized the way white supremacist degradation of black womanhood served to undermine anti-racist struggle. Wells declared: "Among the many things that have transpired to dishearten the Negroes in their effort to attain a level in the status of civilized races, has been the wholesale contemptuous defamation of [black] women." Particularly concerned about the attacks on black women's morality, Wells suggested that within the sphere of white supremacist assault on black womanhood nothing was as hurtful quite as "deeply and keenly as the taunt of immorality; the jest and sneer with which our women are spoken of, and the utter incapacity or refusal to believe there are among us mothers, wives, and maidens who have attained a true, noble, and refining womanhood." When I published my first feminist book in 1981,

Ain't I a Woman: Black Women and Feminism, I included a chapter called "Continued Devaluation of Black Womanhood." Calling attention to the way in which "myths and stereotypes used to characterize black womanhood have their roots in negative anti-woman mythology," I stressed that these negative standpoints "form the basis of most critical inquiry into the nature of black female experience." Devaluation of black womanhood is central to the maintenance of white supremacist capitalist patriarchy.

Black women active in the struggle for black liberation and all social movements advocating women's rights both in the past and in the present have continually resisted this devaluation. Our resistance has intensified as we have struggled to place transforming cultural attitudes about the representation of black women on the agendas of both black liberation movement and contemporary feminist movement. Indeed, militant black female resistance to racist/sexist representations of our reality gained momentum as individual black women asserted leadership in both the production of feminist theory and feminist political practice. Working to critically interrogate and challenge racist/sexist representations, revolutionary feminist black women have offered to all black people, and everyone else, a progressive anti-racist, anti-sexist standpoint that fundamentally alters old ways of thinking about black female reality. Though well received by black women who are struggling to decolonize their minds and educate themselves for political consciousness (and our allies in struggle), these resistance efforts are continually undermined by white supremacist capitalist patriarchal assaults on black womanhood. Those assaults are evident in the mass media which continue to serve as the primary propaganda machine for the dissemination of white supremacist capitalist patriarchal thought and values.

Assailed on the one hand by white patriarchy and on the other hand by sexist black men and racist white women, black women must be ever vigilant in our struggle to challenge and transform the devaluation of black womanhood. Those of us who advocate feminist politics must continually counter representations of our reality that depict us as race traitors. Throughout our history in the United States, patriarchal black nationalism has consistently represented any black female who dares to question sexism and misogyny as a betrayer of the race. From its inception, this thinking has overlapped with assumptions about black womanhood perpetuated by white supremacist thought (for example, notions that black women are somehow more inherently treacherous, devious, lacking in morality and ethics than male counterparts; that we derive benefits and privileges from patriarchy because we are somehow, as sexist thinking would have it, inherently predisposed on the basis of our gender to lie, cheat, and betray). These negative stereotypes about black womanhood usually shape the way we are represented in mainstream mass media. Consequently, a suspicious light is almost always cast on the achievements of individual black women who become self-determining despite the barriers created by institutionalized structures of domination, by race, sex, and class exploitation and/or oppression. Most recently in the wake of an overall attack on feminist politics in our society, black women are once again represented in mainstream media as liars, as lacking in ethical and moral values, as potential traitors. Liberal white male patriarchy has promoted this devaluation as much as its conservative counterpart. The most recent examples of the assault on black womanhood emerge from the heart of American government: the defamation of Anita Hill's character during the Clarence Thomas hearings, President Clinton's refusal to support the appointment of civil rights attorney Lani Guinier, and his insistence that Joycelyn Elders resign her position as surgeon general. These three cases have received global attention. In each one these black women are represented as liars, as uppity, disobedient, disloyal, and out of control. Mainstream mass media would have the world believe that no systematic genocidal assault on black womanhood exists in the United States, that black women are our own worst enemies.

Often white racists are joined in this devaluation of black womanhood by sexist black male peers who continue to act as though all efforts on the part of black women to assert liberatory agency in our lives are really attacks on black manhood, acts of betrayal that are meant to keep the black male down. Orlando Patterson's essay "Blacklash" is a fine example of this type of thinking. While this essay purports to address the gender crisis among African Americans, Patterson cannot approach his topic without first diminishing the work of black women by suggesting that "contemporary African-American feminist thought has badly obscured our understanding of gender relations." Throughout his piece he pits black women and men against one another in an effort to reiterate the sexist/racist assumption that first appeared in the white supremacist rhetoric of slavery which claimed that black women, because of their "gender," are more likely to be given privileges and benefits in the existing social structure. It was this thinking that was expressed in the old-time folk saying "a nigger woman and a white man are de freest things on this earth." Embedded in such thinking is the misogynist assumption that biology gives black females an advantage since they can appeal to the sexual licentiousness of white men to negotiate advancement. This may seem like a networking edge to black males who are mired in sexist thinking but it is simply exploitation in the minds of most black women.

Since contemporary feminist movement began, and created more of a cultural space for feminist black female voices to come out of the shadows and be heard—a space for more of us to gain access to power and privilege within the existing social structure—sexist black men have felt threatened. Yet they do not present the threat as a challenge to the patriarchal mindset they refuse to give up but rather represent black women engaged in feminist politics as usurping benefits and privileges that if bestowed exclusively on black men would benefit racial uplift. The notion that somehow black males are more committed to racial uplift and black liberation struggle than their female counterparts is an idea that has its foundation in patriarchal assumptions of gender values. Black women's roles in struggles for black liberation have always been and continue to be subordinated to those of black males. Sexist black men (and their female allies) want to keep it that way. They have no difficulty supporting those white men and women who promote gender divisiveness among black people, who pit black women and men against one another. Concurrently, in separatist black nationalist locations, black women are continually represented as race traitors who must be disciplined and kept in place by strong non-emasculated black men. Haile Gerima's popular film *Sankofa* gave viewers an Afrocentric representation of the betraying black woman who redeems herself when she submits to reeducation by a strong black male teacher/healer. In this same film, the bi-racial black male (child of a strong black mother and the white colonizer) can assume his rightful place as warrior challenging the system only after he murders the black female "matriarch." Again and again the rhetoric of black nationalism which supports patriarchy suggests that the "death" of strong black women whether literal or symbolic is needed for the redemption of black masculinity, which is then made synonymous with redemption of the race.

All the recent mass media focus on black males, labeling

them as an "endangered species," reinscribes white supremacist capitalist patriarchal scapegoating of black womanhood
by the constant insistence that black women are to "blame"
for the dilemmas black males face and not white supremacy
and/or patriarchy. Whether it is a small academic journal like
Transition publishing articles with undocumented data that
suggest black professional women are earning more than
black men or a similar representation in the magazine section
of the *New York Times*, the message is the same—black
women are gaining benefits at the expense of black men.
Such thinking promotes divisiveness between black women
and men. It continues racist/sexist devaluation of black
women as well as condoning violent repression as a means
of keeping uppity black women in check. This assault is usually overtly directed at professional black women yet it con-
verges with the more vicious sustained and insidious assault
on single black mothers, especially those who receive welfare.

Before Daniel Patrick Moynihan launched his patriarchal
attack on black women in 1960 when he prepared a report
for President Johnson's War on Poverty, which blamed
black female–headed households for the dilemmas black males
faced in this society and not racist assault, sexist black men
from slavery times on had created a paradigm for black racial
uplift that was fundamentally based on the assumption that
acquisition of patriarchal power and privilege was the standard by which black liberation would be judged. Recent mass
media focus on black female–headed households reinscribes
Moynihan's perspective. Once again black feminist thinkers
and our allies in struggle must militantly challenge sexist/
racist representation that would have everyone believe that
black women are responsible for the many dilemmas black
families are facing. Black women are blamed for poverty,
joblessness, black male aggression, and violence both inside

and outside the home. Drawing on the work of black women scholars who have consistently critiqued Moynihan's notion of black matriarchy, feminist activists in the recently published anthology *The Coming of Black Genocide* launch a fresh critique of this racist/sexist doctrine, calling attention to the fact that it converged with black male sexist thought:

> Another reason that Moynihan-ism never died is that it played on the chords of sexism within the Black community. Don't forget that the White House only agreed to risk that public conference because Moynihan had gotten private agreement from many Black [male] leaders. His sexist theories about the harmful Black "matriarchy" were borrowed A to Z from the writings of Black sociologist E. Franklin Frazier of Howard University. Even that zingy line that most angered Black women—of their families being only "a tangle of pathology"—was only Moynihan quoting E. Franklin Frazier.... Moynihanism was a last grope by the patriarchal ruling class, to explore a sucker's alliance with Black bourgie men against Black women and children. It wasn't just a white thing.

Currently conservative and liberal sexist black male political leaders and scholars are primary advocates of a reformist patriarchal vision of racial uplift that not only scapegoats black women, particularly black single mothers, but aggressively works to deny welfare benefits. Their sexism and misogyny is once again masked by a polemical rhetoric of care and concern about black families.

In her excellent work *The Rising Song of African-American Women* insurgent black woman intellectual and activist Barbara Omolade offers a critical analysis of this assault on black womanhood both from within black community and without in her chapter "It's a Family Affair," pointing out that "black women who do need welfare are subjected to a system whose implicit assumption is that it's a crime for men not to support women and children and for women not to force men to support them. That system blames Black women for 'allowing' men to impregnate them without benefit of marriage or money. Welfare policies confuse the economic issue of how to support a family with the personal issues of sexuality and procreation, and this confusion shapes the perception of Black female-headed households as lacking men rather than money." Concurrently, embedded in all the critiques of black female-headed households is the assumption that somehow these individuals are actively seeking to prevent black men from assuming the roles patriarchal masculinity would have them perform. In actuality, the absence of adult black male presence in female-headed households as either providers or authority figures does not mean that patriarchal thinking and overvaluation of maleness are not the norm in those domestic households. Single black women raised in this society have internalized sexist thinking as much as any other group. The fact that economic circumstance coupled with planned or unplanned pregnancies may lead them to head households does not mean that they do not support male domination or teach patriarchal values to their children. In fact, the vast majority of black male children raised in such environments offer poignant passionate testimony about the way they are socialized by single black mothers to embrace patriarchal notions of masculinity, whether they can realistically actualize these identities or not.

For the most part, liberal and radical black women active in feminist movement have not joined together to embrace those forms of feminist activism that would effectively challenge white supremacist capitalist patriarchy's assault on single black mothers. Unfortunately, too many of these women hold bourgeois values and are as suspicious and condemnatory of poor black women as their male counterparts. Needless to say the masses of white women who had no difficulty championing Anita Hill when she rightly exposed Clarence Thomas as a sexual harasser (a case they felt was tied to their own class interests and feminist concerns) offer little activist zeal to challenge and counter the denigration of poor single mothers, especially black females.

Until progressive women and men engaged in anti-racist, anti-sexist work fully recognize that continued devaluation of black womanhood undermines these struggles neither movement can progress. We must vigilantly challenge negative representations of black women, understanding that they both shape public policy and determine attitudes towards us in everyday life. All too often progressive white women and men who are committed to a feminist vision fall prey to liberal sentimental overvaluing of black male pain in ways that lead them to accept sexist behavior from this group that they would rigorously challenge in interactions with white peers. These folks often stand idly by as sexist black men assault the dignity and integrity of black womanhood. Concurrently, those individual black males who have embraced feminist politics in ways that enable them to divest of both sexist thinking and action must play a primary role in challenging sexist representations of black womanhood, particularly those that are created by black male leaders and thinkers who have access to mass media. All black females gain when we challenge the continued devaluation of black womanhood. The struggle black women began in the nineteenth century to challenge and transform white supremacist capitalist patriarchal ways of seeing black womanhood must continue.

FEMINISM

IT'S A BLACK THING

More black men than ever before acknowledge that sexism is a problem in black life. Yet rarely is that acknowledgment linked with progressive political struggle to end sexism, to critique and challenge patriarchy. While these black men can acknowledge that sexism is an issue, they tend to see it as a "natural" response, one that need not be altered. In more recent years some black males link sexist thinking and action to their sense of victimization by racist exploitation and oppression. Extreme expressions of sexism, misogyny, made visible by overt exploitation of women by men, become in their minds a dysfunctional response to racism rather than a perspective that exists both apart from and in conjunction with racism.

Such thinking enables black males to assume no direct accountability for a politics of sexism that in reality does not have its origin in racist aggression. To see sexism as an outcome of racist victimization is to construct a worldview wherein black males can easily deflect attention away from the power and privileges accorded them by maleness within white supremacist capitalist patriarchy, however relative, even as they simultaneously undermine the seriousness of sexist exploitation by insisting that the problem is ultimately, and always, only racism. This overlapping of the two systems of domination, in ways that deflect attention away from black male accountability for sexist exploitation of black females, was evoked in a recent interview with black male journalist Nathan McCall, highlighting the publication of his autobiographical work *Makes Me Wanna Holler*. McCall comments: "If you hate what's black it doesn't matter if it's a man or a woman. And if it's a woman it's even more convenient because women are subjugated. It's understood that the only folks in this world who are at the mercy of black men are black women." While there are culprits in racist aggression against black males, there are no culprits who subjugate black women in McCall's rhetoric. Female subjugation is presented as "natural," already in place, not something black men create, only something they exploit. McCall shares his understanding of black male sexist aggression towards black females: "A common response to oppression, or abuse, is to become an abuser. Black men don't have the traditional avenues that other men in this society have for expressing what we consider manhood." These assumptions, presented as fact, are dangerous. They belie the reality that white men, and individual men from diverse groups who have access to all the traditional avenues of power and privilege, willingly perpetuate sexism and sexist exploitation and oppression. Concurrently, as long as access to patriarchal power and privilege in all avenues of life is presented as the balm that will heal the wounds inflicted on black men by racist victimization then maintaining sexism will be seen as essential not only to black male freedom but to the well-being of all black people.

When black men like Nathan McCall acknowledge a structure of sexist exploitation and/or oppression in black life that promotes the systematic abuse of black females, without in any way offering a critique or challenge to that structure, they reinscribe the assumption that sexist brutality cannot change or be eradicated. This tacit acceptance of a system they acknowledge to be wrong is a form of complicity. That complicity for seeing sexism in black life yet viewing it unproblematically is often shared by white individuals, even some liberal and progressive white feminists, who ignore and in some cases condone black male sexism when it is articulated as a response to racist aggression.

Linking sexism and racism in ways that condone one as a response to the other in contemporary society pits black males and females against one another. As long as individual black males (and some females) feel that their freedom cannot be attained without the establishment of patriarchal power and privilege, they will see black female struggles for self-determination, our engagement with feminist movement, as threatening. Convinced that the struggle to "save" the black race is really first and foremost about saving the lives of black males, they will not only continually insist that their "sufferings" are greater than those of black females, they will believe that the proud assertion of sexist politics registers a meaningful opposition to racism. Mainstream white culture has shown that it is far more willing to listen and respond to the dilemmas of black men when those dilemmas are articulated not as the harsh aftermath of white supremacist aggression and assault that affects all black folks but instead when these issues are mediated by a discourse of tragic, "failed," emasculated manhood. Within contemporary white supremacist capitalist patriarchy, the discourse of an unrealized wounded black manhood, which is constantly in jeopardy or under assault, that responds to victimization with brutal threatening aggression, is played out in public rhetoric that defines black males as an "endangered" species. Black males who are usually astute in their critique of racist stereotypes of black masculinity have not raised objections to the use of dehumanizing language that links black males to a public rhetoric that is usually evoked to talk about the extinction of wild animals. Instead some black males opportunistically exploited the racist/sexist rhetoric implied in the phrase "endangered species" to call attention to the serious impact of racism on black male lives. However, by not questioning this rhetoric they implicitly endorse the notion that there exists a black "bestial" masculinity, so central to racist/sexist iconography, that must be properly controlled, because it represents a danger to itself and others. Embedded in much of this rhetoric is the assumption that young black males would not represent a "danger" to white society if they could all be in training to be mature patriarchs. Conservative whites, and even some liberals, seem to be able to respond to the real dilemmas that affect black males only if the rhetoric that explains these problems shifts from white accountability to a focus on gender, wherein the creation of a context for "healthy" black masculinity to flourish is perceived to be the remedy and not confronting and changing white supremacy. As a consequence both black males and white society invest in a rhetoric of self-recovery for black males that explicitly perpetuates and maintains sexism and patriarchy.

Much of the recent emphasis on the need for special schools for black boys invests in a rhetoric of patriarchal thinking that uncritically embraces sexist-defined notions of manhood as the cure for all that ails black males. No one talks about the need for black girls to have positive black male role models that would offer them the kind of affirmation and care that could enhance their self-esteem. No one insists that young black males need positive black female role models whom they respect and treat with regard. All the rhetoric that privileges the self-esteem of black male children over that of girls maintains and perpetuates the assumption that sexist-defined sex roles are healthy, are the key to creating a non-dysfunctional black family. A major focus in schools for all black males is a militaristic emphasis on discipline. This seems especially significant since it was Daniel Patrick Moynihan who first suggested in his racist formulations of a theory of black matriarchy a sexist paradigm that would explain black male dysfunction by suggesting that they were castrated and emasculated by strong black females who prevented them from realizing manhood. His suggestion was that black males should enter the military, a world without women, wherein they could self-actualize. It is tragically ironic that black folks who once clearly saw the racism in this attempt to blame the problems black men face living in a white supremacist society on black females are now employing a similar mode of analysis. The notion that schools for all black boys which teach a patriarchal pedagogy, one that emphasizes both coercive discipline and obedience to authority, are a corrective to dysfunctional behavior is one that completely erases the extent to which patriarchal thinking promotes dysfunction. A recent article in *Black Issues in Higher Education* positively highlighted Detroit's African-centered academies for boys. The author states: "Discipline is one of the cornerstones of the academies' overall program. Teachers don't cut youngsters any slack. Students dress in uniforms which are inspected regularly, and must speak clearly and assertively in full sentences, and address adults in a proper manner." While it is positive for young black males and females to learn discipline and self-responsibility, those attitudes, values, and habits of being can be taught with pedagogical strategies that are liberatory, that do not rely on coercive control and punishment to reinforce positive behavior. It is obvious that militaristic models of education effectively teach young males behavior that may lead them to be more positively disciplined, etc. However, there is an extremely negative dimension to this coercive hierarchical model of education that no one talks about. If these young males are being taught to be disciplined within a learning community where they are also learning patriarchal thinking, how will they respond to females who do not conform to their expectations. As adult men will they attempt to subordinate black females using a discipline and punish model. Significantly, all the schools for young black males described in this article are called by the name of important black male figures—Paul Robeson, Malcolm X, or Marcus Garvey. Supporters of these schools, and others like them around the nation, rarely question the teaching of patriarchal perspectives. Even the critics are more concerned with whether there should be "African-centered" schools than with the issue of gender. In white supremacist capitalist patriarchy it is often just assumed that black gender relations will necessarily be retrograde, inferior to those of whites, be they conservative or progressive. Despite the cultural impact of feminist movement, most white and black critics in contemporary mass media do not extend the same critical awareness to gender issues when black folks are the center of attention. Individuals who support separate schools for black boys that emphasize a militaristic patriarchal pedagogy or for that matter any of the folks who push patriarchy using the guise of building strong black families do not have to confront an interrogating public, demanding hard evidence that patriarchy is healing to the psyches of black males who are assaulted by racism. There is no evidence that suggests patriarchal black males who are successful in the arena of work, who are not in prisons, who are not committing crimes on the street, are more humane in their relationships with black females or less powerful males than unsuccessful black males whom society deems dysfunctional and/or criminal. There is plenty of evidence to substantiate the reality that black men who have obtained class power, status, and privilege, like their white counterparts, often dominate females in assaultive coercive ways to maintain sexist power. Concurrently, many of the negative ways black males interact with one another, using coercive violence or assaultive verbal harassment, are behavior patterns reinforced by sexist constructions of masculine identity. Yet the extent to which embracing feminist thinking and practice could transform black male identity is never presented as an option by that public claiming to be concerned about the quality of life for black males in white supremacist capitalist patriarchy.

So far only small numbers of black males willingly engage feminist critique, seeing it from a standpoint that enables them to divest of learned engagement with patriarchal thinking that is fundamentally undermining and disenabling. Many black males accept and perpetuate sexist/racist notions about black manhood not only because they can receive more sympathetic attention from the dominant culture by focusing on a wounded masculinity but because by endorsing sexist thinking they also strengthen their alliances with white males. Throughout the history of black male presence in the United States, masculine physical prowess has been one of the few arenas where they are perceived as heterosexuals. Negative representations of lesbians and gay men abound in black life, precisely because they create a context of fear and condemnation that closes off the possibility that black heterosexuals will study and learn from the critical thinking and writing of black homosexuals. Much of the compelling critique and challenge to black male engagement with sexist thinking, with patriarchy, exists primarily in the work of gay black men. If straight black men never seek this literature and/or repudiate it, they deprive themselves of life-affirming and life-sustaining discussions of black masculinity. Homophobic thinking and action is a barrier that often prevents black males and females from choosing to learn about feminist thinking.

At the peak of contemporary feminist movement black males were one-upping white males by representing themselves as that group of males who had not capitulated to feminist demands that they rethink sexism. That repudiation of feminist thinking was highlighted when black males responded to the feminist fiction writing of black females like Alice Walker by once again flaunting their sexism and accusing her and other black women of being traitors to the race. To support the race, to not be seen as traitors, black women were and are still being told to express racial allegiance by passively accepting sexism and sexist domination. Recent anti-feminist backlash has led to the positive highlighting of black male sexism and phallocentrism. In public spheres of homo-social bonding black males inspire alternately fear and envy in white males by flaunting the "it's a dick thing" masculinity. Willingness to flaunt sexist behavior, coercive masculine domination of females, is one of the ways black males receive respect and admiration as well as rewards from white male peers. Often mainstream white culture condemns black male sexism if it impinges on its freedom even as it rewards it if the targets of that rage remain black females, less powerful black males, and advocates of feminist movement. The production and dissemination of rap music that perpetuates sexist and/or misogynist thinking, that condones the assertion of male domination over females by any means necessary, is a site of cultural production where black males are alternately punished and rewarded for this conduct. The punishment usually takes the form of public critique and censorship. Ultimately, the positive response to sexist and/or misogynist rap music (fame, wealth) reinforces the reality that these attitudes and values will be rewarded in this society. If black males find that they can make much more money flaunting lyrics that are sexist and misogynist, it is mainstream consumer culture that creates the demand for this product. If white supremacist capitalist patriarchy rewards black males for sexist behavior whether in the entertainment, sports, or political arena (i.e., the Thomas hearings) there are few incentives for black males to divest of sexist thinking.

Ultimately, sexist aggression by black males towards black females creates a cultural climate in black life where gender wars and conflicts claim the attention and energy that could be constructively used to create strategies for radical intervention that would challenge and undermine the existing racist and sexist systems of domination. As long as the vast majority of black males are brainwashed into thinking that sexist thinking enhances their lives, white patriarchy need never fear being dismantled by progressive black male insurrection. Nationalist black leaders male and female, whether they be in conservative religious organizations or represent themselves as spokespersons of more radical movements for liberation, continue to suffer failures of insight that lead them to invest in the notion that patriarchy is the only possible system of social organization that can bring stability to black family life and to the race.

Unfortunately, as long as the misguided assumption that patriarchal power compensates black males for the trauma of living in a white supremacist society and experiencing the trauma of perpetual racist assault is accepted without question, then the reproduction of sexist thinking and action will remain the norm in black life. Concurrently the negative consequences of sexist black male domination will remain a taboo subject. Those of us who break the silence will be continually cast as traitors. Until this silence is repeatedly broken, African Americans will never be able to constructively address issues of positive gender identity formation, domestic violence, rape, incest, or black male-on-male violence. We will not be able to challenge and critique sexism if the destructive impact of patriarchal thinking is always denied, covered up, masked as a response to racial victimization.

Individual, progressive black heterosexual males who engage a critique of domination that takes feminist thinking and practice seriously as a radical alternative to the push to institutionalize potentially exploitative and oppressive patriarchal regimes in black life must be more willing to act politically so that their counter hegemonic presence is visible. Working in collective solidarity with black women who are active in progressive movements for black self-determination that incorporate fully a feminist standpoint, these black men represent a vanguard group that could begin and sustain a cultural revolution that could vigilantly contest, challenge, and change sexism and misogyny in black life. All too often the anti-feminist perspective is the only voice that masses of black people have the opportunity to hear. It is this voice that most intimately addresses black folks across class. Progressive black women and men often end up speaking the most to mainstream white culture. While this speaking is necessary intervention, it must be coupled with an equally intense effort to address gender issues with strategies that articulate ways the struggle to end sexism can positively transform black life in diverse black communities. Black males who cling to sexist thinking and fantasies of patriarchal power need to know that a concrete engagement with feminist thinking would allow them to examine the ways their acceptance of patriarchal notions of masculine identity undermine their capacity to live fully and freely. No matter how clearly and passionately black women active in feminist thinking and progressive black liberation struggle critique patriarchal thinking and action, it ultimately deprives black males of the opportunity to construct self and identity in ways that are truly liberatory, that do not require the subordination and domination of anyone else, and ultimately only the testimony of black males can bear witness to this truth. We need to hear more from black males who repudiate domination as the only possible means of social intercourse between themselves and black females. We need to hear from those black males who are not sadomasochistically seduced by images of black females "at the mercy of black men." We need to hear from black males who have turned their gaze away from the colonizer's face and are able to look at gender and race with new eyes. Black men who can hear anew the prophetic words of Malcolm X urging us to change our minds: "We've got to change our own minds about each other. We have to see each other with new eyes. We have to see each other as brothers and sisters. We have to come together with warmth." Any black male or female who seriously contemplates this message of radical black self-determination would necessarily embrace the struggle to end sexism and sexist domination in black life. It is that struggle that offers us the hope of mutual intimacy, of a redemptive love that can extend beyond the limitations of utopian fantasies of family and nation, that can transcend narrowly constructed paradigms of identity formation and fixed sexual practice, a redemptive love that can indiscriminately offer every black male and female the hope that our suffering within white supremacist capitalist patriarchy will cease, that our wounds can be healed, that the struggle for black liberation can be realized in the politics of daily life.

REVOLUTIONARY FEMINISM

AN ANTI-RACIST AGENDA

Throughout the more than twenty years that I have spent writing feminist theory, I have consistently worked to make a clear distinction between revolutionary feminist politics and the more widely accepted version of feminism that has as its primary agenda achieving for white women of privileged classes social and economic equality with men of their class. In my first book, *Ain't I a Woman: Black Women and Feminism*, I suggested that the movement of masses of white women, particularly those from privileged-class backgrounds, into the workforce was not sanctioned simply by feminist thinking but by the very white supremacist capitalist patriarchal economic system that movement claimed to want to dismantle. Coming in the wake of civil rights struggle, of black power movements which were demanding cultural revolution, a sharing of the nation's material resources as well as an end to white supremacy, contemporary white women's liberation movement was easily co-opted to serve the interests of white patriarchy by reconsolidating white power, by keeping resources all in the family.

It should have come as no surprise to any of us that those white women who were mainly concerned with gaining equal access to domains of white male privilege quickly ceased to espouse a radical political agenda which included the dismantling of patriarchy as well as an anti-racist, anti-classist agenda. No doubt white patriarchal men must have found it amusing and affirming that many of the white women who had so vehemently and fiercely denounced domination were quite happy to assume the role of oppressor and/or exploiter if it meant that they could wield power equally with white men. Nor should it have surprised us that those individual white women who remained true to the radical and/or revolutionary vision of feminist politics, who had been among the vanguard of the struggle, were soon marginalized as feminist politics entered the mainstream. For example, many of the radical white women who struggled to establish women's studies in colleges and universities throughout the United States did not have doctoral degrees and were soon let go as patriarchal academic legitimation became more important than sisterhood and solidarity. Often to stay within this system individual white women were compelled to complete further graduate study, a process which was usually depoliticizing, which rewarded abandoning of radical feminist practice.

No critical intervention renewed the spirit of radical feminism that had been sorely diminished by patriarchal co-optation more than the insistence on the part of black women and other women of color that white women interrogate their racial identity and racial privilege. Ironically, many white women appropriated the discourse of race to advance their careers, drawing from the scholarship and critical thinking of black women even as they then bashed us for insisting that any meaningful feminist movement would necessarily have an anti-racist agenda. This bashing is most vehemently expressed in the work of self-proclaimed "white power-feminists" who would have everyone believe that there is no undermining of feminist politics when the central goal of the movement is to allow individual white women access to ruling-class wealth and power. It is this opportunistic appropriation of feminist thinking that consistently corrupts feminist politics, sending the clear message to disenfranchised poor and working-class women and men of all races that feminist movement is not for them. Given this message and the white supremacist agenda that is perpetuated by white power-feminism, it is not surprising that people of color who do not understand the history of the movement, who may not have access to revolutionary feminist thought and praxis, usually see feminism as a threat and do not see the uses these opportunistic white women have made of it. If people of color naively allow our understanding of feminist politics to be shaped by mass media which focus only on white power-feminism then we become complicit, denying ourselves and our diverse communities access to a resistance struggle that would provide strategies for challenging sexist exploitation and oppression in our lives.

To many black folks feminism continues to be seen as synonymous with bourgeois white women. As a consequence any black woman who uses the term risks being seen as a race traitor. The dismissal of black female voices that advocate feminist politics has intensified with the resurgence of narrow nationalist thinking that either invests in supporting the maintenance of patriarchal gender role or insists that embracing an Afrocentric worldview will necessarily return black females and males to an idyllic location where gender hierarchies do not exist. Again and again in my work I have had to reiterate that the racism of white women should be militantly challenged but that it should not act as a barrier preventing black women and men from engaging feminist politics. Even though Karl Marx was clearly racist in his thinking, this has never stopped black folks who seek to radicalize their consciousness around the issue of class from engaging Marxism. Surely it is patriarchal condescension that leads black folks, particularly sexist black men, to assume that black females are incapable of embracing revolutionary feminism in ways that would enhance rather than diminish black liberation, despite the continued overt racism and racist agendas of those groups of white women who can most easily lay claim to the term "feminism" and project their conservative and reactionary agendas. Often this condescension merely masks allegiance to sexism and patriarchal thinking in black life. Certainly, the labeling of black women who engage feminist thinking as race traitors is meant to prevent us from embracing feminist politics as surely as white power-feminism acts to exclude our voices and silence our critiques. In this case, both groups are acting to protect and maintain the privileges, however relative, that they receive in the existing social structure.

It is usually materially privileged white women who identify as feminists, and who have gained greater social equality and power with white men in the existing social structure, who resist most vehemently the revolutionary feminist insistence that an anti-racist agenda must be at the core of our movement if there is ever to be solidarity between women and effective coalitions that cross racial boundaries and unite us in common struggle. These are the women who are determined to leave the issue of race behind. Recently white women producers of an ABC news story on feminist movement went in search of radical/revolutionary feminists to appear on their show. I was called, then dismissed as inappropriate because I would raise the issue of race and racism, thereby—according to them—changing the subject. Similar silencing occurs in predominantly black public settings when race is the topic and black females approach these discussions from a feminist standpoint. We are seen as derailing or shifting the focus, not adding to the depth and complexity of our understanding. In such settings we are usually bashed into silence. Given these contexts it is no wonder that there are few black women who choose to publicly advocate revolutionary feminist politics. Indeed, the black female who engages issues of gender, even perhaps challenges sexism, can gain a hearing as long as she does not encourage black folks to embrace revolutionary feminism. Individual radical black women feminists who gain a public hearing usually do so by turning their backs on black constituencies, focusing their attention on white audiences. Often anti-feminist backlash is the excuse they give for not struggling to promote feminist politics in diverse black communities. Yet usually when one examines the history of their engagement, there is no record of any meaningful attempt to educate black communities for critical consciousness when it comes to the issue of feminism. Unfortunately the individual black women who do address gender issues in black settings tend to espouse liberal or conservative politics. They present the same old reformist social-equality white women's liberation agenda in blackface. Like their white female counterparts, these opportunistic black women are primarily concerned with gaining access to privilege within the existing structure.

Revolutionary feminist thinkers must consistently challenge white power-feminism so that our radical agendas are not completely erased by those white women who continue to support racism and white supremacy. Increasingly, more and more individual white revolutionary feminist activists are critiquing the racism of their white peers with the same militancy as their women-of-color peers. Let's be clear. It was individual black women and women of color who were and remain at the forefront of the struggle to maintain an antiracist revolutionary feminist agenda. It is a meaningful and powerful expression of solidarity and sisterhood that individual radical white women are daring to challenge courageously the racism of their peers. The essays in the collection *The Coming of Black Genocide*, a reprinting of articles from *Bottomfish Blues*, is a fine example. Described in the introduction as an underground Amazon publication, it has two main themes: to "radically challenge white women's complicity in both the on-going Black Genocide and the patriarchy's war against women." Reiterating the analysis first given by black women thinkers, myself included (who are never acknowledged or cited in this text), the anonymous authors courageously make connections between white supremacist perpetuation of black genocide and the women's movement for white equality. Their analysis is worth quoting at length:

> If the just-starting women's liberation movement had survived it would have divided white society, and would have seriously endangered the plans for Black Genocide. Born out of the sparks from Black liberation, with its own revolutionary pulse, women's liberation would have been guerilla movement behind enemy lines. It might have sabotaged the machinery of genocide. Just as the student antiwar movement did to the invasion of Vietnam. . . . The power structure neutralized women's liberation by smothering it under the "neutra-sweet" women's movement for white equality. And then pretended that they were both the same thing.

It is unfortunate that the revolutionary feminist thinkers who wrote these essays do not identify the work of those black women and other women of color engaged in feminist movement from its inception to the present day, work that has helped shape and clarify their thinking. This oversight makes it appear that they came "naturally" to divest of white supremacist thinking and allegiances rather than having developed this radical standpoint and practice via a process of education for critical consciousness about race and racism that is fundamentally rooted in the feminist pedagogy of black women. Without naming this input they can easily be seen as yet another group of radical white folks appropriating feminist critical discourse on race in ways that deny the vanguard activism of black women. By so doing they undermine a politics of solidarity.

The crude racism and white supremacy that surface in white power-feminism send the message that solidarity between white women and black women can never be a reality. To counter that message, those white women who are fundamentally committed to advocating revolutionary feminist thinking, which has as a core agenda anti-racist struggle, must dare to make their voices heard. Often the individual white women who have divested of white supremacy, and who show themselves again and again to be our allies in the struggle to end racism, rarely receive the limelight. Mass media certainly do not highlight their work. Concurrently, they do not shine a spotlight on individual black women or women of color who courageously work in solidarity educating and furthering the liberation of white women by helping them decolonize their minds and actions and engaging them as comrades as they struggle to divest fully of racist thought and behavior. It is a utopian dream to imagine that white women will divest of white supremacist thinking in isolation without critical engagement and dialectical exchange with non-white peers. It is concrete interaction between groups that is the proving ground, where our commitments to anti-racist behavior are tested and realized. While white women can and must assume a major voice speaking to and about anti-racist struggle to other white women, it is equally important that they learn to speak with and, if need be, make it necessary to speak for women of color in ways that do not reinscribe and perpetuate white supremacy.

This revolutionary interdependency is usefully outlined in Mab Segrest's book *Memoir of a Race Traitor*. She daringly critiques the way an ethic of competition can lead white women to seek the upper hand in all their relations, including those across race. Segrest contends:

> As a child of Europeans, a woman whose families have spent many generations on these shores, some of them in relative material privilege, my culture raised me to compete for grades, for jobs, for money, for self-esteem. As my lungs breathed in competition, they breathed out the stale air of individualism, delivering the toxic message: You are on your own. Being "queer" only amplified the problem. Traveling across race and class and cultural boundaries, my ear eventually became tuned to different vibrations so that I began to hear, first as a murmur, then as clearly articulated sound: We . . . are . . . in . . . this . . . together. My lungs relaxed some, my chest gasped the clearer air.

Women and men of all races who are committed to revolutionary feminist movement, who want to end sexism and sexist exploitation and oppression, recognize that we create and sustain the conditions for solidarity and coalition building by vigilantly challenging the ethic of competition, replacing it with a communal ethic of collective benefit. Those white women who write about race in ways that mask the debt they owe to black women and women-of-color thinkers often do so because they are working within structures that affirm competition, that encourage folks to make it appear that their ideas always come from some space of original thought. The ethic of competition does not place value on collaboration or dialectical exchange. It does not create an atmosphere where individuals who have white privilege and authority in relation to the discourse of race and racism can link their work to anti-racist struggle by repudiating the need to erase, render invisible, and/or devalue the work of non-white peers.

Honoring the engagement with black peers that enhanced her capacity to break with white supremacist thinking and fully commit to anti-racist struggle Segrest shares:

> Lenny taught me that fascism was about isolation, about political movements deliberately breaking down the human bonds between people so that they give blind allegiance to a leader or an ideology. Reverend Lee showed me how to go after the lost, to defy the isolation imposed by denial, terror and ideologies of hate. But I was lost myself, and I found myself, in part at least, in the acts of searching out others. It made me a different person—but not a better person—than either of my parents. To differentiate myself, I have had to accept the gifts they gave me, which paradoxically, I could not do until I was sure I am my own person. "When people have to choose, they go with their own race," my mother had said, but she was wrong. It is not a matter of choosing one race or family and betraying one another. The choice is for justice! community! humanity! the glimpse that we are all one organism. . . .

It is this understanding of revolutionary interdependency that must be shared if we are to reclaim a vision of feminist sisterhood that proudly acknowledges feminist commitment to anti-racist struggle. Advocates of revolutionary feminist movement are among that group of women and men who do not despair about the capacity of white folks to divest of white supremacy because we have engaged in resistance and seen the reality of solidarity emerge in the context of mutual commitment and struggle. These stories must be told to counter the mounting despair, to counter the claims of white power-feminism. There will be no feminist revolution without an end to racism and white supremacy. When all women and men engaged in feminist struggle understand the interlocking nature of systems of domination, of white supremacist capitalist patriarchy, feminist movement will regain its revolutionary progressive momentum.

TEACHING RESISTANCE

THE RACIAL POLITICS OF MASS MEDIA

W hen I began the process of education for critical consciousness to radicalize my thinking and action, I relied on the writings and life practices of Malcolm X, Paulo Freire, Albert Memmi, Frantz Fanon, Amical Cabral, Walter Rodney, and a host of other thinkers. The work of these teachers and political mentors led me to think about the absence of a discourse on colonialism in the United States. When thinking about the kind of language commonly evoked to talk about black experience in white supremacist capitalist patriarchal North America, I was often struck by the pervasive use of euphemisms, words like "Jim Crow," "Uncle Tom," "Miss Ann," etc. These colorful terms obscured the underlying structures of domination that kept white supremacy in place. By socializing white and black citizens in the United States to think of racism in personal terms, individuals could think of it as having more to do with inherent prejudicial feelings than with a consciously mapped-out strategy of domination that was systematically maintained. Even though African Americans in the United States had no country, whites took over and colonized; as a structure of domination that is defined as the conquest and ownership of a people by another, colonialism aptly describes the process by which blacks were and continue to be subordinated by white supremacy.

In the beginning black folks were most effectively colonized via a structure of ownership. Once slavery ended, white supremacy could be effectively maintained by the institutionalization of social apartheid and by creating a philosophy of racial inferiority that would be taught to everyone. This strategy of colonialism needed no country, for the space it sought to own and conquer was the minds of whites and blacks. As long as a harsh brutal system of racial apartheid was in place, separating blacks from whites by laws, coercive structures of punishment, and economic disenfranchisement, many black people seemed to intuitively understand that our ability to resist racist domination was nurtured by a refusal of the colonizing mindset. Segregation enabled black folks to maintain oppositional worldviews and standpoints to counter the effects of racism and to nurture resistance. The effectiveness of those survival strategies was made evident by both civil rights movements and the militant resistance that followed in their wake. This resistance to colonialism was so fierce, a new strategy was required to maintain and perpetuate white supremacy. Racial integration was that strategy. It was the setting for the emergence of neo-colonial white supremacy.

Placed in positions of authority in educational structures and on the job, white people could oversee and eradicate organized resistance. The new neo-colonial environment gave white folks even greater access and control over the African-American mind. Integrated educational structures were the locations where whites could best colonize the minds and imaginations of black folks. Television and mass media were the other great neo-colonial weapons. Contemporary African Americans often ponder how it is possible for the spirit of resistance to be so diminished today even though the structures of our lives continue to be shaped and informed by the dictates of white supremacy. The spirit of resistance that remained strong from slavery to the militant sixties was displaced when whites made it seem as though they were truly ready to grant black folks social equality, that there were indeed enough resources to go around, that the imperialist wealth of this country could be equitably shared. These assumptions were easy to believe given the success of sixties black militant struggle. By the time the bubble burst, collectively black folks had let our guard down and a more insidious colonization of our minds began to take place. While the Eurocentric biases taught to blacks in the educational system were meant to socialize us to believe in our inherent inferiority, it was ultimately the longing to have access to material rewards granted whites (the luxury and comfort represented in advertising and television) that was the greatest seduction. Aping whites, assimilating their values (i.e., white supremacist attitudes and assumptions) was clearly the way to achieve material success. And white supremacist values were projected into our living rooms, into the most intimate spaces of our lives by mass media. Gone was any separate space apart from whites where organized militant resistance could emerge. Even though most black communities were and remain segregated, mass media bring white supremacy into our lives, constantly reminding us of our marginalized status.

With the television on, whites were and are always with us, their voices, values, and beliefs echoing in our brains. It is this constant presence of the colonizing mindset passively consumed that undermines our capacity to resist white supremacy by cultivating oppositional worldviews. Even though

most African Americans do not identify with the experiences
of whites in real life or have intimate relationships with them,
these boundaries are crossed when we sit facing the television. When television was first invented and many black folks
could not afford TVs or did not have the luxury of time to
consume representations of whiteness all day long, a barrier
still existed between the value system of the dominant white
culture and the values of most black folks. That barrier was
torn down when televisions entered every living room. Movies function in a similar way. Not surprising, when black
Americans were denied easy access to white movies, black
cinema thrived. Once the images of whiteness were available
to everyone there was no black movie-going audience starv-
ing for black images. The hunger to see black folks on the
screen had been replaced by the desire to be close to the
Hollywood image, to whiteness. No studies have been done
that I know of which look at the role mass media have played
since 1960 in perpetuating and maintaining the values of
white supremacy. Constantly and passively consuming white
supremacist values both in educational systems and via pro-
longed engagement with mass media, contemporary black
folks, and everyone else in this society, are vulnerable to a
process of overt colonization that goes easily undetected. Acts
of blatant racism are rarely represented in mass-media images. Most television shows suggest via the liberal dialogues
that occur between white characters, or racially integrated
casts, that racism no longer serves as a barrier. Even though
there are very few black judges in the United States, television courtroom dramas cast black characters in these roles
in ways so disproportionate to the reality that it is almost
ludicrous. Yet the message sent to the American public and
folks all over the world watching American TV is that our
legal system has triumphed over racial discrimination, that

not only is there social equality but that black folks are often the ones in power. I know of no studies that have examined the role television has played in teaching white viewers that racism no longer exists. Many white folks who never have intimate contact with black folks now feel that they know what we are like because television has brought us into their homes. Whites may well believe that our presence on the screen and in their intimate living spaces means that the racial apartheid that keeps neighborhoods and schools segregated is the false reflection and that what we see on television represents the real.

Currently black folks are often depicted on television in situations where they charge racist victimization and then the viewer is bombarded with evidence that shows this to be a trumped-up charge, that whites are indeed far more caring and able to be social equals than "misguided" blacks realize. The message that television sends then is that the problem of racism lies with black people—that it exists in our minds and imaginations. On a recent episode of *Law and Order* a white lawyer directs anger at a black woman and tells her, "If you want to see the cause of racism, look in the mirror." Television does not hold white people responsible for white supremacy; it socializes them to believe that subjugation and subordination of black people by any means necessary is essential for the maintenance of law and order. Such thinking informed the vision of white folks who looked at the tape showing the brutal beating of Rodney King by a group of white men and saw a scenario where he was threatening white lives and they were merely keeping the peace.

Movies also offer us the vision of a world where white folks are liberal, eager to be social equals with blacks. The message of films like *Grand Canyon, Lethal Weapon, The Bodyguard*, and a host of other Hollywood films is that whites and blacks live together in harmony. Contemporary Hollywood films that show strife between races situate the tension around criminal behavior where black characters may exist as good or bad guys in the traditional racist cowboy scenario but where most whites, particularly heroic ones, are presented as capable of transcending the limitations of race.

For the most part television and movies depict a world where blacks and whites coexist in harmony although the subtext is clear; this harmony is maintained because no one really moves from the location white supremacy allocates to them on the race-sex hierarchy. Denzel Washington and Julia Roberts may play opposite one another in *The Pelican Brief* but there will not be a romance. True love in television and movies is almost always an occurrence between those who share the same race. When love happens across boundaries as in *The Bodyguard, Zebrahead,* or *A Bronx Tale,* it is doomed for no apparent reason and/or has tragic consequences. White and black people learning lessons from mass media about racial bonding are taught that curiosity about those who are racially different can be expressed as long as boundaries are not actually crossed and no genuine intimacy emerges. Many television viewers of all races and ethnicities were enchanted by a series called *I'll Fly Away* which highlighted a liberal white family's struggle in the South and the perspective of the black woman who works as a servant in their home. Even though the series is often centered on the maid, her status is never changed or challenged. Indeed she is one of the "stars" of the show. It does not disturb most viewers that at this moment in history black women continue to be represented in movies and on television as the servants of whites. The fact that a black woman can be cast in a dramatically compelling leading role as a servant does not intervene on racist/sexist stereotypes, it reinscribes them.

Hollywood awarded its first Oscar to a black person in 1939 when Hattie McDaniel won as Best Supporting Actress in *Gone With the Wind*. She played the maid. Contemporary films like *Fried Green Tomatoes* and *Passion Fish*, which offer viewers progressive visions of white females, still image black women in the same way—as servants. Even though the black female "servant" in *Passion Fish* comes from a middle-class background, drug addiction has led to her drop in status. And the film suggests that working secluded as the caretaker of a sick white woman redeems the black woman. It was twenty-four years after McDaniel won her Oscar that the only black man to ever receive this award won Best Actor. Sidney Poitier won for his role in the 1960s film *Lilies of the Field*. In this film he is also symbolically a "mammy" figure, playing an itinerant worker who caretakes a group of white nuns. Mass media consistently depict black folks either as servants or in subordinate roles, a placement which still suggests that we exist to bolster and caretake the needs of whites. Two examples that come to mind are the role of the black female FBI agent in *The Silence of the Lambs*, whose sole purpose is to bolster the ego of the white female lead played by Jodie Foster. And certainly in all the *Lethal Weapon* movies Danny Glover's character is there to be the buddy who because he is black and therefore subordinate can never eclipse the white male star. Black folks confront media that include us and subordinate our representation to that of whites, thereby reinscribing white supremacy.

While superficially appearing to present a portrait of racial social equality, mass media actually work to reinforce assumptions that black folks should always be cast in supporting roles in relation to white characters. That subordination is made to appear "natural" because most black characters are consistently portrayed as always a little less ethical and moral than whites, not given to rational reasonable action. It is not surprising that it is those black characters represented as didactic figures upholding the status quo who are portrayed as possessing positive characteristics. They are rational, ethical, moral peacemakers who help maintain law and order.

Significantly, the neo-colonial messages about the nature of race that are brought to us by mass media do not just shape whites' minds and imaginations. They socialize black and other non-white minds as well. Understanding the power of representations, black people have in both the past and present challenged how we are presented in mass media, especially if the images are perceived to be "negative," but we have not sufficiently challenged representations of blackness that are not obviously negative even though they act to reinforce white supremacy. Concurrently, we do not challenge the representations of whites. We were not outside movie theaters protesting when the white male lead character in *Paris Trout* brutally slaughters a little black girl (even though I can think of no other image of a child being brutally slaughtered in a mainstream film) or when the lead character in *A Perfect World* played by Kevin Costner terrorizes a black family who gives him shelter. Even though he is a murderer and an escaped convict, his character is portrayed sympathetically whereas the black male father is brutally tortured presumably because he is an unloving, abusive parent. In *A Perfect World* both the adult white male lead and the little white boy who stops him from killing the black man are shown to be ethically and morally superior to black people.

Films that present cinematic narratives that seek to intervene in and challenge white supremacist assumption, whether they are made by black or white folks, tend to receive negative attention or none at all. John Sayles's film *The Brother from Another Planet* successfully presented a black male

character in a lead role whose representation was oppositional. Rather than portraying a black male as a sidekick of
a more powerful white male, or as a brute and sex fiend, he
offered us the image of a gentle, healing, angelic black male
spirit. John Waters's film *Hairspray* was able to reach a larger
audience. In this movie, white people choose to be anti-
racist, to critique white privilege. Jim Jarmusch's film *Mystery Train* is incredibly deconstructive of racist assumptions.
When the movie begins we witness a young Japanese couple
arriving at the bus station in Memphis who begin to speak
Japanese with a black man who superficially appears to be
indigent. Racist stereotypes and class assumptions are challenged at this moment and throughout the film. White privilege and lack of understanding of the politics of racial
difference are exposed. Yet most viewers did not like this
film and it did not receive much attention. Julie Dash's film
Daughters of the Dust portrayed black folks in ways that
were radically different from Hollywood conventions. Many
white viewers and even some black viewers had difficulty
relating to these images. Radical representations of race in
television and movies demand that we be resisting viewers
and break our attachment to conventional representations.
These films, and others like them, demonstrate that film and
mass media in general can challenge neo-colonial representations that reinscribe racist stereotypes and perpetuate white supremacy. If more attention were given these films, it would
show that aware viewers long for mass media that act to challenge and change racist domination and white supremacy.

Until all Americans demand that mass media no longer
serve as the biggest propaganda machine for white supremacy, the socialization of everyone to subliminally absorb white
supremacist attitudes and values will continue. Even though
many white Americans do not overtly express racist thinking,

it does not mean that their underlying belief structures have not been saturated with an ideology of difference that says white is always, in every way, superior to that which is black. Yet so far no complex public discourse exists that explains the difference between that racism which led whites to enjoy lynching and murdering black people and that wherein a white person may have a black friend or lover yet still believe black folks are intellectually and morally inferior to whites.

Mainstream media's endorsement of *The Bell Curve* by Richard J. Herrnstein and Charles Murray reflects the American public's willingness to support racist doctrine that represents black people as genetically inferior. Anti-racist white male thinker and activist Edward Herman reminds us of the danger of such acceptance in his essay "The New Racist Onslaught":

> Built on black slavery, with segregation and poverty helping reinforce stereotypes after 1865, racism has deep and persistent roots in this country. Today, racist Bob Grant has a radio audience of 680,000 in New York City, and racist Rush Limbaugh has a supportive audience of millions (extending to Supreme Court Justice Clarence Thomas). Reagan with his repeated imagery of black welfare mothers exploiting the taxpayer, Bush with Willie Horton and the menace of "quotas," and a slew of code words bandied about by politicians, show that polarizing racist language and political strategies are acceptable and even integral parts of mainstream culture today.

When black psyches are daily bombarded by mass media representations that encourage us to see white people as more caring, intelligent, liberal, etc., it makes sense that many of us begin to internalize racist thinking.

Without an organized resistance movement that focuses on the role of mass media in the perpetuation and maintenance of white supremacy, nothing will change. Boycotts remain one of the most effective ways to call attention to this issue. Picketing outside theaters, turning off the television set, writing letters of protest are all low-risk small acts that can become major interventions. Mass media are neither neutral nor innocent when it comes to spreading the message of white supremacy. It is not far-fetched for us to assume that many more white Americans would be anti-racist if they were not socialized daily to embrace racist assumptions. Challenging mass media to divest of white supremacy should be the starting point of a renewed movement for racial justice.

BLACK BEAUTY AND
BLACK POWER

INTERNALIZED RACISM

No social movement to end white supremacy addressed the issue of internalized racism in relation to beauty as intensely as did the black power revolution of the sixties. For a time at least this movement challenged black folks to examine the psychic impact of white supremacy. Reading Frantz Fanon and Albert Memmi, our leaders began to speak of colonization and the need to decolonize our minds and imaginations. Exposing the myriad ways white supremacy had assaulted our self-concept and our self-esteem, militant leaders of black liberation struggle demanded that black folks see ourselves differently—see self-love as a radical political agenda. That meant establishing a politics of representation which would both critique and integrate ideals of personal beauty and desirability informed by racist standards and put in place progressive standards, a system of valuation that would embrace a diversity of black looks.

Ironically, as black leaders called into question racist-defined notions of beauty, many white folks expressed awe and wonder that there existed in segregated black life color-caste systems wherein the lighter one's skin the greater one's individual social value. Their surprise at the way color caste functioned in black life exposed the extent to which they chose to remain willfully ignorant of how systemic white supremacist thinking is established and maintained. Construction of color-caste hierarchies by white racists in nineteenth-century life is well documented in their history and literature. That contemporary white folks are ignorant of this history reflects the way the dominant culture seeks to deny, via erasure, a history of race relations that documents their accountability. This denial allows no space for accountability, no space for whites in contemporary culture to know and acknowledge the primary role whites played in the formation of color castes. All black folks, even those who know very little, if anything at all, about North American history, slavery, Reconstruction, etc., know that racist white folks often treated lighter-skinned black folks better than their darker counterparts and that this pattern was mirrored in black social relations. Individual black folks who grow to maturity in all-white settings that may have allowed them to remain ignorant of color-caste systems are soon initiated when they have contact with other black people.

Issues of skin color and caste were highlighted by militant black struggle for rights. The slogan "black is beautiful" worked to intervene in and alter those racist stereotypes that had always insisted black was ugly, monstrous, undesirable. One of the primary achievements of black power movement was the critique and in some instances dismantling of color-caste hierarchies. This achievement often goes unnoticed and undiscussed largely because it created major unseen and usually undocumented changes in the psyches of black folks, particularly those of us from working-class and/or poor backgrounds who did not have access to public forums where we could announce and discuss these changes. Coming of age before black power, most black folks faced the implications of color caste either through devaluation or overvaluation. In other words to be born light meant that one was born with an advantage, recognized by everyone. To be born dark was to start life handicapped, with a serious disadvantage. At the onset of contemporary feminist movement I had only recently stopped living in a segregated black world and begun life in predominantly white settings. I remember countering white female insistence that when a child is newly born and coming out of the womb the first concern is to identify gender, whether male or female, by calling attention to the reality that the initial concern for most black parents is skin color—this concern being a direct reflection of the correlation between skin color and success.

Militant black liberation struggle challenged this sensibility. It made it possible for black people to have an ongoing public discourse about the detrimental impact of internalized racism as regards skin color and beauty standards. Darker-skinned blacks, who had historically borne the brunt of devaluation based on color, were recognized as having been wronged by assaultive white supremacist aesthetic values. New beauty standards were set that sought to value and embrace the different complexions of blackness. Suddenly, the assumption that each individual black person, irrespective of sexual preference, would also seek a lighter partner was called into question. When our militant charismatic black male revolutionary leader Malcolm X chose to marry a darker-skinned woman, he set different standards. These changes had a profound impact on black family life. The needs of children who suffered various forms of discrimination and were psychologically wounded in families and/or public school systems because they were not the right color could be addressed. For example, parents of a dark-skinned child who when misbehaving at school would be called a devil or evil and unjustly punished now had recourse to material written by black psychologists and psychiatrists documenting the detrimental effects of the color-caste system. In all areas of black life the call to see black as beautiful was empowering. Large numbers of black women stopped chemically straightening our hair since there was no longer any negative stigma attached to wearing one's hair with its natural texture. Those folks who had often stood passively by while observing other black folks being mistreated on the basis of skin color felt for the first time that it was politically appropriate to intervene. I remember when I and my siblings challenged our grandmother, who could pass for white, about the disparaging comments she made about dark-skinned people, including her grandchildren. Even though we were in a small southern town, we were deeply affected by the call to end color-caste hierarchies. This process of decolonization created powerful changes in the lives of all black people in the United States. It meant that we could now militantly confront and change the devastating psychological consequences of internalized racism.

Even when contemporary collective militant black struggle for self-determination began to wane, alternative ways of seeing blackness and defining beauty continued to flourish. These changes diminished as assimilation became the process by which black folks could successfully enter the mainstream. Once again the fate of black folks rested with white power. If a black person wanted a job and found it easier to get it if he or she did not wear a natural hairstyle etc. this was perceived by many to be a legitimate reason to change. And of course many black and white folks felt that the gains in civil rights, racial integration, and the lifting of many long-standing racial taboos (for example, interracial relationships and the resistance to segregated housing) meant that militant struggle was no longer needed. Since freedom for black folks had been defined as gaining the rights to enter mainstream society, to assume the values and/or economic standing of white privileged classes, it logically follows that it did not take long for interracial interaction in the areas of education and jobs to reinstitutionalize, in less overt ways, a system wherein individual black folks who were most like white folks in the way they looked, talked, dressed, etc., would find it easier to be socially mobile. To some extent the dangers of assimilation to white standards were obscured by the assumption that our ways of seeing blackness had been fundamentally changed. Aware black activists did not assume that we would ever return to social conditions where black folks would once again be grappling with issues of color. While leaders like Eldridge Cleaver, Malcolm X, Huey Newton, and many others repeatedly made the issue of self-love central to black liberation struggle, once many rights were gained new activists did not continue the emphasis on decolonization. Many folks just assumed we had collectively resisted and altered color castes.

Few black activists were vigilant enough to see that concrete rewards for assimilation would undermine subversive oppositional ways of seeing blackness. Yet racial integration meant that many black folks were rejecting the ethic of communalism that had been a crucial survival strategy when racial apartheid was the norm and were embracing liberal individualism. Being free was seen as having the right to satisfy individual desire without accountability to a collective body. Consequently, black folks could now feel that the way they wore their hair was not political but simply a matter of choice. Seeking to improve class mobility, to make it in the white world, black folks began to backtrack and assume once again the attitudes and values of internalized racism. Some folks justified their decisions to compromise and assimilate white aesthetic standards by seeing it as simply "wearing the mask" to get over. This was best typified by those black females who wore straight "white looking" wigs to work covering natural hairdos. Unfortunately, black acceptance of assimilation meant that a politics of representation affirming white beauty standards was being reestablished as the norm.

Without an organized ongoing collective movement for black self-determination, militant conscious black critical thinkers and/or activists began to constitute a subculture. A revolutionary militant stance, one that seriously critiqued capitalism and imperialism, was no longer the message black masses internalized. Given these circumstances the radicalization of a leader like Martin Luther King went unnoticed by most black folks; his passionate critiques of militarism and capitalism were not heard. He continues to be remembered primarily for those earlier stages of political work wherein he supported a bourgeois model of assimilation and social mobility. Those black activists who remained in the public eye did not continue a militant critique and interrogation of white standards of beauty. While radical activists like Angela Davis who had major public forums continued to wear natural hair and be individually black identified, they did not make continued decolonization of our minds and imaginations central to their political agendas. They did not continually call for a focus on black self-love, on ending internalized racism.

Towards the end of the seventies, black folks were far less interested in calling attention to the perpetuation of racism and beauty standards. No one interrogated radical activists who began to straighten their hair, etc. It was assumed that internalized racial self-hatred was no longer and the way we wore our hair was merely an expression of liberal individualism. Heterosexual black male leaders openly chose their partners and spouses using the standards of the color-caste system. During the most militant stages of black power movement they had never really stopped allowing racist notions of beauty to define female desirability even as they preached a message of self-love and an end to internalized racism. This hypocrisy also played a major role in creating a framework where color-caste systems could become once again the accepted norm.

Resurgence of interest in black self-determination as well as growing overt white supremacy created a context in the eighties where attention could be given the issue of decolonization, of internalized racism. Mass media carried stories about the fact that black children had low self-esteem, that they preferred white images over black ones, that black girls liked white dolls better than black ones. This news was all presented with awe and wonder as though everyone was unaware that any political context could exist for the repudiation and devaluation of blackness. Yet the politics of racial assimilation had always operated as a form of backlash intended to undermine black self-determination. Not all black people closed our eyes to this reality. However, we did not have the access to mass media and public forums that would have made it possible for us to launch a sustained challenge to internalized racism. Most of us continued to fight against the internalization of white supremacist thinking on whatever fronts we found ourselves. As a professor I continually interrogate these issues in the classroom and as a writer in my books.

Nowadays, in some circles it is fashionable to mock black power struggle and see it solely as a failed social movement. It is easy for folks to make light of the slogan "black is beautiful." Yet this contemporary mockery does not change the reality that the interrogation of internalized racism embedded in this slogan and the many concrete challenges that took place in all areas of black life did produce radical changes even though they were undermined by white supremacist backlash. Most folks refuse to see the intensity of this backlash and place responsibility on radical black activists for having too superficial an agenda. The primary justifiable critique we can make of militant black liberation struggle is its failure to institutionalize sustained strategies of critical resistance. Collectively and individually we must all assume accountability for the resurgence of color-caste hierarchies in black life.

White supremacist capitalist patriarchal assaults on movements for black self-determination aimed at ending internalized racism were most effectively launched by mass media. Institutionalizing a politics of representation which ended years of racial segregation put black people on the screen even as the images produced were mirrored stereotypes. These representations undermined black self-determination. The affirmation of assimilation as well as racist white aesthetic standards became one of the most effective ways to undermine efforts to transform internalized racism in the psyches of the black masses. When these racist stereotypical images were coupled with a concrete reality whereby assimilated black folks were the ones receiving greater material reward, the culture was ripe for a resurgence of color-caste hierarchy.

Color-caste hierarchies embrace the issues of both skin color and hair texture. Since lighter-skinned black people often are genetically connected to intergenerational pairings of both white and black people, they tend to look more like whites. Females who were the offsprings of generations of interracial mixing are more likely to have long straight hair.

The exploitative and/or oppressive nature of color-caste systems in white supremacist society has always had a gendered component. A mixture of racist and sexist thinking informs the way color-caste hierarchies detrimentally affect the lives of black females differently than they do black males. Light skin and long straight hair continue to be traits that define a female as beautiful and desirable in the racist white imagination and in the colonized black mindset. Darker-skinned black females must work to develop positive body self-esteem in a society that continually devalues their image. To this day the image of black female bitchiness, evil temper, and treachery continues to be represented by someone with dark skin. Light-skinned women are never represented as Sapphires, only dark-skinned females occupy this devalued position. We see these images continually in mass media whether they be presented to us in television sitcoms (like the popular show *Martin*), on cop shows (the criminal "bad" black woman is usually dark), and in movies made by black and white directors alike. Spike Lee graphically portrayed conflict over skin color in his film *School Daze* not via male characters but by staging a dramatic fight between light-skinned women and their darker counterparts. His film merely exploited the issue. It was not critically subversive or oppositional. And in many theaters black audiences loudly expressed their continued investment in color-caste hierarchies by "dissing" darker-skinned female characters.

Throughout the history of white supremacy in the United States, racist white men have regarded the bi-racial white and black female as a sexual ideal. Black men have taken their cues from white men in this regard. Stereotypically portrayed as embodying a passionate sensual eroticism as well as a subordinate feminine nature, the bi-racial–looking black woman as well as the bi-racial woman has been and remains the standard other black females are measured against. Even when darker-skinned black women are given "play" in mass media, television, and movies their characters are usually subordinated to lighter-skinned females who are deemed more desirable. For a time films that portrayed the bi-racial–looking black woman as a "tragic mulatto" were passé but contemporary films like the powerful drama *One False Move* return this figure to center stage. Whereas the impact of militant black liberation struggle had once impressed upon white-dominated fashion magazines and black magazines to show diverse images of black female beauty, in more recent times it has been acceptable to simply highlight and valorize the image of the bi-racial–looking black woman and the bi-racial woman. Black women models like Naomi Campbell find that they have a greater crossover success if their images are altered by long straight wigs, weaves, or bonded hair so that they resemble the "wannabes"—folks who affirm the equation of whiteness with beauty by seeking to take on the characteristic look of whiteness. This terrain of "drag" wherein the distinctly black-looking female is made to appear in a constant struggle to transform herself to look like a white female is a space only a brown-skinned black woman can occupy. Bi-racial–looking black women and bi-racial women already occupy a distinctly different, more valued place within the beauty hierarchy. Once again as in the days of slavery and racial apartheid, white fascination with racial mixing determines the standard of valuation, especially when the issue is valuation of black female bodies. A world that can recognize the dark-skinned Michael Jordan as a symbol of black beauty scorns and devalues the beauty of Tracy Chapman. Black male pop icons, especially comedians, mock her looks. And while folks comment on the fact that light-skinned and/or bi-racial women have become the stars of most movies that depict black folks, no one has organized public forums to talk about the way this mass media focus on color undermines our efforts to decolonize our minds and imaginations. Just as whites now privilege lighter skin in movies and fashion magazines, particularly with female characters, folks with darker skin face media that subordinate their image. Dark skin is stereotypically coded in the racist, sexist, and/or colonized imagination as masculine. Hence, a male's power is enhanced by dark looks while a female's dark looks diminish her femininity. Irrespective of people's sexual preferences, the color-caste hierarchy functions to diminish the desirability of darker-skinned females. Being seen as desirable does not simply affect one's ability to attract partners, it enhances class mobility in public arenas—in educational systems and in the workforce.

Fundamentally the tragic consequences of color-caste hierarchy are evident among the very young who are striving to construct positive identity and healthy self-esteem. Black parents testify that black children learn early to devalue dark skin. One black mother in an interracial marriage was shocked when her four-year-old girl expressed the desire that her mom be white like herself and her dad. She had already learned that white was better. She had already learned to negate the blackness in herself. Yet her black mother had been unaware that her daughter was internalizing racist attitudes and values. In high schools all around the United States, darker-skinned black girls must resist the societal socialization that encourages them to see themselves as ugly. They must resist this socialization in order to construct healthy self-esteem. Concurrently they must resist the efforts of peers to devalue and berate them. This is just one of the tragic implications of black reinvestment in color-caste hierarchies. Had there never been a shift in color consciousness among black people, no one would have paid special attention to the reality that many black children seem to be having as much difficulty learning to love blackness in this racially integrated time of multiculturalism as folks had during periods of intense racial apartheid.

Kathe Sandler's documentary film *A Question of Color* examines the way black liberation politics of the sixties challenged color caste even as she shows recent images of activists who returned to conventional racist-defined notions of beauty. This shift is most signaled by changes in hairstyles. Sandler's film is an important intervention because it creates a cultural context wherein serious discussion of color castes can once again become an integral part of public discourse. Unfortunately, Sandler does not offer suggestions and strategies for how we can deal with this problem now. Merely describing the problems of color caste is not an act of critical intervention. Change will come only as we know the ways these hierarchies create a crisis of consciousness that must be addressed politically if we are not to return to an old model of class and caste where those blacks who are most privileged will be light skinned and/or bi-racial and act as mediators between the white world and a disenfranchised disadvantaged mass of black folks with dark skin. Right now there is a new wave of young well-educated bi-racial folks who identify as black and who benefit from this identification socially as well as when they enter the workforce. Although they realize the implicit racism at work when they are valued more by whites than darker-skinned blacks, the ethic of opportunistic liberal individualism sanctions this complicity. Ironically, they may be among those who critique color caste even as they accept the "perks" that come from the culture's reinvestment in color-caste hierarchies.

Until black folks begin to collectively critique and question the politics of representation that systematically devalue blackness, the devastating effects of color caste will continue to inflict psychological damage on masses of black folks. To intervene and transform those politics of representation informed by colonialism, imperialism, and white supremacy we have to be willing to challenge the effort of mainstream culture to erase racism by suggesting it does not really exist. Recognizing the power of mass media images to define social reality we need lobbyists in the governments, organized groups who sponsor boycotts, etc., to create awareness of these concerns and to demand change. Progressive non-black allies in struggle must join the effort to call attention to internalized racism. Everyone must break through the wall of denial that would have us believe hatred of blackness emerges from troubled individual psyches and acknowledge that it is systematically taught through processes of socialization in white supremacist society. That black folks who have internalized white supremacist attitudes and values are as much agents of this socialization as their racist non-black counterparts. Progressive black leaders and/or critical thinkers who are committed to a politics of cultural transformation that would constructively change the lot of the black underclass, and thus positively impact the culture as a whole, need to make decolonizing our minds and imaginations central when we educate for critical consciousness. Learning from the past, we need to remain critically vigilant, willing to interrogate our work as well as our habits of being to ensure that we are not perpetuating internalized racism. Currently, more conservative black political agendas, like the Nation of Islam and certain strands of Afrocentrism, are the only groups who make self-love central as a strategy to capture the imagination of the masses.

Revolutionary struggle for black self-determination must become a real political movement in our lives if we want to counter conservative thinking and offer life-affirming practices to masses of black folks who are daily wounded by white supremacist assaults. Those wounds will not heal if left unattended.

HEALING OUR WOUNDS

LIBERATORY MENTAL HEALTH CARE

U nwilling to embrace a psychology of victimhood for fear that black life in the United States would be forever seen as pathological, nineteenth- and early-twentieth-century black critical thinkers and/or activists chose to embrace a psychology of triumph. They emphasized the myriad ways black folks managed to survive with grace, elegance, and beauty despite the harsh brutality of living in a white supremacist nation. Passionately devoted to the political goal of racial uplift, they highlighted the achievements of exceptional individuals. They cited their lives and work as evidence that we were not only equal to white people but perhaps superior because so many of us managed to start from nothing and invent powerful creative selves. They did not talk about the psychological casualties. Such thinking must have inspired W. E. B. Du Bois to declare:

> If in America it is to be proven for the first time in modern history that not only are Negroes capable of evolving great figures like Frederick Douglass but are a

nation stored with wonderful possibilities of culture then their destiny is not a servile imitation of Anglo Saxon culture but a stalwart originality which shall unswervingly follow Negro ideals. That is to say that Negro ideals would be retained and assured by the group through the development of Negro genius, of Negro literature and art and of Negro spirit.

When early-twentieth-century scholars tried to develop a discourse about black life that attempted to construct paradigms which suggested that all black experience could be understood by a pathological reading, this line of thinking was countered by black folks.

Emphasis on racial uplift, though crucial to efforts to intervene on and challenge white supremacy, nevertheless created a culture of shame wherein any aspect of black life that could be seen as evidence of mental disorder, of pathology, had to be hidden or viewed as utterly aberrant. It is this untalked-about culture of shame that has made it practically impossible for African Americans to acknowledge the ways in which living in a white supremacist society and being the constant targets of racist assault and abuse are fundamentally psychologically traumatic. For black folks to acknowledge that we are collectively wounded by racial trauma would require severing our attachment to an unproblematized tradition of racial uplift where that trauma had been minimized in the effort to prove that we were not collectively dehumanized by racist oppression and exploitation. This desperate need to "prove" to white folks that racism had not really managed to wreak ongoing psychological havoc in our lives was and is a manifestation of trauma, an overreactive response. It was this type of psychological response to white supremacy as a weapon of domestic cultural colonization that Frantz Fanon, a black psychiatrist from Martinique, had described in *The Wretched of the Earth* as a situation of depersonalization where "colonized people find that they are reduced to a body of individuals who only find cohesion when in the, presence of the colonizing nation." To break with a colonizing mentality, black folks must acknowledge the need for racial uplift via cultural production and the development of black genius even as we also engage a politics of resistance that can address the psychological trauma we experience, both in the past and in the present, as we struggle to create self and identity within white supremacist society.

While contemporary young black folks eschew identification with the movement for racial uplift, they seek to replace a narrative of triumph that denies adversity with a narrative of pleasure and cool, as in "we are too busy having fun inventing our funky black selves to be in pain and we certainly never feel self-hatred." In public discourse, black woman journalist Lisa Jones celebrates this perspective in her collection of essays *Bulletproof Diva: Tales of Race, Sex, and Hair* wherein she pokes fun at me and other black critical thinkers who want to call public attention to self-hatred engendered by internalized racism in an essay mockingly titled "Make Self-Love." Jones flippantly declares that "there is a body of evidence that speaks to our subjugation and one that speaks to our triumph . . . it's your choice which cloak you wear." Unable to break with the very binary choices I have been critiquing, she, like many other folks, is unable to see that we can claim our triumph and our pain without shame. Younger generations of black folks long to highlight pleasure as a way of masking, suppressing any acknowledgment of pain. Clearly, we must make a critical distinction between black pleasure and black agency. At times when we have had no agency, no real control over even the most basic aspects of our lives (i.e., control over our bodily functions) we have still known pleasure.

It is not surprising that the individuals who most want to highlight pleasure are educationally privileged young black thinkers who can border-cross as much as they like, move in and out of blackness when it feels good and pays well, that are the most eager to deny the existence of black self-hatred or even profound debilitating life-threatening psychological pain. They pitch their discourse of black pleasure to an audience of white consumers who are more than eager to tune out any expressions of black pain. Many of the privileged black folks who are the most uncomfortable with the use of a term like "self-hatred" were the very children who were raised in settings where they longed to self-erase and be white. If that is not a destructive, potentially hateful gesture, what is? Of course once it became cool to be black their problems were solved, or so it seemed. However, they were often not claiming blackness as a gesture of self-love but rather as a way of saying to envious whites "now the tables are turned—you long to be black but I *am* black." Note that the fixation here is still on how white people see us and not on how we see ourselves—in other words black identity as performance art. I have no attachment to the term "self-hatred" but when black folks use it to express their pain, I have no need to silence them by stopping the discussion to talk about semantics. Finally, the words we use mean nothing if we are not creating a cultural context where black pain can speak and be directly attended to without being served up as tasty melodrama for those who desire only to "eat the other." This voyeuristic cannibalism is enacted by black consumers as well, who are pleasured by glamorized representations of genocidal black self-destructiveness.

Contrary to Jones's insistence that we need to expend energy challenging "the notion that there are masses of folks out there hating themselves," the need to create a context where our pain can be reclaimed from a voyeuristic ethnographic note-taking that turns it into spectacle by either mocking, trivializing, or sentimentalizing it is urgent. More important than anyone's witty insistence that if they "don't think black folks hate themselves," such feelings must not exist. It is striking that the will to denial so often comes from those who have the greatest access to structures of healing, so that whatever wounds may have existed in their lives can have been attended to. Unfortunately, if those of us who are culturally privileged, who have the advantage of knowing lots of black folks who are not mired in self-hate, use that privilege to erase and diminish the many black folks, often among the underclass and poor, who give testimony to self-hatred engendered by internalized racism, we are simply enacting a more sophisticated form of cultural imperialism. In other words, we are acting as though as a privileged black elite you can take what you want from black culture; the cool that you need to enhance your shit can be appropriated like any other resource and you can leave the rest. It is this class-based cultural neo-colonialism that acts to censor and silence any effort on the part of black folks to name our pain, whatever its source, and to heal our wounds.

Collective failure to address adequately the psychic wounds inflicted by racist aggression is the breeding ground for a psychology of victimhood wherein learned helplessness, uncontrollable rage, and/or feelings of overwhelming powerlessness and despair abound in the psyches of black folks yet are not attended to in ways that empower and promote wholistic states of well-being. Until African Americans, and everyone else in the United States, are able to acknowledge the psychic trauma inflicted upon black folks by racist aggression and assault, there will be no collective cultural understanding of the reality that these wrongs cannot be redressed simply by programs for economic reparation, equal opportunity in the workforce, or attempts to create social equality between the races. Like all mental health disorders, the wounded African-American psyche must be attended to within the framework of programs for mental health care that link psychological recovery with progressive political awareness of the way in which institutionalized systems of domination assault, damage, and maim. Such programs will never emerge as long as African Americans rely on existing structures within education and mental health care to address these concerns.

Within institutions shaped by white supremacist capitalist patriarchal biases, there is little hope that individuals who are interested in developing psychological theories and practices that address the dilemmas facing African Americans will find support. When this reality is linked to a culture of shame within diverse black communities that silences attempts by black folks to name our woundedness, a climate of repression and suppression prevails. In more recent years this culture of shame, and the psychological policing that it promotes, has been most challenged by the writings of black women. The breaking of this collective silence has its most sustained expression in the work of black women writers, particularly fiction writers. Works like Alice Walker's *The Color Purple* and Toni Morrison's first novel, *The Bluest Eye* (published before Walker's book), as well as the more widely acclaimed *Beloved*, all address issues of psychic trauma. Significantly, many of the works by contemporary black women writers began to overtly address psychological trauma in the wake of contemporary feminist movement sanctioning the disclosure of private matters and secrets in public space. Feminist activists called attention to the way in which the separation of public and private was necessary for the maintenance of institutionalized patriarchal domination which condones exploitation and oppression of women, particularly when it happens in domestic space. Feminist focus on reproductive rights, domestic violence, rape, and child abuse, particularly incest, as well as on patterns of domination in sexual and intimate relations, intervened in the cultural silence that had once deemed these topics taboo. Contemporary black women writers were able to enter that space and create a literature addressing subjects that to some extent were still taboo in writing deemed specifically about race.

Unlike contemporary writing by white women of this time, which did not highlight issues of race, the work of black women writers necessarily evoked the interconnectedness of race, gender, and class. Classic works of American fiction by black women writers were rediscovered. Suddenly folks who had not previously read them recognized that throughout the history of our writing, black females have addressed trauma. Indeed, it was Ann Petry's heroine Lutie in the forties novel *The Street* who articulated that most black folks were holding an anger at racism so intense it constantly threatened to implode, to destroy us from the inside out. Speaking of the collective trauma black folks experience Lutie declares: "Everyday we are choking down that rage." The focus on psychological trauma in contemporary black women's fiction was so attentive to issues of gender that the interrelatedness of race and gender might have been overlooked had negative public response to this work not generated ongoing discussion and debate. Concurrently, in nonfiction writing by black women engaged in feminist thinking (particularly the work of writers like Audre Lorde, Toni Bambara, Barbara Smith, Michele Wallace, myself, and many others), there was a consistent demand for an interrogation of our personal histories that would allow for the breaking of silences, the revelation of our woundedness and strategies for healing. Unfortunately, this call to break silences was not welcomed by many black folks or mainstream culture. It did not serve as the catalyst for the production of a substantial body of critical work that would examine black folks' construction of self and identity in relation to the politics of white supremacy in daily life. While our words and writings have been listened to and affirmed by black and non-black audiences when we speak about gender, either directly or indirectly to the trauma of male domination, when the issue is race there is still a tendency to defer to the words and writings of black men. Concurrently, black male thinkers have shown and continue to show greater reluctance to articulate and confront issues of psychological pain.

Collectively, the black male response both to feminist thinking and practice and to the focus on individual trauma was generally negative. While large numbers of black women were engaging ourselves in recovery movements and seeking various forms of therapy and self-help, in general black males were not eager to embrace an analysis of the impact of white supremacy on our lives that included a recognition of both psychic trauma and the need for psychological recovery. The group of black males who were most responsive to this focus were black gay men. As individuals, they were more willing to take a critical look at childhood and family relations, acknowledging destructive habits formed there that could be traced to the internalization of white supremacist attitudes and values. Powerful contemporary straight black male leaders and/or critical thinkers, whether activists or scholars, have not raised the issue of mental health even though those issues had been raised by their peers in the sixties. Even though their work was Eurocentric, patriarchal, and mired in the rhetoric of neo-colonialism, black male psychiatrists Grier and Cobbs with their popular work *Black Rage* published at the peak of black power movement presented analysis of the impact of racist exploitation and oppression on the black psyche rooted in psychoanalytical concerns. No doubt patriarchal black male fear that breaking the silences and making public the psychic pain of black folks would render us vulnerable to attack prevented such work from gathering momentum. Sadly, by now there should be an incredible body of psychoanalytical and psychological material, written from a progressive standpoint, about black mental health that looks at the connection between concrete victimization and mental disorders, yet this work does not exist.

No matter how many million Americans, of all races, fall in love with the novels of Alice Walker or Toni Morrison and identify with the psychological havoc wreaked in the lives of the characters, there is still a collective cultural refusal to assume any accountability for the psychological wounding of black people that continues into the present day. The success of a novel like *Beloved* is tied to the fact that it highlights the trauma of slavery and Reconstruction. Slavery has come to be recognized as a holocaust experience. Even though books like *Beloved*, along with works by black male novelists like David Bradley's *The Chaneysville Incident*, call attention to the trauma of slavery and its aftermath, readers are not compelled to relate that understanding to concrete contemporary circumstances. Indeed, for some readers the focus on slavery deflects attention away from current situations of racialized trauma or allows them to trivialize contemporary pain. Concurrently, much of the contemporary nonfiction writing by black scholars, particularly males, downplays the significance of trauma in order to emphasize triumph over adversity. When Elaine Brown published *A Taste of Power*, her autobiographical account of activism in the black power movement, she documented a world where progressive political visions of resisting white supremacy and promoting black self-determination were rarely linked to a concern for mature psychological development. Her story, like that of many others, paints a portrait of radical political agendas undermined by individuals who were sometimes trapped by intense psychological disorders that distorted their vision and judgment. Revolutionary mental health care was not on the militant agenda.

Currently, conventional mental health care professionals who attend to the needs of black folks often reject any analysis that takes into account a political understanding of our personal pain. This may be true of black mental health care workers as well as everyone else. While there is a growing body of self-help literature that is addressed specifically to black folks, it does not connect political injustice with psychological pain. For example, even though there are many self-help books for black folks that look at the issue of low self-esteem, expressed in the extreme by self-hatred, sometimes overtly relating it to internalized racism, such works rarely talk about a healing process that would include radical politicization and social activism. When I wrote *Sisters of the Yam: Black Women and Self-Recovery* the intent was to highlight the connections among psychological trauma, mental disorders, and the madness of forming self and identity in white supremacist capitalist patriarchy. While I wanted to emphasize the importance of individual work for self-recovery, I also wanted to link that work to progressive action for political change.

The resurgence of deeply rooted internalized racism, most overtly manifested in contemporary black life by skin-color politics, is just one indication of our collective failure to heal psychological wounds. In *Sisters of the Yam* I raise questions about negative habits of being that may have emerged as forms of political resistance and/or in the days of extreme racial apartheid and question whether these survival strategies are useful in our contemporary situation or whether they actually promote mental illness. For example, dissimulation— the practice of taking on any appearance needed to manipulate a situation—is a form of masking that black folks have historically used to survive in white supremacist settings. As a social practice it promoted duplicity, the wearing of masks, hiding true feelings and intent. While this may have been useful in daily relations with all-powerful white exploiters and oppressors during a situation of extreme racial apartheid when our lives were constantly at risk, as a paradigm for social relations it has undermined bonds of love and intimacy by encouraging the overvaluation of duplicity, lying, masking, etc. Until progressive black critical thinkers, especially those who specialize in mental health care, distinguish between habits of survival used to withstand racist assault that are no longer useful and those that were and remain constructive, there can be no collective development of resistance strategies that outline concrete ways to create healthy minds. By not addressing our psychological wounds, by covering them, we create the breeding ground for pervasive learned helplessness and powerlessness. This lack of agency nurtures compulsive addictive behavior and promotes addiction. Rarely do discussions of drug, alcohol, and food addiction in black life link these problems to any desire to escape from psychological pain that is the direct consequence of racist assault and/or our inability to cope effectively with that assault. Yet if this reality is not considered then the root causes of genocidal addiction may remain unaddressed.

Similarly, young black children would not be emotionally crippled by psychological problems that emerge from low self-esteem, caused by the internalization of racist thinking, if African Americans had institutionalized progressive mental health care agendas that would address these issues so that they would not be passed from generation to generation. The reenactment of unresolved trauma happens again and again if it is not addressed. Psychological woundedness prevents African Americans from engaging in movements for liberation and self-determination that would enhance the quality of our lives as well as our interactions with non-black people. Only as African Americans break with the culture of shame that has demanded that we be silent about our pain will we be able to engage wholistic strategies for healing that will break this cycle.

Without surrendering the meaningful legacy of triumph over adversity that has been such a dynamic aspect of black experience in the United States, we must always make a place for the acknowledgment of unresolved, recurring psychological pain. Despite the incredible changes in the structure of racism in this country, we still live within a white supremacist capitalist patriarchal society that must attack and assault the psyches of black people (and other people of color) to perpetuate and maintain itself. And we still suffer. When African Americans begin to collectively name and confront this suffering in ways that are constructively healing, we will be better able to share our reality with those allies in struggle who are not black but are equally committed to transforming this society, to ending racist domination. Relationships between blacks and whites, Asians, Native Americans, etc. will not undergo the positive change that is needed to establish solidarity and meaningful coalition unless we build collective awareness and engagement with strategies for empowerment that enable us all to break with a colonizing mentality that promotes mental illness. None of us can create successful revolutionary movements for social change if we begin from the standpoint of woundedness. As African Americans make mental health care a more central aspect of our efforts to resist white supremacy and transform society in ways that promote black self-determination, we will replace the culture of shame with an ongoing culture of resistance. Addressing our individual and collective suffering, we will find ways to heal and recover that can be sustained, that can endure from generation to generation.

LOVING BLACKNESS AS POLITICAL RESISTANCE

We have to change our own mind. . . . We've got to change our own minds about each other. We have to see each other with new eyes. We have to come together with warmth. . . .

—MALCOLM X

The course I teach on black women writers is a consistent favorite among students. The last semester that I taught this course we had the usual passionate discussion of Nella Larsen's novel *Passing*. When I suggested to the class that Clare, the black woman who has passed for white all her adult life and marries a wealthy white businessman with whom she has a child, is the only character in the novel who truly desires "blackness" and that it is this desire that leads to her murder, no one responded. Clare boldly declares that she would rather live for the rest of her life as a poor black woman in Harlem than as a rich white matron downtown. I asked the class to consider the possibility that to love blackness is dangerous in a white supremacist culture—so threatening, so serious a breach in the fabric of the social order, that death is the punishment. It became painfully ob-

146

vious by the lack of response that this group of diverse students (many of them black people) were more interested in discussing the desire of black folks to be white, indeed were fixated on this issue. So much so that they could not even take seriously a critical discussion about "loving blackness."

They wanted to talk about black self-hatred, to hear one another confess (especially students of color) in eloquent narratives about the myriad ways they had tried to attain whiteness, if only symbolically. They gave graphic details about the ways they attempted to appear "white" by talking a certain way, wearing certain clothing, and even choosing specific groups of white friends. Blond white students seized the opportunity to testify that they had never realized racism had this impact upon the psyches of people of color until they started hanging out with black friends, taking courses in black studies, or reading Toni Morrison's *The Bluest Eye*. And better yet, they never realized there was such a thing as "white privilege" until they developed non-white connections.

I left this class of more than forty students, most of whom see themselves as radical and progressive, feeling as though I had witnessed a ritualistic demonstration of the impact white supremacy has on our collective psyches, shaping the nature of everyday life, how we talk, walk, eat, dream, and look at one another. The most frightening aspect of this ritual was the extent to which their fascination with the topic of black self-hatred was so intense that it silenced any constructive discussion about loving blackness. Most folks in this society do not want to openly admit that "blackness" as sign primarily evokes in the public imagination of whites (and all the other groups who learn that one of the quickest ways to demonstrate one's kinship within a white supremacist order is by sharing racist assumptions) hatred and fear. In a white supremacist context "loving blackness" is rarely a political stance that is reflected in everyday life. When present it is deemed suspect, dangerous, and threatening.

The oppositional black culture that emerged in the context of apartheid and segregation has been one of the few locations that has provided a space for the kind of decolonization that makes loving blackness possible. Racial integration in a social context where white supremacist systems are intact undermines marginal spaces of resistance by promoting the assumption that social equality can be attained without changes in the culture's attitudes about blackness and black people. Black progressives suffered major disillusionment with white progressives when our experiences of working with them revealed that they could want to be with us (even to be our sexual partners) without divesting of white supremacist thinking about blackness. We saw that they were often unable to let go the idea that whites are somehow better, smarter, more likely to be intellectuals, and even that they were kinder than black folks. Decolonized progressive black individuals are daily amazed by the extent to which masses of black people (all of whom would identify themselves as anti-racist) hold to white supremacist ways of thinking, allowing this perspective to determine how they see themselves and other black people. Many black folks see us as "lacking," as inferior when compared to whites. The paucity of scholarly work looking at the issue of black self-hatred, examining the ways in which the colonization and exploitation of black people is reinforced by internalized racial hatred via white supremacist thinking, is awesome. Few black scholars have explored extensively black obsession with whiteness.

Black theologian James Cone has been one of the few insurgent black intellectuals who has consistently called for critical interrogation of "whiteness" while simultaneously problematizing constructions of white identity within white supremacist culture. In his early work *A Black Theology of Liberation*, Cone urges folks to understand blackness as an "ontological symbol" that is the quintessential signifier of what oppression means in the United States. Cone calls upon whites, blacks, and all other non-black groups to stand against white supremacy by choosing to value, indeed to love, blackness. Boldly stating his case, Cone suggests:

> Most whites, some despite involvements in protests, do believe in "freedom in democracy," and they fight to make the ideals of the Constitution an empirical reality for all. It seems that they believe that, if we just work hard enough at it, this country can be what it ought to be. But it never dawns on these do-gooders that what is wrong with America is not its failure to make the Constitution a reality for all, but rather its belief that persons can affirm whiteness and humanity at the same time. This country was founded for whites and everything that has happened in it has emerged from the white perspective.... What we need is the destruction of whiteness, which is the source of human misery in the world.

Not surprisingly, many of Cone's readers were disturbed by his evocation of a binary approach. At first glance it can appear to be a mere reversal of white racist paradigms. Blackness in much of his early work is identified with that which is good, righteous, positive and whiteness with all that is bad, negative, sinful.

Cone wanted to critically awaken and educate readers so that they would not only break through denial and acknowledge the evils of white supremacy, the grave injustices of racist domination, but be so moved that they would righteously and militantly engage in anti-racist struggle. Encouraging readers to break with white supremacy as an epistemological standpoint by which they come to know the world, he insisted that "whiteness" as a sign be interrogated. He wanted the public to learn how to distinguish that racism which is about overt prejudice and domination from more subtle forms of white supremacy. In his early work, he frequently chose a rhetoric that would "shock" so as to forcefully impress on the reader's consciousness the seriousness of the issues. Unfortunately, many readers were turned off by his rhetorical stance, his emphasis on binary opposition, and could not hear the wisdom in his call for a critique of whiteness. By focusing on his personal style, many readers willingly allowed themselves to dismiss and/or ignore the extent to which (all polemical rhetoric aside) his discourse on whiteness was a necessary critical intervention, calling for ongoing interrogation of conventional ways of thinking about race or about strategies to eradicate racism.

Cone was suggesting the kind of shift in positionality that has become a crucial and widely accepted tenet of anti-racist struggle advocated in much recent critical work on the subject of race, especially the work that emerges from feminist theory, cultural studies, and postcolonial discourse. Whether they are able to enact it as a lived practice or not, many white folks active in anti-racist struggle today are able to acknowledge that all whites (as well as everyone else within white supremacist culture) have learned to overvalue "whiteness" even as they simultaneously learn to devalue blackness. They understand the need, at least intellectually, to alter their thinking. Central to this process of unlearning white supremacist attitudes and values is the deconstruction of the category "whiteness."

It is much more acceptable nowadays, and even fashionable, to call for an interrogation of the meaning and significance of "whiteness" in contemporary critical discussions of race. While Cone's analysis was sometimes limited by a discourse that invested in binary oppositions (refusing to cut white folks any slack), the significant critical intervention that he made was the insistence that the logic of white supremacy would be radically undermined if everyone would learn to identify with and love blackness. Cone was not evoking the notion of racial erasure—that is, the sentimental idea (often voiced by religious folks) that racism would cease to exist if everyone would just forget about race and just see each other as human beings who are the same. Instead he insisted that the politics of racial domination have necessarily created a black reality that is distinctly different from that of whites, and from that location has emerged a distinct black culture. His prophetic call was for whites to learn how to identify with that difference—to see it as a basis for solidarity.

This message can be heard in current feminist writing on race. Moving away from the notion that an emphasis on sameness is the key to racial harmony, aware feminist activists have insisted that anti-racist struggle is best advanced by theory that speaks about the importance of acknowledging the way positive recognition and acceptance of difference is a necessary starting point as we work to eradicate white supremacy. Critically discussing Richard Rorty's book *Contingency, Irony and Solidarity*, philosopher Ron Scaap, in his essay "Rorty: Voice and the Politics of Empathy," makes the point that liberals often give lip service to a vision of diversity and plurality while clinging to notions of sameness where we are all one, where (to use Michael Jackson's lyrics) "it doesn't matter if you're black or white." Scaap suggests,

> Liberals may pride themselves in their ability to tolerate others but it is only after the other has been redescribed

as oneself that the liberal is able to be "sensitive" to the question of cruelty and humiliation. This act of redescription is still an attempt to appropriate others, only here it is made to sound as if it were a generous act. It is an attempt to make an act of consumption appear to be an act of acknowledgment.

Many unlearning racism workshops focus on helping white individuals to see that they too are wounded by racism and as a consequence have something to gain from participating in anti-racist struggle. While in some ways true, a construction of political solidarity that is rooted in a narrative of shared victimization not only acts to recenter whites, it risks obscuring the particular ways racist domination impacts on the lives of marginalized groups. Implicit in the assumption that even those who are privileged via racist hierarchy suffer is the notion that it is only when those in power get in touch with how they too are victimized will they rebel against structures of domination. The truth is that many folks benefit greatly from dominating others and are not suffering a wound that it is in any way similar to the condition of the exploited and oppressed.

Anti-racist work that tries to get these individuals to see themselves as "victimized" by racism in the hopes that this will act as an intervention is a misguided strategy. And indeed we must be willing to acknowledge that individuals of great privilege who are in no way victimized are capable, via their political choices, of working on behalf of the oppressed. Such solidarity does not need to be rooted in shared experience. It can be based on one's political and ethical understanding of racism and one's rejection of domination. Therefore we can see the necessity for the kind of education for critical consciousness that can enable those with power and privilege rooted in structures of domination to divest without having to see themselves as victims. Such thinking does not have to negate collective awareness that a culture of domination does seek to fundamentally distort and pervert the psyches of all citizens or that this perversion is wounding.

In his work, Cone acknowledges that racism harms whites yet he emphasizes the need to recognize the difference between the hurt oppressors feel and the pain of the oppressed. He suggests:

> The basic error of white comments about their own oppression is the assumption that they *know* the nature of their enslavement. This cannot be so, because if they really knew, they would liberate themselves by joining the revolution of the black community. They would destroy themselves and be born again as beautiful black persons.

Since it is obvious that white folks cannot choose at will to become "black," that utopian longing must be distinguished from a solidarity with blackness that in rooted in actions wherein one ceases to identify with whiteness as symbol of victimization and powerlessness.

Recently, I gave a talk highlighting ways contemporary commodification of black culture by whites in no way challenges white supremacy when it takes the form of making blackness the "spice that can liven up the dull dish that is mainstream white culture." At the end of the talk a white woman who sounded very earnest asked me: "Don't you think we are all raised in a culture that is racist and we are all taught to be racist whether we want to be or not?" Note that she constructs a social framework of sameness, a homogeneity of experience. My response was to say that all white people (and everyone else in this society) can choose to be actively anti-racist twenty-four hours a day if they so desire and none of us is a passive victim of socialization. Elaborating on this point, I shared how I was weary of the way in which white people want to deflect attention away from their accountability for anti-racist change by making it seem that everyone has been socialized to be racist against their will. My fear is that this often becomes another apology for racism, one which seeks to erase a vision of accountability and responsibility which could truly empower. It was apparent that the white woman who asked the question was dissatisfied with my response. When I suggested that she was less interested in what I had to say and perhaps had her own agenda, she stated that the point she really wanted to make was that "blacks are just as racist as whites—that we are all racists." When I critically interrogated this statement, explaining the difference between prejudicial feelings (which blacks and whites alike harbor towards one another as well as other groups) and institutionalized white supremacist domination, she promptly left.

A vision of cultural homogeneity that seeks to deflect attention away from or even excuse the oppressive, dehumanizing impact of white supremacy on the lives of black people by suggesting black people are racist too indicates that the culture remains ignorant of what racism really is and how it works. It shows that people are in denial. Why is it so difficult for many white folks to understand that racism is oppressive not because white folks have prejudicial feelings about blacks (they could have such feelings and leave us alone) but because it is a system that promotes domination and subjugation? The prejudicial feelings some blacks may express about whites are in no way linked to a system of domination that affords us any power to coercively control the lives and well-being of white folks. That needs to be understood.

Concurrently, all social manifestations of black separatism are often seen by whites as a sign of anti-white racism, when they usually represent an attempt by black people to construct places of political sanctuary where we can escape, if only for a time, white domination. The ideas of conservative black thinkers who buy into the notion that blacks are racist are often evoked by whites who see them as native informants confirming this as fact. Shelby Steele is a fine example of this tendency. I believe that his essays were the most Xeroxed pieces of writing by white folks in the academy who wanted to share with black colleagues that they have been right all along when they suggested that black folks were racist. Steele suggests that any time black people choose to congregate solely with one another we are either supporting racial separatism because of deeply ingrained feelings of inferiority or a refusal to see racial differences as unimportant (i.e., to accept the notion that we are all the same). Commenting on the issue of self-segregation in *The Content of Our Character*, he declares: "There is a geopolitics involved in this activity, where race is tied to territory in a way that mimics the whites only/colored only designations of the past." At no point in his analysis does Steele suggest that blacks might want to be away from whites to have a space where we will not be the object of racist assaults.

Every aware black person who has been the "only" in an all-white setting knows that in such a position we are often called upon to lend an ear to racist narratives, to laugh at corny race jokes, to undergo various forms of racist harassment. And that self-segregation seems to be particularly intense among those black college students who were often raised in material privilege in predominantly white settings where they were socialized to believe racism did not exist, that we are all "just human beings," and then suddenly leave home and enter institutions and experience racist attacks. To a great extent they are unprepared to confront and challenge white racism, and often seek the comfort of just being with other blacks.

Steele's refusal to acknowledge this pain—this way that white supremacy manifests itself in daily social interaction—makes it appear that black individuals simply do not like socializing with whites. The reality is that many black people fear they will be hurt if they let down their guard, that they will be the targets of racist assault since most white people have not unlearned racism. In classroom settings, I hear so many narratives of black students who accepted the notion that racism did not exist, who felt there was nothing wrong with being with white friends and sharing similar interests, only to find themselves in circumstances where they had to confront the racism of these people. The last story I heard was from a young black woman talking about always being with white buddies in high school. One day they were all joy-riding in someone's car, and they came across a group of young black males crossing the street. Someone in the car suggests they should "just run those niggers down." She talked about her disbelief that this comment had been made, her hurt. She said nothing but she felt that it was the beginning of an estrangement from white peers that has persisted. Steele's writing assumes that white people who desire to socialize with black people are not actively racist, are coming from a position of goodwill. He does not consider the reality that goodwill can coexist with racist thinking and white supremacist attitudes.

Throughout my tenure as a Yale professor, I was often confronted with white students who would raise the issue of why it is black students sit together in the cafeteria, usually at one table. They saw this as some expression of racial separatism, exclusion, etc. When I asked them why they never raised the issue of why the majority of tables are white students self-segregating, they invariably said things like, "We sit together with folks with whom we share common interests and concerns." They were rarely at the point where they could interrogate whether or not shared "whiteness" allowed them to bond with one another with ease.

While it has become "cool" for white folks to hang out with black people and express pleasure in black culture, most white people do not feel that this pleasure should be linked to unlearning racism. Indeed there is often the desire to enhance one's status in the context of "whiteness" even as one appropriates black culture. In his essay "A Place Called Home: Identity and the Cultural Politics of Difference," Jonathan Rutherford comments:

> Paradoxically, capital has fallen in love with difference: advertising thrives on selling us things that will enhance our uniqueness and individuality. It's no longer about keeping up with the Joneses, it's about being different from them. From World Music to exotic holidays in Third World locations, ethnic tv dinners to Peruvian hats, cultural difference *sells*.

It makes perfect sense that black people and other people of color often self-segregate to protect themselves from this kind of objectifying interaction.

Steele never sees the desire to create a context where one can "love blackness" as a worthy standpoint for bonding, even if such bonding must take the form of self-segregation. Luckily, there are individual non-black people who have divested of their racism in ways that enable them to establish bonds of intimacy based on their ability to love blackness without assuming the role of cultural tourists. We have yet to have a significant body of writing from these individuals that gives expression to how they have shifted attitudes and daily vigilantly resist becoming reinvested in white supremacy. Concurrently, black folks who "love blackness"—that is, who have decolonized our minds and broken with the kind of white supremacist thinking that suggests we are inferior, inadequate, marked by victimization, etc.—often find that we are punished by society for daring to break with the status quo. On our jobs, when we express ourselves from a decolonized standpoint, we risk being seen as unfriendly or dangerous.

Those black folks who are more willing to pretend that "difference" does not exist, even as they self-consciously labor to be as much like their white peers as possible, will receive greater material rewards in white supremacist society. White supremacist logic is thus advanced. Rather than using coercive tactics of domination to colonize, it seduces black folks with the promise of mainstream success if only we are willing to negate the value of blackness. Contrary to James Cone's hope that whites would divest of racism and be born again in the spirit of empathy and unity with black folks, we are collectively asked to show our solidarity with the white supremacist status quo by overvaluing whiteness, by seeing blackness solely as a marker of powerlessness and victimization. To the degree that black folks embody by our actions and behavior familiar racist stereotypes, we will find greater support and/or affirmation in the culture. A prime example of this is white consumer support of misogynist rap which reproduces the idea that black males are violent beasts and brutes.

In Nella Larsen's *Passing*, Clare chooses to assume a white identity because she sees blackness only as a sign of victimization and powerlessness. As long as she thinks this, she has a sustained bond with the black bourgeoisie who often self-segregate even as they maintain contempt for blackness, especially for the black underclass. Clare's bond with Irene, her black bourgeois friend, is broken when she seeks to define blackness positively. In *Passing* it is this bourgeois class and the world of whiteness Clare's husband embodies that turn against her when she attempts to reclaim the black identity she has previously denied. When the novel ends we do not know who has murdered her, the black bourgeois friend or the white husband. She represents a "threat" to the conservative hierarchical social order based on race, class, and gender that they both seek to maintain.

Despite civil rights struggle, the 1960s black power movement, and the power of slogans like "black is beautiful," masses of black people continue to be socialized via mass media and nonprogressive educational systems to internalize white supremacist thoughts and values. Without ongoing resistance struggle and progressive black liberation movements for self-determination, masses of black people (and everyone else) have no alternative worldview that affirms and celebrates blackness. Rituals of affirmation (celebrating black history, holidays, etc.) do not intervene on white supremacist socialization if they exist apart from active anti-racist struggle that seeks to transform society.

Since so many black folks have succumbed to the post-1960s notion that material success is more important than personal integrity, struggles for black self-determination that emphasize decolonization, loving blackness, have had little impact. As long as black folks are taught that the only way we can gain any degree of economic self-sufficiency or be materially privileged is by first rejecting blackness, our history and culture, then there will always be a crisis in black identity. Internalized racism will continue to erode collective struggle for self-determination. Masses of black children will continue to suffer from low self-esteem. And even though they may be motivated to strive harder to achieve success because they want to overcome feelings of inadequacy and lack, those successes will be undermined by the persistence of low self-esteem.

One of the tragic ironies of contemporary black life is that individuals succeed in acquiring material privilege often by sacrificing their positive connection to black culture and black experience. Paule Marshall's novel *Praisesong for the Widow* is a fictional portrayal of such tragedy. A young black couple, Avey and Jay, start their family life together empowered by their celebration and affirmation of black culture, but this connection is eroded as Jay strives for material success. Along the way, he adopts many mainstream white supremacist ways of thinking about black folks, expressing disdain for the very culture that had been a source of joy and spiritual fulfillment. Widowed, her children grown, Avey begins a process of critical remembering where she interrogates their past, asking herself:

> Would it have been possible to have done both? That is, to have wrested, as they had done over all those years, the means needed to rescue them from Halsey Street and to see the children through, while preserving, safeguarding, treasuring those things that had come down to them over the generations, which had defined them in a particular way. The most vivid, the most valuable part of themselves!

To recover herself and reclaim the love of blackness, Avey must be born again. In that state of rebirth and reawakening, she is able to understand what they could have done, what it would have called for: "Awareness. It would have called for an awareness of the worth of what they possessed. Vigilance. The vigilance needed to safeguard it. To hold it like a jewel high out of the envious reach of those who would either destroy it or claim it as their own." To recover herself, Avey has to relearn the past, understand her culture and history, affirm her ancestors, and assume responsibility for helping other black folks to decolonize their minds.

A culture of domination demands of all its citizens self-negation. The more marginalized, the more intense the demand. Since black people, especially the underclass, are bombarded by messages that we have no value, are worthless, it is no wonder that we fall prey to nihilistic despair or forms of addiction that provide momentary escape, illusions of grandeur, and temporary freedom from the pain of facing reality. In his essay "Healing the Heart of Justice," written for a special issue of *Creation Spirituality* highlighting the work of Howard Thurman, Victor Lewis shares his understanding of the profound traumatic impact of internalized oppression and addiction on black life. He concludes:

> To value ourselves rightly, infinitely, released from shame and self-rejection, implies knowing that we are claimed by the totality of life. To share in a loving community and vision that magnifies our strength and banishes fear and despair, here, we find the solid ground from which justice can flow like a mighty stream. Here, we find the fire that burns away the confusion that oppression heaped upon us during our childhood weakness. Here, we can see what needs to be done and find the

strength to do it. To value ourselves rightly. To love one another. This is to heal the heart of justice.

We cannot value ourselves rightly without first breaking through the walls of denial which hide the depth of black self-hatred, inner anguish, and unreconciled pain.

Like Paule Marshall's character Avey, once our denial falls away we can work to heal ourselves through awareness. I am always amazed that the journey home to that place of mind and heart, where we recover ourselves in love, is constantly within reach and yet so many black folks never find the path. Mired in negativity and denial we are like sleepwalkers. Yet, if we dare to awaken, the path is before us. In *Hope and History*, Vincent Harding asks readers to consider: "In a society increasingly populated by peoples of color, by those who have known the disdain and domination of the Euro-American world, it would be fascinating to ponder self-love as a religious calling." Collectively, black people and our allies in struggle are empowered when we practice self-love as a revolutionary intervention that undermines practices of domination. Loving blackness as political resistance transforms our ways of looking and being, and thus creates the conditions necessary for us to move against the forces of domination and death and reclaim black life.

BLACK ON BLACK PAIN

CLASS CRUELTY

Class difference is an aspect of black identity that is often overlooked. It is not just white people who refuse to acknowledge different class status among blacks; many of us want to ignore class. A major difference in the agendas set by the movement for civil rights and militant struggles for black power was caused by different class perspectives. Even though the civil rights movement engaged masses of poor and working-class black people, the values shaping this struggle were fundamentally bourgeois. Assimilating the values of white privileged classes was the idea of freedom civil rights struggle supported. Even though the call was for social equality between the races, black leaders were also motivated by a desire to gain access to middle-class incomes and lifestyles. It was this desire for upward class mobility that led black male patriarchs at the forefront of the bus boycott to publicly ignore the courage of lower-class black females who refused to give up their bus seats and to focus on Rosa Parks. This class betrayal is discussed in *Night Vision*, in the chapter "Women and Children in the Armed

Struggle." The role played by poor and lower-class black females like Epsie Worthy, who did not receive public acclaim because they were not of the acceptable class status, is acknowledged. For example, one black female was deemed unfit because she was young, angry, poor, and lived with her alcoholic father. Rosa Parks, on the other hand, was more acceptable because she was seen by men as respectable: "It takes nothing away from Rosa Parks' courage and years of dedication to see that she was not the first, not the catalyst, but was the symbol reluctantly chosen by men for a struggle that other New Afrikan women had already started months ago. It was fighting women, who weren't respectable, who were 'too hot, too Black' for the men of the Civil Rights movement, who first broke the chains and opened the way." This is just one example of the way in which bourgeois class values have dominated civil rights struggle in the United States.

Temporarily at least that hold was broken by militant black struggle in the sixties. A powerful but often forgotten aspect of this struggle was the profound critique of capitalism, as an economic and social order that would never fully allow black liberation. That critique of capitalism is virtually absent from any aspect of contemporary black liberation struggle. Even those individual black Leftists who offer a class analysis do not provide any concrete vision for social change that speaks to what conditions might be put in place to allow a fierce critique of the existing economic structure, an alternative, and strategies for resistance even as we live and work within a capitalist framework. It is rare for a contemporary black leader to make any suggestions about ways to live well and be self-determining in the midst of a capitalist system that is continually increasing the size of the black poor and destitute even as we remain critical of capitalism. Even though rapper Ice-T can offer a class analysis in his collection of short essays *The Ice Opinion* he does not engage a serious critique of capitalism. He can share this insight: "The ghetto is set up like a concentration camp. The government has broken the system down to a series of financially segregated villages. South Central is not a black community, it's a poor community. You live there 'cause you're broke, not because you're black." Then he proceeds to praise capitalism, identifying it as the only way out. However, his relationship to wealth is not one where he conceptualizes using his resources in a radical way. He helps his buddies and supports the philanthropic causes that matter to him. This is what the socially aware wealthy have always done in the United States. Ice-T does not talk about sharing resources, buying land away from utterly economically depressed communities and building housing. Few monied black Americans seem interested in sharing their resources in radical ways. There are no examples of cooperative black communities where resources are shared, no utopian communities that promote living simply (the growing of food, nonwasteful use of natural resources). The ethic of liberal individualism has so deeply permeated the psyches of black folks in America of all classes that we have little support for a political ethic of communalism that promotes the sharing of resources. While folks continue to share resources within family and extended kinship structures, the sense of a communal accountability that transcends these ties has severely diminished.

Tragically, it has diminished at a time when larger numbers of black folks than ever before are entering the ranks of the economically privileged. Sadly, most of these black folks use their resources in many of the same ways as their white counterparts. Monied black folks have not organized to create progressive black educational institutions. While they may contribute funding to existing structures which advance bourgeois values, it is not clear if any economically well-off black folks contribute large sums to radical causes. The ethic of liberal individualism, more than the accumulation of wealth and class privilege, legitimizes the refusal to share resources. When all black people lived in segregated communities, it was much easier for the well-to-do to be vigilant about sharing resources, often because it was in their class interests to do so. Once racial integration was the norm, it was much easier for well-off blacks to leave segregated communities and move to areas where they would not be reminded of an ethic of communalism. Breaking their bonds of solidarity with underprivileged blacks enhances the likelihood that they can fully assimilate into mainstream, class-privileged white culture. Often these black folks are not interested in bonding with the white poor and working class. For the most part their lifestyles usually mean they will have no ongoing relations with underprivileged black folks outside kinship structures.

Class divisions among blacks in a racially desegregated society have been the breeding grounds for those who are privileged to internalize contempt and hatred of the black poor and underclass. The connectedness of capitalism and the perpetuation of racist exploitation makes class a subject privileged blacks seek to avoid. More than other groups of black folks, they emphasize racism as a system of domination without drawing attention to class. They do not want to call attention to the way in which class power mediates the extent to which they will suffer from racist exploitation and aggression. Instead it is in their class interests to emphasize the way racism inhibits their progress. Since their social and professional relations are much more likely to be orchestrated within a framework where they primarily interact with white folks who share their class standing, it is those relations they seek to change in a positive way and not their relations with the black underprivileged.

Indeed the growing body of academic work on the topic of race and racism emerging from black scholars is revealing in that it demonstrates clearly that the dialogue is perceived to be between whites and blacks who share similar class standing and class interests. When a black intellectual begins a collection of essays on race by sharing an anecdote about his or her inability to stop a taxi, in the interests of documenting the way racism obscures class in some situations, he or she is speaking to those who presumably do not have this knowledge, in other words to a white audience. The fact that so many black scholars, thinkers, and writers are primarily directing their work towards a white audience would not be so problematic if there were a large body of work that was more inclusive or addressed specifically to black audiences. It is equally problematic that so much of the work is assuming the role of explaining blackness, particularly the experiences of the black poor and underclass, to privileged-class audiences that are mainly white. The attitudes, assumptions, and critical thoughts about underprivileged blacks shared by privileged blacks are presented as though there is no danger of class biases potentially distorting their perspectives. Since the black poor and underclass do not have the same power of access to mass media, educational institutions, etc., they cannot talk back to that growing body of privileged-class blacks who are not only explaining their reality but seeking to determine the political agendas that should be important for black life. It is easy for these black leaders and/or scholars to act not only as though they speak for economically disenfranchised blacks but as though they know best what is needed to remedy their lot in life. The control privileged-class blacks garner daily over any public discourse and public policy about black life is dangerous not only in that it makes us the "gatekeepers" who determine what should or should not be said but also it means that there is no structure of accountability. It becomes practically impossible to engage in any meaningful critical dialogue. Since most privileged-class blacks are not committed to radical and/or revolutionary politics they can effectively police the voices of those of us who speak from dissenting standpoints, making it difficult for us to gain a wider public audience.

Concurrently, the growing class power and public voice of conservative and liberal well-to-do black folks easily obscures the class cruelty these individuals enact both in the way they talk about underprivileged blacks and the way they represent them. The existence of that class cruelty and its fascist dimensions have been somewhat highlighted by the efforts of privileged-class blacks to censor the voices of black youth, particularly gangsta rappers who are opposing bourgeois class values by extolling the virtues of street culture and street vernacular. Significantly, the attack on urban underclass black youth culture and its gangster dimensions (glamorization of crime, etc.) is usually presented via a critique of sexism. Since most privileged-class blacks have shown no interest in advancing feminist politics, the only organized effort to end sexism and sexist oppression, this attack on sexism seems merely gratuitous, a smoke screen that deflects away from the fact that what really disturbs bourgeois folks is the support of rebellion, unruly behavior, and disrespect for their class values. In reality, they and their white counterparts fear the power these young folks have to change the minds and life choices of youth from privileged classes. If only underclass black folks were listening to gangsta rap, there would be no public effort to silence and censor this music. The fear is that it will generate class rebellion.

In some circles conservative blacks mediate their relationships with the existing white power structure by assuming the role of policing underclass black culture. These conservatives have no trouble uniting to suppress the public discourses that challenge their class values emerging from alternative and/or underclass black youth culture. Without shame they repudiate racial solidarity, to call for the "extermination" of underclass black youth whom they see always and only as troublemakers. Their lack of racial solidarity and concern for the impact of white supremacy on the lives of underprivileged black youth positively mediates their relations to whites. They do not care about the erosion of racial solidarity among blacks.

Ironically, white consumer demand for the commodification of blackness has led more assimilated non-black–identified black folks who have class privilege to engage themselves with interpreting and reinventing the blackness they once repudiated. They come "back to blackness" because it is opportunistically lucrative for them to do so. Class differences have always existed among black folks but class warfare has not. Racial bonding in the interest of challenging white supremacy had suppressed class tensions. Those tensions are mounting. These divisions serve the interest of neo-colonial white supremacy, for they lead to the formation of a new black bourgeoisie who work to strengthen the imperialism and capitalism of mainstream white culture while simultaneously advancing their own class interests.

Amical Cabral's account of the struggle for national liberation in Guinea provides useful paradigms for understanding the class strife that is brewing among African Americans. Understanding that liberatory change often advances the petty bourgeoisie, he shared the insight that the only way to curtail internal contradictions and prevent the betrayal of liberatory objectives was to strengthen the revolutionary consciousness of the privileged classes. Cabral insisted that "the revolutionary petty bourgeoisie must be capable of committing suicide as a class, to be restored to life in the condition of a revolutionary worker completely identified with the deepest aspirations of the people to which he belongs." When we consider that many of the African Americans who are fast swelling the ranks of a privileged-class elite were once engaged in the radical struggle for black liberation and self-determination, it is certainly evident that they were not able to sustain their loyalty to the black underclass, whose mass participation in civil rights struggle has allowed them to have that access to class privilege. These individuals "disidentify" with underprivileged classes. Their lack of empathy and identification is rooted in opportunistic protection of their class interests and/or in a failure to understand the needs and concerns of the black poor and underclass.

In order both to intervene in the class cruelty shown underprivileged blacks by unenlightened black folks from privileged classes and to create a cultural context for renewing bonds of solidarity between black folks, across classes, that is based not on identity politics but on shared commitment to ending white supremacy, critical dialogues must take place about class. The silence around class contradictions and tensions in black life must be broken. The voices of underprivileged black folks and their allies in struggle from privileged-class groups must not be censored or silenced. Vigilant interrogation of our intentionality and political commitment to black liberation must guide black intellectuals when we engage in public discourse about blackness that centralizes the experience of the poor and underclass. If we fail to interrogate our standpoints, we may unwittingly undermine and betray allegiances to those who are less privileged. That vigilance is particularly needed at a time when there are so many material rewards offered us by mainstream white culture when we participate in the commodification of blackness in ways that betray radical commitment to social justice, to ending racism. Class cruelty, the black on black pain, that is emerging as class warfare in black life will not cease as long as we remain silent about class differences. White supremacy is strengthened by the breakdown in political solidarity among black folks that cuts across class. In the long run all black folks will suffer if those among us who are privileged abandon the struggle for racial justice and by our example encourage the poor and underclass to do likewise. By recognizing a mutual political interdependency that transcends differences in class status, that is rooted in the recognition that ultimately we are all diminished if white supremacy continues to dominate our lives, aware black folks may come together across class to share resources and to participate in collective struggle.

MARKETING BLACKNESS

CLASS AND COMMODIFICATION

Concluding Paul Fussell's playful discussion of the serious issue of social status in *Class* is a discussion of a category outside the conventional structures titled "The X Way Out." Folks who exist in category X, he reports, "earn X-personhood by a strenuous effort of discovery in which curiosity and originality are indispensable." They want to escape class. Describing the kind of people who are Xs Fussell comments:

> The old fashioned term bohemians gives some idea; so does the term the talented. Some Xs are intellectual, but a lot are not: they are actors, musicians, artists, sport stars, "celebrities," well-to-do former hippies, confirmed residers abroad, and the more gifted journalists.... They tend to be self employed, doing what social scientists call autonomous work.... X people are independent-minded, free of anxious regard for popular shibboleths, loose in carriage and demeanor. They adore the work they do.... Being an X person is like having much of

the freedom and some of the power of a top-out-of-sight
or upper class person, but without the money. X category
is a sort of unmonied aristocracy.

Even though I grew up in a southern black working-class
household, I longed to be among this X group. Radicalized
by black liberation struggle and feminist movement, my
struggle to make that longing compatible with revolution
began in college. It was there that I was subjected to indoc-
trination that would prepare me to be an acceptable member
of the middle class. Then, as now, I was fundamentally anti-
bourgeois. To me this did not mean that I did not or do not
like beautiful things or desire material well-being. It meant
that I did not or do not sit around longing to be rich, that
I believe hedonistic materialism to be a central aspect of an
imperialist colonialism that perpetuates and maintains white
supremacist capitalist patriarchy. Since this is the ideological
framework that breeds domination, a culture of repression,
repudiation of the ethic of materialism is central to transformation of our society as we now know it. While I do not
believe that any of us really exist in a category outside class,
in that free space of X, I do believe that those of us who
repudiate domination must be willing to divest of class elitism. That it would be useful if progressive folks who oppose
domination in all its forms, who manage to accumulate material plenty and/or wealth, would share their understanding of
ways this status informs their commitment to radical social
change, their political allegiances, publicly naming the means
by which they hold that class privilege in ways that do not
exploit or impinge on the freedom and welfare of others.
  Lately, when I find myself among groups of black academics and/or intellectuals wherein I raise the issue of class,
suggesting that we need to spend more time talking about

class differences among black people, everyone refuses to speak to the issues of race and class. Most are unwilling to acknowledge that class positionality shapes our perspectives and standpoints. This refusal seems to be rooted in a history of class privilege wherein privileged black folks, writers, artists, intellectuals, and/or academics have been able to set the agenda for any public discourse on black culture. That agenda has rarely included a willingness to problematize the issue of class. Among these groups of black folks there is a tacit assumption that we all long to be upper class, and if at all possible, rich. Throughout my years in college and graduate school, black professors were among those committed to policing and punishing the rest of us in the interest of maintaining privileged class values. My twenty years of working as a professor in the academy has not altered this perception. I still find that most black academics, irrespective of their politics, whether they identify as conservative, liberal, or radical, religiously uphold privileged-class values in the manner and style in which they teach, when it comes to habits of being, to mundane matters like dress, language, decorum, etc. Increasingly I find these same attitudes in the world of black cultural production outside academic settings. These values tend to be coupled with a particular brand of class opportunism that has come to be socially acceptable, a sign that one is not so naive or stupid to actually believe that there could be any need to repudiate capitalism or the ethic of materialism.

To a grave extent the commodification of blackness has created the space for an intensification of opportunistic materialism and longing for privileged-class status among black folks in all classes. Yet when the chips are down, it is usually the black folks who already have some degree of class privilege who are most able to exploit the market in blackness as commodity for individual material gain. Ironically, however, the sign of blackness in much of this cultural marketplace is synonymous with the underclass, so that individuals from backgrounds of privilege must either pretend to be "down" or create from the standpoint of what could be called "darky nostalgia" or the overseer's vision of blackness. When I recently commented to several black women scholars doing work in feminist literary criticism that I thought it was useful to talk about ways the shifting class positionality of writers like Alice Walker and Toni Morrison informs their writing style, content, construction of character, etc., they responded with hostility—as though my suggestion that we talk about the way in which privileged-class status shapes black perspective was in some way meant to suggest these writers were not "black," were not "authorities." Since I do not believe in monolithic constructions of blackness and am not a nationalist, I want to call attention to the real and concrete ways class is central to contemporary constructions of black identity. It not only determines the way blackness is commodified, it shapes political standpoint. These differences in no way negate a politics of solidarity that seeks to end racist exploitation and oppression while simultaneously creating a context for black liberation and self-determination; however, they do make it clear that this united front must be forged in struggle and does not emerge solely because of shared racial identity.

To confront class in black life in the United States means that we must deconstruct the notion of an essential binding blackness and be able to critically examine ways the desire to be accepted into privileged-class groups within mainstream society undermines and at times destroys commitment to a politics of cultural transformation that consistently critiques domination. Such a critique would necessarily include the challenge to end class elitism and call for replacing the ethic of individualism with a vision of communalism. In his collection of essays *Reconstructing Memory* Fred Lee Hord calls attention to the way his students at a predominantly black institution make it clear that they are interested in achieving material success and "that if black communal struggle is in conflict with the pursuit of that dream, there will be no struggle." Like Hord, I believe that black experience has been and continues to be one of internal colonialism and that "the cultural repression of American colonial education serves to distort." I would add that the contemporary commodification of blackness has become a dynamic part of that system of cultural repression. Opportunistic longings for fame, wealth, and power now lead many black critical thinkers, writers, academics, and/or intellectuals to participate in the production and marketing of black culture in ways that are complicit with the existing oppressive-exploitative structure. That complicity begins with the equation of black capitalism with black self-determination.

The global failings of socialism have made it easier for individuals within the United States to reject visions of communalism or participatory economics that would redistribute this society's resources in more just and democratic ways. Just as it makes it easy for folks who want to be seen as progressive to embrace a socialist vision even as their habits of being affirm class elitism, passive acceptance of domination, and oppression. In keeping with the way class biases frame discussions of blackness, privileged African-American critics are more than willing to discuss the "nihilism" of the underclass, the pervasive hopelessness, while they ignore the intense "nihilism" of many black folks who have always known material privilege yet who have no sense of agency, no conviction that they can make meaningful changes in the existing social structure. Their "nihilism" does not lead to self-destruction in the classic sense; it may simply lead to symbolic murder of the self that longs to end domination so they can be born again as hard-core opportunists eager to make it within the existing system. Academics are among this group. I confront that hard-core cynicism whenever I raise the issue of class. My critical comments about the way class divisions among black people are creating a climate of fascism and repression tend to be regarded by cynics as merely an expression of envy and longing. Evidently many black folks, especially the bourgeoisie, find it difficult to believe that we are not all eagerly embracing an American dream of wealth and power, that some of us might prefer to live simply in safe comfortable multiethnic neighborhoods rather than in mansions or huge houses, that some of us have no desire to be well-paid tokens at ruling-class white institutions, or that there might even exist for some of us aspects of black life and experience that we hold sacred and are not eager to commodify or sell to captive colonized imaginations. I say this because several times when I have tried, at academic conferences, to talk in a more complex way about class, I have been treated as though I am speaking about this only because I have not really "made it." And on several occasions individual black women have regarded me with patronizing contempt—as though I, who am a well-paid member of the professional-managerial academic class, have no right to express concern about black folks of all classes, to critique the mindless embracing of an ethic of materialism. In both instances, the individuals in question came from privileged-class backgrounds. When it is assumed that I have "made it," my individual success is seen as stripping me of any "authority" to speak about the dilemmas of those who are poor and destitute, especially if what I am saying contradicts the prevailing bourgeois black discourse.

A dimension of making it for many black critics, academics, and/or intellectuals is the assertion of control over the discourse and circulation of ideas about black culture. When their viewpoints are informed by class biases there is little recourse for contestation since they have greater access to white-dominated mass media. A consequence of this is that there is no progressive space for black thinkers to engage in debate and dissent. Concurrently, black thinkers who may have no commitment to diverse black communities, who may regard black folks who are not of their class with contempt and disrespect, are held up in mass media as spokespersons even if they have never shown themselves to be at all concerned with a critical pedagogy that seeks to address black audiences as well as other folks.

Commodification of blackness strips away that component of cultural genealogy that links living memory and history in ways that subvert and undermine the status quo. When the discourse of blackness is in no way connected to an effort to promote collective black self-determination it becomes simply another resource appropriated by the colonizer. It is then possible for white supremacist culture to be perpetuated and maintained even as it appears to be more welcoming, more inclusive. To deflect away from the reality that no attempt to radicalize consciousness through cultural production will be heralded and promoted, colonizers find it useful to create a structure of representation that enables them to project an image that is meant to suggest racist domination is no longer a norm, that all blacks can get ahead if they are just smart enough and work hard. Those individual black folks who are privileged either by birth or by assimilation become the primary representations of the insistence that the American dream is intact, that it can be fulfilled. This holds true in academic circles and in all arenas of cultural production. No matter the extent to which Spike Lee calls attention to injustice, the fact that he can become rich in America while still young leads many folks to ignore the attempts he makes at social critique (when the issue is racism) and see him only as an example of the existing system working. And since his agenda is to succeed within that system as much as possible, he must "work" it by reproducing conservative and even stereotypical images of blackness so as not to alienate that crossover audience. His work cannot be revolutionary and generate wealth at the same time. Yet it is in his class interest to make it seem as though he, and his work, embodies the "throw down ghetto" militant blackness that is the desired product. Not only must his middle-class origins be downplayed, so must his newfound wealth. Similarly, when Allen and Albert Hughes, young bi-racial black males from a privileged-class background, make the film *Menace II Society*, fictively highlighting not the communities they live in but the world of the black underclass, audiences oppose critique by insisting that the brutal dehumanizing images of black family life that are portrayed are "real" or "that's just the way it is." They refuse to see that while there may be aspects of reality portrayed in the film, the film is not a documentary, that it is not offering a view of daily life but is a fiction. The refusal to see the class positionality of the filmmakers informing those aspects of black underclass life they choose to display is rooted in denial, not only of class differences, but of a conservative politics of representation in mainstream cinema that makes it easier to offer a vision of black underclass brutality rather than any other aspect of that community's daily life.

Privileged black folks who are pimping black culture for their own opportunistic gain tend to focus on racism as though it were the great equalizing factor. For example, when a materially successful black person tells the story of how no cab will stop for him because of color he claims unity with the masses of black folks who are daily assaulted by white supremacy. Yet this assertion of shared victimhood obscures the fact that this racial assault is mediated by the reality of class privilege. However "hurt" or even "damaged" the individual may be by his failure to acquire a taxi immediately, that individual is likely to be more allied with the class interests of individuals who share similar status (including whites) than with the needs of those black folks whom racist economic aggression renders destitute, who do not even have the luxury to consider taking a taxi. The issue of course is audience. Since all black folks encounter some form of racial discrimination and/or aggression every day, we do not need stories like this to remind us that racism is widespread. Nonblack folks, especially whites, are the group that most wants to insist that class power and material privilege free individual black folks from the stereotypes associated with the black poor and as a consequence from the pain of racial assault. They, and colonized black folks who live in denial, are the audience that must be convinced that race matters.

Black bourgeois opportunists, who are a rising social class both in the academy and in other spheres of cultural production, are unwittingly creating a division where "within class, race matters." This was made evident in the *Newsweek* cover story "The Hidden Rage of Successful Blacks." A vast majority of the black folks interviewed seemed most angry that they are not treated as equals by whites who share their class. There was little rage directed at the systemic white supremacy that assaults the lives of all black folks, but in particular those who are poor, destitute, and/or uneducated, and who do not call for militant resistance. While it may help convince mainstream society that racism and racist assault inform interpersonal dynamics in this society daily for

black individuals from privileged classes to publicly acknowledge the ways we are hurt, this appeal tends to erase class
privilege. It obscures the extent to which it can be effectively
used to mediate our daily lives so that we can avoid racist
assault in ways that materially disadvantaged individuals cannot. Those black individuals, myself included, who primarily
work and/or live in predominantly white settings where liberalism structures social decorum do not confront unmediated
fierce white racist assault. This lived experience has had the
potentially dangerous effect of creating in some of us a mindset that denies the impact of white supremacy, its assaultive
nature. It is not surprising that black folks in these settings
are more positive about racial integration, cultural mixing,
and border crossing than folks who live in the midst of intense racial apartheid.

By denying or ignoring the myriad ways class positionality
informs perspective and standpoint, individual black folks
who have class privilege are not challenged to interrogate
the ways class biases shape their representations of black
life. For example, why does so much contemporary African-
American literature highlight the circumstances and conditions of underclass black life in the South and urban cities
when it is usually written by folks whose experiences are just
the opposite? The point of raising this question is not to
censor but rather to urge critical thought about a cultural
marketplace wherein blackness is commodified in such a way
that fictive accounts of underclass black life, in whatever setting, may be more lauded, more marketable than other
visions because mainstream conservative white audiences desire these images. As rapper Dr. Dre calls it: "People in the
suburbs, they can't go to the ghetto so they like to hear about
what's going on. Everybody wants to be down." The desire
to be "down" has not only promoted conservative appropria-

tion of specific aspects of underclass black life; that reality is dehumanized via a process of commodification wherein no correlation is made between mainstream hedonistic consumerism and the reproduction of a social system that perpetuates and maintains an underclass.

Without a sustained critique of class power and class divisions among black folks, what is represented in mass media, in cultural production, will merely reflect the biases and standpoints of a privileged few. If that few have not decolonized their minds and choose to make no connection between the discourse of blackness and the need to be engaged in ongoing struggle for black self-determination, there will be few places where progressive visions can emerge and gain a hearing. Coming from a working-class background into the academy, and other arenas of cultural production, I am always conscious of a dearth of perspectives from individuals who do not have a bourgeois mindset. It grieves me to observe the contempt and utter disinterest black individuals from privileged classes often show in their interactions with disadvantaged black folks, or their allies in struggle, particularly those of us whose backgrounds are poor and working class, even if they have built their careers focusing on "blackness," mining the lives of the poor and disadvantaged for resources. It angers me when that group uses its class power and its concomitant conservative politics to silence, censor, and/or de-legitimize counter hegemonic perspectives on blackness.

Irrespective of class background or current class positionality, progressive black individuals whose politics include a commitment to black self-determination and liberation must be vigilant when we do our work. Those of us who speak, write, and act in other ways from privileged-class locations must self-interrogate constantly so that we do not unwittingly

become complicit in maintaining existing exploitative and oppressive structures. None of us should be ashamed to speak
about our class power or lack of it. Overcoming fear, even
the fear of being immodest, and acting courageously to bring
issues of class—especially radical standpoints—into the discourse of blackness is a gesture of militant defiance, one that
runs counter to bourgeois insistence that we think of "money"
in particular and class in general as private matters. Progressive black folks who work to live simply because we respect
the earth's resources, who repudiate the ethic of materialism
and embrace communalism, must gain a public voice. Those
of us who are still working to mix the vision of autonomy
evoked by the X category with our dedication to struggling
to end domination in all its forms, who cherish openness,
honesty, radical will, creativity, and free speech, and who are
possessed by no longing to have power over, to build nations,
or even mini-academic empires, are working to project alternative politics of representation—working to free the "black
image" so it is not enslaved to any exploitative and/or oppressive agenda.

OVERCOMING
WHITE SUPREMACY

A COMMENT

Black people in the United States share with black people in South Africa and with people of color globally both the pain of white supremacist oppression and exploitation and the pain that comes from resistance and struggle. The first pain wounds us, the second pain helps heal our wounds. It often troubles me that black people in the United States have not risen en masse to declare solidarity with our black sisters and brothers in South Africa. Perhaps one day soon—say, Martin Luther King's birthday—we will enter the streets at a certain hour, wherever we are, to stand for a moment, naming and affirming the primacy of black liberation.

As I write, I try to remember when the word "racism" ceased to be the term which best expressed for me exploitation of black people and other people of color in this society and when I began to understand that the most useful term was "white supremacy." It was certainly a necessary term when confronted with the liberal attitudes of white women active in feminist movement who were unlike their racist ancestors—white women in the early women's rights movement who did not wish to be caught dead in fellowship with black women. In fact, these women often requested and longed for the presence of black women. Yet when present, what we saw was that they wished to exercise control over our bodies and thoughts as their racist ancestors had—that this need to exercise power over us expressed how much they had internalized the values and attitudes of white supremacy.

It may have been this contact or contact with fellow white English professors who want very much to have "a" black person in "their" department as long as that person thinks and acts like them, shares their values and beliefs, is in no way different, that first compelled me to use the term "white supremacy" to identify the ideology that most determines how white people in this society (irrespective of their political leanings to the right or left) perceive and relate to black people and other people of color. It is the very small but highly visible liberal movement away from the perpetuation of overtly racist discrimination, exploitation, and oppression of black people which often masks how all-pervasive white supremacy is in this society, both as ideology and as behavior. When liberal whites fail to understand how they can and/or do embody white supremacist values and beliefs even though they may not embrace racism as prejudice or domination (especially domination that involves coercive control), they cannot recognize the ways their actions support and affirm the very structure of racist domination and oppression that they profess to wish to see eradicated.

Likewise, "white supremacy" is a much more useful term for understanding the complicity of people of color in upholding and maintaining racial hierarchies that do not involve force (i.e., slavery, apartheid) than the term "internalized racism"—a term most often used to suggest that black people have absorbed negative feelings and attitudes about blackness held by white people. The term "white supremacy" enables us to recognize not only that black people are socialized to embody the values and attitudes of white supremacy, but that we can exercise "white supremacist control" over other black people. This is important, for unlike the term "uncle tom," which carried with it the recognition of complicity and internalized racism, a new terminology must accurately name the way we as black people directly exercise power over one another when we perpetuate white supremacist beliefs. Speaking about changing perspectives on black identity, writer Toni Morrison said in a recent interview: "Now people choose their identities. Now people choose to be Black." At this historical moment, when a few black people no longer experience the racial apartheid and brutal racism that still determine the lot of many black people, it is easier for that few to ally themselves politically with the dominant racist white group.

Assimilation is the strategy that has provided social legitimation for this shift in allegiance. It is a strategy deeply rooted in the ideology of white supremacy and its advocates urge black people to negate blackness, to imitate racist white people so as to better absorb their values, their way of life. Ironically, many changes in social policy and social attitudes that were once seen as ways to end racial domination have served to reinforce and perpetuate white supremacy. This is especially true of social policy that has encouraged and promoted racial integration. Given the continued force of racism, racial integration translated into assimilation ultimately serves to reinforce and maintain white supremacy. Without an ongoing active movement to end white supremacy, without ongoing black liberation struggle, no social environment can exist in the United States that truly supports integration. When black people enter social contexts that remain unchanged, unaltered, in no way stripped of the framework of white supremacy, we are pressured to assimilate. We are rewarded for assimilation. Black people working or socializing in predominantly white settings whose very structures are informed by the principles of white supremacy who dare to affirm blackness, love of black culture and identity, do so at great risk. We must continually challenge, protest, resist while working to leave no gaps in our defense that will allow us to be crushed. This is especially true in work settings where we risk being fired or not receiving deserved promotions. Resisting the pressure to assimilate is a part of our struggle to end white supremacy.

When I talk with audiences around the United States about feminist issues of race and gender, my use of the term "white supremacy" always sparks a reaction, usually of a critical or hostile nature. Individual white people and even some non-whites insist that this is not a white supremacist society, that racism is not nearly the problem it used to be (it is downright frightening to hear people argue vehemently that the problem of racism has been solved), that there has been change. While it is true that the nature of racist oppression and exploitation has changed as slavery has ended and the apartheid structure of Jim Crow has legally changed, white supremacy continues to shape perspectives on reality and to inform the social status of black people and all people of color. Nowhere is this more evident than in university settings. And often it is the liberal folks in those settings who are unwilling to acknowledge this truth.

Recently in a conversation with a white male lawyer at his home where I was a guest, he informed me that someone had commented to him that children are learning very little history these days in school, that the attempt to be all-inclusive, to talk about Native Americans, blacks, women, etc. has led to a fragmented focus on particular representative individuals with no larger historical framework. I responded to this comment by suggesting that it has been easier for white people to practice this inclusion rather than change the larger framework; that it is easier to change the focus from Christopher Columbus, the important white man who "discovered" America, to Sitting Bull or Harriet Tubman, than it is to cease telling a distorted version of U.S. history which upholds white supremacy. Really teaching history in a new way would require abandoning the old myths informed by white supremacy like the notion that Columbus discovered America. It would mean talking about imperialism, colonization, about the Africans who came here before Columbus (see Ivan Van Sertima's *They Came Before Columbus*). It would mean talking about genocide, about the white colonizers' exploitation and betrayal of Native Americans; about ways the legal and governmental structures of this society from the Constitution on supported and upheld slavery, apartheid (see Derrick Bell's *And We Are Not Saved*). This history can be taught only when the perspectives of teachers are no longer shaped by white supremacy. Our conversation is one of many examples that reveal the way black people and white people can socialize in a friendly manner, be racially integrated, while deeply ingrained notions of white supremacy remain intact. Incidents like this make it necessary for concerned folks, for righteous white people, to begin to fully explore the way white supremacy determines how they see the world, even as their actions are not informed by the type of racial prejudice that promotes overt discrimination and separation.

Significantly, "assimilation" was a term that began to be

more commonly used after the revolts against white supremacy in the late 1960s and early 1970s. The intense, passionate rebellion against racism and white supremacy of this period was crucial because it created a context for politicization, for education for critical consciousness, one in which black people could begin to confront the extent of our complicity, our internalization of white supremacy, and begin the process of self-recovery and collective renewal. Describing this effort in his work *The Search for a Common Ground*, black theologian Howard Thurman commented:

> "Black is Beautiful" became not merely a phrase—it was a stance, a total attitude, a metaphysics. In very positive and exciting terms it began undermining the idea that had developed over so many years into a central aspect of white mythology: that black is ugly, black is evil, black is demonic. In so doing it fundamentally attacked the front line of the defense of the myth of white supremacy and superiority.

Clearly, assimilation as a social policy upholding white supremacy was strategically an important counterdefense, one that would serve to deflect the call for radical transformation of black consciousness. Suddenly the terms for success (that is, getting a job, acquiring the means to provide materially for oneself and one's family) were redefined. It was not enough for black people to enter institutions of higher education and acquire the necessary skills to effectively compete for jobs previously occupied solely by whites; the demand was that blacks become "honorary whites," that black people assimilate to succeed.

The force that gave the social policy of assimilation power to influence and change the direction of black liberation struggle was economic. Economic distress created a climate wherein militancy—overt resistance to white supremacy and racism (which included the presentation of self in a manner that suggests black pride)—was no longer deemed a viable survival strategy. Natural hairstyles, African dress, etc. were discarded as signs of militancy that might keep one from getting ahead. A similar regressive, reactionary move was taking place among young white radicals, many of whom had been fiercely engaged in Left politics, who suddenly began to seek reincorporation into the liberal and conservative mainstream. Again the force behind their reentry into the system was economic. On a very basic level, changes in the cost of housing (as in the great apartment one had in 1965 for $100 a month cost $400 by 1975) had a frightening impact on college-educated young people of all ethnicities who thought they were committed to transforming society, but who were unable to face living without choice, without the means to escape, who feared living in poverty. Coupled with economic forces exerting pressure, many radicals despaired of the possibility that this white supremacist capitalist patriarchy could really be changed.

Tragically, many radical whites who had been allies in the black liberation struggle began to question whether the struggle to end racism was really that significant, or to suggest that the struggle was over, as they moved into their new liberal positions. Radical white youth who had worked in civil rights struggles, protested the war in Vietnam, and even denounced U.S. imperialism could not reconstruct their ties to prevailing systems of domination without creating a new layer of false consciousness—the assertion that racism was no longer pervasive, that race was no longer an important issue. Similarly, critiques of capitalism, especially those that urged individuals to try and live differently within the framework of capitalism, were also relegated to the back burner as people "discovered" that it was important to have class privilege so that one could better help the exploited.

It is no wonder that black radicals met these betrayals with despair and hopelessness. What had all the contemporary struggle to resist racism really achieved? What did it mean to have this period of radical questioning of white supremacy, of black is beautiful, only to witness a few years later the successful mass production by white corporations of hair care products to straighten black hair? What did it mean to witness the assault on black culture by capitalist forces which stress the production on all fronts of an image, a cultural product that can "cross over"—that is, that can speak more directly to the concerns, to the popular imagination of white consumers, while still attracting the dollars of black consumers. And what does it mean in 1987 when television viewers watch a morning talk show on black beauty, where black women suggest that these trends are only related to personal preferences and have no relation to racism; when viewers witness a privileged white male, Phil Donahue, shaking his head and trying to persuade the audience to acknowledge the reality of racism and its impact on black people? Or what does it mean when many black people say that what they like most about the Bill Cosby show is that there is little emphasis on blackness, that they are "just people"? And again to hear reported on national news that little black children prefer playing with white dolls rather than black dolls? All these popular narratives remind us that "we are not yet saved," that white supremacy prevails, that the racist oppression and exploitation which daily assaults the bodies and spirits of black people in South Africa assaults black people here.

Years ago when I was a high school student experiencing racial desegregation, there was a current of resistance and militancy that was so fierce. It swept over and through our bodies as we—black students—stood, pressed against the red brick walls, watching the National Guard with their guns, waiting for those moments when we would enter, when we would break through racism, waiting for the moments of change—of victory. And now even within myself I find that spirit of militancy growing faint; all too often it is assaulted by feelings of despair and powerlessness. I find that I must work to nourish it, to keep it strong. Feelings of despair and powerlessness are intensified by all the images of black self-hate that indicate that those militant 1960s did not have sustained radical impact—that the politicization and transformation of black consciousness did not become an ongoing revolutionary practice in black life. This causes such frustration and despair because it means that we must return to this basic agenda, that we must renew efforts at politicization, that we must go over old ground. Perhaps what is more disheartening is the fear that the seeds, though planted again, will never survive, will never grow strong. Right now it is anger and rage (see Audre Lorde's "The Uses of Anger" in *Sister Outsider*) at the continued racial genocide that rekindles within me that spirit of militancy.

Like so many radical black folks who work in university settings, I often feel very isolated. Often we work in environments predominantly peopled by white folks (some of whom are well-meaning and concerned) who are not committed to working to end white supremacy, or who are unsure about what that commitment means. Certainly feminist movement has been one of the places where there has been renewed interest in challenging and resisting racism. There too it has been easier for white women to confront racism as overt exploitation and domination, or as personal prejudice, than to confront the encompassing and profound reality of white supremacy.

In talking about race and gender recently, the question most often asked by white women has to do with white women's response to black women or women of color insisting that they are not willing to teach them about their racism—to show the way. They want to know: What should a white person do who is attempting to resist racism? It is problematic to assert that black people and other people of color who are sincerely committed to struggling against white supremacy should be unwilling to help or teach white people. Challenging black folks in the nineteenth century, Frederick Douglass made the crucial point that "power accedes nothing without demand." For the racially oppressed to demand of white people, of black people, of all people that we eradicate white supremacy, that those who benefit materially by exercising white supremacist power, either actively or passively, willingly give up that privilege in response to that demand, and then to refuse to show the way, is to undermine our own cause. We must show the way. There must exist a paradigm, a practical model for social change that includes an understanding of ways to transform consciousness that are linked to efforts to transform structures.

Fundamentally, it is our collective responsibility as radical black people and people of color, and as white people, to construct models for social change. To abdicate that responsibility, to suggest that change is just something an individual can do on his or her own or in isolation with other racist white people, is utterly misleading. If as a black person I say to a white person who shows a willingness to commit herself or himself to the struggle to end white supremacy that I refuse to affirm or help in that endeavor, it is a gesture that undermines my commitment to that struggle. Many black people have essentially responded in this way because we do not want to do the work for white people, and most importantly we cannot do the work, yet this often seems to be what is asked of us. Rejecting the work does not mean that we cannot and do not show the way by our actions, by the information we share. Those white people who want to continue the dominant-subordinate relationship so endemic to racist exploitation by insisting that we "serve" them—that we do the work of challenging and changing their consciousness—are acting in bad faith. In his work *Pedagogy in Progress: The Letters to Guinea-Bissau*, Paulo Freire reminds us:

> Authentic help means that all who are involved help each other mutually, growing together in the common effort to understand the reality which they seek to transform.

It is our collective responsibility as people of color and as white people who are committed to ending white supremacy to help one another. It is our collective responsibility to educate for critical consciousness. If I commit myself politically to black liberation struggle, to the struggle to end white supremacy, I am not making a commitment to working only for and with black people; I must engage in struggle with all willing comrades to strengthen our awareness and our resistance. (See *The Autobiography of Malcolm X* and *The Last Year of Malcolm X—The Evolution of a Revolutionary* by George Breitman.) Malcolm X is an important role model for those of us who wish to transform our consciousness for he was engaged in ongoing critical self-reflection, in changing both his words and his deeds. In thinking about black response to white people, about what they can do to end racism, I am reminded of that memorable example when Malcolm X expressed regret about an incident with a white female college student who asked him what she could do and he told her: "nothing." He later saw that there was much

that she could have done. For each of us, it is work to educate ourselves to understand the nature of white supremacy
with a critical consciousness. Black people are not born into
this world with innate understanding of racism and white
supremacy. (See John Hodge, ed., *Cultural Bases of Racism
and Group Oppression*.)

In recent years, particularly among women active in feminist movement, much effort to confront racism has focused
on individual prejudice. While it is important that individuals
work to transform their consciousness, striving to be anti-
racist, it is important for us to remember that the struggle
to end white supremacy is a struggle to change a system, a
structure. Hodge emphasizes in his book "the problem of
racism is not prejudice but domination." For our efforts to
end white supremacy to be truly effective, individual struggle
to change consciousness must be fundamentally linked to
collective effort to transform those structures that reinforce
and perpetuate white supremacy.

BEYOND BLACK ONLY

BONDING BEYOND RACE

A frican Americans have been at the forefront of the struggle to end racism and white supremacy in the United States since individual free black immigrants and the larger body of enslaved blacks first landed here. Even though much of that struggle has been directly concerned with the plight of black people, all the gains received from civil rights work have had tremendous positive impact on the social status of all non-white groups in this country. Bonding between enslaved Africans, free Africans, and Native Americans is well documented. Freedom fighters from all groups (and certainly there were many traitors in all three groups who were co-opted by rewards given by the white power structure) understood the importance of solidarity—of struggling against the common enemy, white supremacy. The enemy was not white people. It was white supremacy.

Organic freedom fighters, both Native and African American, had no difficulty building coalitions with those white folks who wanted to work for the freedom of everyone. Those early models of coalition building in the interest of dismantling white supremacy are often forgotten. Much has happened to obscure that history. The construction of reservations (many of which were and are located in areas where there are not large populations of black people) isolated communities of Native Americans from black liberation struggle. And as time passed both groups began to view one another through Eurocentric stereotypes, internalizing white racist assumptions about the other. Those early coalitions were not maintained. Indeed the bonds between African Americans struggling to resist racist domination, and all other people of color in this society who suffer from the same system, continue to be fragile, even as we all remain united by ties, however frayed and weakened, forged in shared anti-racist struggle.

Collectively, within the United States people of color strengthen our capacity to resist white supremacy when we build coalitions. Since white supremacy emerged here within the context of colonization, the conquering and conquest of Native Americans, early on it was obvious that Native and African Americans could best preserve their cultures by resisting from a standpoint of political solidarity. The concrete practice of solidarity between the two groups has been eroded by the divide-and-conquer tactics of racist white power and by the complicity of both groups. Native American artist and activist of the Cherokee people Jimmie Durham, in his collection of essays *A Certain Lack of Coherence*, talks about the sixties as a time when folks tried to regenerate that spirit of coalition: "In the 1960s and '70s American Indian, African-American and Puerto Rican activists said, as loudly as they could, 'This country is founded on the genocide of one people and the enslavement of another.' This statement, hardly arguable, was not much taken up by white activists." As time passed, it was rarely taken up by anyone. Instead the fear that one's specific group might receive more attention has led to greater nationalism, the showing of concern for one's racial or ethnic plight without linking that concern to the plight of other non-white groups and their struggles for liberation.

Bonds of solidarity between people of color are continuously ruptured by our complicity with white racism. Similarly, white immigrants to the United States, both past and present, establish their right to citizenship within white supremacist society by asserting it in daily life through acts of discrimination and assault that register their contempt for and disregard of black people and darker-skinned immigrants. Concurrently, darker-skinned immigrants mimic this racist behavior in their interactions with black folks. In her editorial "On the Backs of Blacks" published in a recent special issue of *Time* magazine Toni Morrison discusses the way white supremacy is reinscribed again and again as immigrants seek assimilation into this society:

> All immigrants fight for jobs and space, and who is there to fight but those who have both? As in the fishing ground struggle between Texas and Vietnamese shrimpers, they displace what and whom they can.... In race talk the move into mainstream America always means buying into the notion of American blacks as the real aliens. Whatever the ethnicity or nationality of the immigrant, his nemesis is understood to be African-American.... So addictive is this ploy that the fact of blackness has been abandoned for the theory of blackness. It doesn't matter anymore what shade the newcomer's skin is. A hostile posture toward resident blacks must be struck at the Americanizing door before it will open....

Often people of color, both those who are citizens and those who are recent immigrants, hold black people responsible for the hostility they encounter from whites. It is as though they see blacks as acting in a manner that makes things hard for everybody else. This type of scapegoating is the mark of the colonized sensibility which always blames those victimized rather than targeting structures of domination.

Just as many white Americans deny both the prevalence of racism in the United States and the role they play in perpetuating and maintaining white supremacy, non-white, non-black groups, Native, Asian, Hispanic Americans, all deny their investment in anti-black sentiment even as they consistently seek to distance themselves from blackness so that they will not be seen as residing at the bottom of this society's totem pole, in the category reserved for the most despised group. Such jockeying for white approval and reward obscures the way allegiance to the existing social structure undermines the social welfare of all people of color. White supremacist power is always weakened when people of color bond across differences of culture, ethnicity, and race. It is always strengthened when we act as though there is no continuity and overlap in the patterns of exploitation and oppression that affect all our lives.

To ensure that political bonding to challenge and change white supremacy will not be cultivated among diverse groups of people of color, white ruling groups pit us against one another in a no-win game of "who will get the prize for model minority today." They compare and contrast, affix labels like "model minority," define boundaries, and we fall into line. Those rewards coupled with internalized racist assumptions lead non-black people of color to deny the way racism victimizes them even as they actively work to disassociate themselves from black people. This will to disassociate is a gesture of racism.

Even though progressive people of color consistently critique these standpoints, we have yet to build a contemporary mass movement to challenge white supremacy that would draw us together. Without an organized collective struggle that consistently reminds us of our common concerns, people of color forget. Sadly, forgetting common concerns sets the stage for competing concerns. Working within the system of white supremacy, non-black people of color often feel as though they must compete with black folks to receive white attention. Some are even angry at what they wrongly perceive as a greater concern on the part of the dominant culture for the pain of black people. Rather than seeing the attention black people receive as linked to the gravity of our situation and the intensity of our resistance, they want to make it a sign of white generosity and concern. Such thinking is absurd. If white folks were genuinely concerned about black pain, they would challenge racism, not turn the spotlight on our collective pain in ways that further suggest that we are inferior. Andrew Hacker makes it clear in *Two Nations* that the vast majority of white Americans believe that "members of the black race represent an inferior strain of the human species." He adds: "In this view, Africans—and Americans who trace their origins to that continent—are seen as languishing at a lower evolutionary level than members of other races." Non-black people of color often do not approach white attention to black issues by critically interrogating how those issues are presented and whose interests these representations ultimately serve. Rather than engaging in a competition that sees blacks as winning more goodies from the white system than other groups, non-black people of color who identify with black resistance struggle recognize the danger of such thinking and repudiate it. They are politically astute enough to challenge a rhetoric of resistance that is based on competition rather than a capacity on the part of non-black groups to identify with whatever progress blacks make as being a positive sign for everyone. Until non-black people of color define their citizenship via commitment to a democratic vision of racial justice rather than investing in the dehumanization and oppression of black people, they will always act as mediators, keeping black people in check for the ruling white majority. Until racist anti-black sentiments are let go by other people of color, no transformation of white supremacy will take place. Concurrently, when black people have internalized white supremacist attitudes and values, revealing the same prejudicial feelings towards non-black people of color, especially immigrants, and complain that these groups are receiving too much attention, they undermine freedom struggle. When this happens people of color are all acting in complicity with existing exploitative and oppressive structures.

As more people of color raise our consciousnesses and refuse to be pitted against one another, the forces of neo-colonial white supremacist domination must work harder to divide and conquer. The most recent effort to undermine progressive bonding between people of color is the institutionalization of "multiculturalism." Positively, multiculturalism is presented as a corrective to a Eurocentric vision of model citizenship wherein white middle-class ideals are presented as the norm. Yet this positive intervention is then undermined by visions of multiculturalism that suggest everyone should live with and identify with their own self-contained cultural group. If white supremacist capitalist patriarchy is unchanged then multiculturalism within that context can only become a breeding ground for narrow nationalism, fundamentalism, identity politics, and cultural, racial, and ethnic separatism. Each separate group will then feel that it must protect its own interests by keeping outsiders at bay, for the group will always appear vulnerable, its power and identity sustained by exclusivity. When people of color think this way, white supremacy remains intact. For even though demographics in the United States would suggest that in the future the nation will be more populated by people of color, and whites will no longer be the majority group, numerical presence will in no way alter white supremacy if there is no collective organizing, no efforts to build coalitions that cross boundaries. Already, the white Christian Right is targeting large populations of people of color to ensure that the fundamentalist values they want this nation to uphold and represent will determine the attitudes and values of these groups. The role Eurocentric Christianity has played in teaching non-white folks Western metaphysical dualism, the ideology that undergirds binary notions of superior/inferior, good/bad, white/black, cannot be ignored. While progressive organizations are having difficulty reaching wider audiences, the white-dominated Christian Right organizes outreach programs that acknowledge diversity and have considerable influence. Just as the white-dominated Christian church in the United States once relied on biblical references to justify racist domination and discrimination, it now deploys a rhetoric of multiculturalism to invite non-white people to believe that racism can be overcome through a shared fundamentalist encounter. Every contemporary fundamentalist white male–dominated religious cult in the United States has a diverse congregation. People of color have flocked to these organizations because they have felt them to be places where racism does not exist, where they are not judged on the basis of skin color. While the white-dominated mass media focus critical attention on black religious fundamentalist groups like the Nation of Islam, and in particular Louis Farrakhan, little critique is made of white Christian fundamentalist outreach to black people and other people of color. Black Islamic fundamentalism shares with the white Christian Right support for coercive hierarchy, fascism, and a belief that some groups are inferior and others superior, along with a host of other similarities. Irrespective of the standpoint, religious fundamentalism brainwashes individuals to not think critically or see radical politicization as a means of transforming their lives. When people of color immerse themselves in religious fundamentalism, no meaningful challenge and critique of white supremacy can surface. Participation in a radical multiculturalism in any form is discouraged by religious fundamentalism.

Progressive multiculturalism that encourages and promotes coalition building between people of color threatens to disrupt white supremacist organization of us all into competing camps. However, this vision of multiculturalism is continually undermined by greed, one group wanting rewards for itself even at the expense of other groups. It is this perversion of solidarity the authors of *Night Vision* address when they assert: "While there are different nationalities, races and genders in the U.S., the supposedly different cultures in multiculturalism don't like to admit what they have in common, the glue of it all—parasitism. Right now, there's both anger among the oppressed and a milling around, edging up to the next step but uncertain what it is fully about, what it means. The key is the common need to break with parasitism." A progressive politics of solidarity that embraces both a broad-based identity politics which acknowledges specific cultural and ethnic legacies, histories, etc. as it simultaneously promotes a recognition of overlapping cultural traditions and values as well as an inclusive understanding of what is gained when people of color unite to resist white supremacy is the only way to ensure that multicultural democracy will become a reality.

KEEPING A LEGACY
OF SHARED STRUGGLE

Recently teaching women's studies courses for two months at a European university, engaging in intense discussions about race and racism, I found myself speaking much more about anti-Semitism than I ever did in the United States. Emphasizing connections between the global development of anti-Semitism and anti-black racism, I often referred to Ronald Sanders's book *Lost Tribes and Promised Lands: The Origins of American Racism*. Within the European context to talk of white supremacy one must necessarily look at the history of Jews (white and non-white) in the world and make sense of that history in relationship to the development of racist thinking about black people. These discussions led me to reflect often on the growing antagonism between white Jewish people and black folks in the United States. (There are black Jews either by birth or conversion. To respect their culture and faith throughout this essay when I am speaking about white Jews that is the term I will use. Usually folks refer solely to the experiences of white Jews [i.e., when scholars and writers talk about the relationship between blacks and Jews].)

I remember heated arguments in classrooms at Oberlin when black students would talk about white people and white culture and Jewish students would speak out and insist that they not be included in this category of whiteness. What these discussions always revealed was that we lacked a complex language to talk about white Jewish identity in the United States and its relationship to blackness and black identity. It was hard and painful for some Jewish students to acknowledge that in a white supremacist society like the United States where race/ethnicity is often defined solely by skin color, the fact of whiteness can subsume allegiance to Jewish identity, religion, etc. and overdetermine one's actions in daily life, or how one is treated. To some extent these students believe so deeply in the notion of democracy and individual rights that they are convinced that if they choose not to identify as "white" no one will see them that way. Their fierce denial of any allegiance or participation in constructions of whiteness seemed to evoke an equally fierce desire on the part of black students to insist that not only was the fact of whiteness more obvious than Jewishness, but that it was the denial of this reality that made it possible for Jewish students to be complicit with racism and remain unaware of the nature of that participation. When such conflicts arise it is always useful to send students to read *Yours in Struggle: Three Feminist Perspectives on Anti-Semitism and Racism*, especially the sections by Elly Bulkin.

In her section Bulkin asserts that she assumes that "all non-Jews, even those without institutional power, have internalized the norm of anti-Semitism in this culture and are capable of being anti-Semitic, whether through hostility or ignorance." Agreeing with this assumption, I have always deemed it significant that Bulkin chose to highlight that we are all capable of anti-Semitic thought and action, rather than to assert as some folks do that we are all "naturally" anti-Semitic because we are born into an anti-Semitic culture. By focusing on our "capability," she reminds us that we are able to act in ways that fundamentally resist and oppose anti-Semitism. Growing up in the segregated South the fundamental lesson that I was taught via the black Baptist church was that Jews all over the world had suffered exploitation and oppression, that we identified with them and took their struggle to be our own because of shared experience. Most importantly, we were taught that anti-Semitism and anti-black racism were fundamentally connected. One could not be raised in hard-core Klan country and not be aware of this connection. It was deeply embedded in our consciousness as southern blacks that we had to oppose anti-Semitism—always.

Given these teachings, we knew as children that white Jews born and raised in the South often suffered at the hands of white supremacists. We also knew that in high school it bolstered the image of the "Jew" in the eyes of white supremacists when white Jewish students would make a point of acting in a racist way towards black folks. Like us, many of these young Jews had been taught in the context of home and religious experience to identify with the oppressed, and therefore to recognize their connections with black folks. So early on, we all experienced contradictions in how we thought and how we behaved. Jewish white students who might be the most racist in front of other southern white folks might in a different context act in a non-racist manner. When we "reported" these contradictions in our segregated religious contexts, we were taught that no matter the actions of individual Jews, we were called by our faith and our destiny as a people to stand in solidarity with them.

Perhaps it was solely due to the backwoods provincial nature of my region and upbringing, but it was not until I left the South for college that I first heard black folks make anti-Semitic remarks. These were northern black folks who behaved and acted in ways that were completely alien to me. Indeed, it was those early years of college that shook up my notions of monolithic black identity. I learned that not all black folks thought the same way or shared the same values. And I learned that we did not always think alike on the subject of the relationship between blacks and Jews. I learned that not all black people were Christians. I learned this from the followers of Elijah Muhammad who sold their papers and spread their teachings on campus. And it was there as an undergraduate that I developed deep friendships and political alliances with young white Jews. Then, we did not feel that there was a need to define the nature of our solidarity; we accepted the bonds of history, a continuum of shared struggle. It was only when we began to look beyond our small circles of intimacy and fellowship that we had to think critically about the relationship between blacks and white Jews. Within feminist circles we focused our discussions on the relationships among women, not directing them to a larger audience. This may be why folks act as though women thinkers have no worthwhile perspectives to offer on the subject. Usually when relations between "blacks and Jews" are talked about what is really evoked is the relationship between black men and white Jewish men.

The discussion of black-Jewish relationships in the United States has mainly been an exchange between male thinkers. It has often been dominated by northern voices. *Yours in Struggle* was published in 1984 and it did not lead to a growth of literature by black women (some of whom are Jewish) and white Jewish women. It was impossible to read

Henry Louis Gates's recent *New York Times* editorial "Black Demagogues and Pseudo-Scholars" and not notice that all the critical thinkers mentioned are male. However, I assume that he includes black females when he asserts: "While anti-Semitism is generally on the wane in this country, it has been on the rise among black Americans. A recent survey finds not only that blacks are twice as likely as whites to hold anti-Semitic views but—significantly—that it is among the younger and more educated blacks that anti-Semitism is most pronounced." This assertion is dangerously provocative. I wanted to know how, when, and who had conducted such a survey. And whether or not this was equally true for blacks in different regions—if there were any differences of opinions based on gender. Unlike Gates, I do not believe that anti-Semitism is on the wane in this country. Anyone who has followed the campaign of David Duke and the rise in white supremacist groups would do well to question such an assertion. Since I see anti-Semitism as connected to anti-black racism, which is on the rise, I can only assume that anti-Semitism is also gaining new ground. From my perspective, it is precisely the rise in conservative thinking that advocates and supports white supremacy that has created a climate where anti-Semitism and racism are both flourishing.

In his piece Gates paints a graphically harsh portrait of black anti-Semitism that does not include a concomitant picture of black resistance to anti-Semitism. By so doing he runs the risk of further perpetuating a schism between blacks and Jews. Though his critique of recent black anti-Semitic thought and his citing of specific scholars is useful, his article tends to construct a monolithic black community that can be and is easily duped by outspoken black males (mostly self-appointed leaders) who are pushing anti-Semitic thinking. And even though Gates cites work written by white males as central to the development of anti-Semitic thought among some blacks, he does not identify them as "white" influences, which really does distort the issue. There is a profound link between white fascism in this society and black fascism, white conservatism and black conservatism. Black folks who are anti-Semitic are not just under the influence of "crazed" black male leaders; they are also guided by the anti-Semitism that is rampant in the culture as a whole. To refuse to see this as a force that shapes the thinking of conservative black folks, in conjunction with that anti-Semitic teaching that is an aspect of some Afrocentric thought, is to fail to understand the problem. And if we do not accurately name how anti-Semitism is taught to young black minds we will not be able to honestly confront, challenge, and change the situation. Concurrently, if black anti-Semitism is to be eradicated and not merely evoked in ways that pit one group of black folks against another, that make one group of black folks the "darlings" among white Jews and another the "enemy," we must create critical spaces for dialogue where the aim is not to cast "blame" but to look more deeply at why two groups that should and must maintain solidarity are drifting apart.

In my classrooms I can see that one of the primary tensions between young educated black students (some of whom are Jewish) and white Jews is engendered by the feeling (whether rooted in fact or fantasy) on the part of blacks that many Jews who have class privilege, who are able to use white-skin privilege in a white supremacist society like this one, no longer identify with the oppressed (if they ever did) and more importantly often act in a "colonizing" manner in relation to black experience. As with other black folks in the larger society who no longer see Jews as allies in struggle, they feel the legacy of solidarity has been betrayed. Contrary to the Gates piece, they see Jews as breaking that connection in the interest of further assimilation into mainstream white culture. Their hostility at this perceived betrayal is often expressed via anti-Semitic comments. Yet, when probed, I find they do not see the dangerous connection between making these comments and complicity with those who would institutionalize exploitation and oppression of Jews globally. Not only do they not recognize how systems of domination are maintained, they are ignorant of the ways those of us who are relatively "powerless" can act as agents upholding forms of oppression inimical to our own interest.

However wrong-minded, it is not surprising that black youth, many of whom are from materially privileged backgrounds, who feel their chances of gaining economic success are continually thwarted by systems of racial injustice make the mistake of targeting their rage at white Jews. This is part of the way racism works—it is easier to "scapegoat" Jews (especially when one has concrete racist encounters) than to target larger structures of white supremacy. To seriously challenge this anti-Semitism we must have a better knowledge of institutionalized white supremacy. That includes consciously understanding the way white supremacist culture promotes black anti-Semitism. For example, from whom do young black folks get the notion that Jews control Hollywood? This stereotype trickles down from mainstream white culture. It is just one of many. In his *New York Times* article, Gates never acknowledges a link between white Christian fundamentalism that perpetuates anti-Semitic thinking and the fundamentalist thinking of narrow black nationalists. It is a distortion of reality to act as though any form of black anti-Semitism, however virulent, exists in isolation from the anti-Semitism that is learned whenever anyone absorbs without question the values of mainstream white culture, values that are taught via mass media, etc.

Indeed, if we were to investigate why masses of black youth all over the United States know who Louis Farrakhan is, or Leonard Jeffries, we would probably find that white-dominated mass media have been the educational source, not those black bookstores that Gates writes about. Again I want to state strongly that the anti-Semitism expressed by such leaders in public forums is irrevocably linked to the anti-Semitism of those whites who provide the forums but who are not overtly spreading anti-Semitic thinking. It would be a grave mistake for white Jewish readers of the Gates piece to come away imagining that the group that they must see as enemies and armor themselves against is young educated black folks, or black people in general. It is significant that narrow nationalist black leaders who push anti-Semitic thought tend to also push sexist domination of women. The majority are male unless they are the female followers of Farrakhan. It would have been interesting had the Gates piece raised the question of gender for it is not apparent whether black women, young and old, educated or not, are as taken with the black male scholars and leaders he identifies as spreading anti-Semitic thinking as are black males.

The only black woman mentioned in the Gates piece is evoked as a figure of ridicule. Referred to as the "dread-locked woman" who spoke "angrily" at a dialogue between blacks and white Jews saying to one of the white female organizers: "I don't want an apology. I want reparations. Forty acres and a mule, plus interest." Whether one is speaking in a heated manner to an audience that includes white Jews or not, why is the rage of black folks about white supremacy made to appear ridiculous, even if the direction that rage is targeted at is not an appropriate one? Surprisingly, even though Gates evokes Martin Luther King to emphasize the need for us all to remember that white Jews and black

Americans are "caught in an inescapable network of mutuality," this understanding does not lead to the recognition that since both groups are accountable for perpetuating conflict, hostility, and xenophobic/racist thinking about the other, then both groups must work to create the space for dialogue and reconciliation.

Many black folks want white Jews to confront and change their racism. Elly Bulkin writes passionately and honestly about the need for white Jews to confront anti-black racism, acknowledging that "we do not yet know how to raise the issues of Jewish oppression and racism in the best possible way, or, given the history and complexity of both, in ways that will assure us not only that we have done it well, but that we are likely to be heard." The existence of Jewish racism does not justify or excuse black anti-Semitism. However, to honestly name and assume accountability for it does heighten our awareness that not all Jews have been or are friends and allies to black folks. It allows us to face the reality that there are real circumstances in which Jewish racism manifested in daily life encounters leads some black folks to see white Jews as enemies and to imagine that they gain power over this threat by expressing anti-Semitic thought. Gates suggests that "many Jews are puzzled by the recrudescence of black anti-Semitism in view of the historic alliance" but he does not respond to this puzzlement by sharing that it is for some black folks a defense against anti-black racism on the part of Jews.

Solidarity between blacks and white Jews must be mutual. It cannot be based on a notion of black people as needy victims that white Jews "help." It cannot be based on gratitude extended by blacks to white Jews for those historical moments when they have been steadfast comrades in struggle furthering black liberation. It has to be rooted in a recognition on the part of both groups of shared history, shared struggle, and the ways in which our past and future destinies both connect and diverge. It has to be rooted in an ongoing political recognition that white supremacy relies on the maintenance of anti-black racism and anti-Semitism, hence there will never be a time when these two struggles will not be connected. No matter how many or how strong the ties Jewish political parties make with white South Africa, thereby condoning the maintenance of white supremacy, this reality will remain. Wherever there is white supremacy, there will be anti-Semitism and racism.

The failure of blacks and white Jews to engage in critical dialogue that does not reflect prevailing racist hierarchy has meant that it is unclear in what context either group can be critical of the other without being labeled racist or anti-Semitic. Where is the context where blacks can come together with white Jews and talk critically about Jewish appropriation and commodification of black culture? Where is the context where Jews can come together with black non-Jews and talk about the sense of betrayal of a historical legacy of solidarity? What is the context in which black people can be critical of Zionist policies that condone the colonization and exploitation of Palestinians? Where is the context in which Jews can question black folks about our attitudes and opinions about Israel, about Jewish nationalism? Unless these contexts exist we will not be able to create the kind of critical thinking and writing that can challenge and transform black anti-Semitism or white Jewish racism. Targeting our critiques solely at anti-Semitic black leaders (who represent a small fragment of black populations) does not enable masses of blacks and white Jews to understand both the historical and present-day connections among the growth of white supremacy, the development of anti-Semitic thought and practice globally, and the spread of anti-black racism. It is this knowledge that would enable folks from both groups to understand why solidarity between us must be nurtured and sustained.

Black people are not more responsible for eradicating strains of anti-Semitism in black life than in the culture as a whole. However, we must stand against anti-Semitism wherever we encounter it. It is the task facing any of us who work for freedom. To honor our bond of inescapable mutuality, black people and white Jews must share in the *collective work* of creating theory and practice that can counter the anti-Semitic biases of the culture, in whatever location those biases speak themselves. Working to eradicate anti-Semitism we are equally working to end racism.

WHERE IS THE LOVE

POLITICAL BONDING BETWEEN
BLACK AND WHITE WOMEN

A s ridiculous as it may seem, I was thrilled to be asked to appear on a popular talk show as the "expert" on the topic of whether or not black women and white women can be friends. My pleasure emerged from the assumption that it is crucial for those of us who advocate progressive politics, an end to racist and sexist domination, to make our voices heard. When I arrived at the television station, I found that even though I had answered an unequivocal yes to the question of whether white and black women can be friends, with the added comment that interviews and discussions with folks had shown that for the most part we are *not* friends, I was viewed as hostile to the idea. As the show began taping, whenever I spoke about some of the negative ways white women and black women perceive each other and interact with one another, I was yelled at by an audience of black and white folks who were insisting that nothing I was saying was accurate. When I suggested that one could travel all around the United States and sit in shopping malls and the group one would not see hanging out together would be white females and black females, the audience responded negatively. Vehemently shouting their disagreement, they were not willing to engage the idea that serious barriers separate us from one another.

When a young white woman from Alabama attempted to share her failed experience of befriending a black woman neighbor who not only rejected her overtures but was consistently hostile, the audience refused to listen to her articulate the problems which exist between the two groups. An individual black woman who felt that there could not be friendship between white and black females described how her friendship with a white woman ended in betrayal when the latter chose a white boyfriend who would not accept a white girlfriend's having black friends; the audience responded by telling her she should not generalize from one experience. Then the studio brought on a mystery guest, a white woman active in the Nazi party who shared her belief that black females are inferior manlike subhumans who have nothing in common with their white counterparts. At this point the audience went berserk. The taping of the program stopped and it was not aired. Throughout the taping both the audience and the other participants had difficulty focusing on the topic. They kept wanting to talk about race and racism in more general ways. At this point, I suggested that the refusal to take the topic seriously was in itself an indication of the way sexist and racist thinking merge to create a context where this subject could not be taken seriously or discussed respectfully. Ironically, even though the audience was eager to insist that white women and black women are friends, the fact remains that this same audience was not able to see those friendships as worthy of attention and discussion. They insisted on changing the subject.

Prior to appearing at the taping, I spoke with a number of people across race, gender, and geographic location about the show. In every case they responded by saying the topic was "silly" or "stupid." Across many boundaries of identity, class, and lived experience, folks insisted that this topic was not important because it is obvious that the two groups are friends. In fact, friendships between white and black women are not common. Not much about patterns of bonding across race in American life suggests that black females and white females find it at all easy to socialize with one another or bond as friends. Most people seem to be in denial about how few bonds of affection and ties bind black and white women together.

Feminist movement is the one political location where bonding between black women and white women has been raised as an important political issue. When there were only a few black women active in the movement, lack of connection between the two groups was mainly raised around the issue of absence of diversity at feminist gatherings. However, as more black women joined the movement, recognition of a lack of connection was given more serious attention. A commonly heard complaint from white women organizers was that they were unable to attract black women to meetings. When I first became active in feminist movement, I joined the struggle in conjunction with young white female college-student peers. Amid civil rights struggle, black power movement, and anti-war protest, we were collectively trying to educate ourselves for critical consciousness so that we would be aware of progressive political agendas. Like many individual black women who received scholarships at predominantly white institutions, I moved in a circle of friends and associates that were white. We were not trying to ignore the history of racism in the United States, the way it had created a structure of social apartheid. We wanted to face the issues and make a world where there was no racism, where we could choose our friends based on shared sensibility rather than factors of race. We spent hours talking about our differences, working hard to create friendships that we felt were revolutionary because they were in opposition to the status quo. We were concerned with creating the social conditions which would allow white and black women to be close, conditions which had emerged in civil rights struggle, in feminist movement.

Now, after more than twenty years of active engagement with feminist movement, it is more evident to me than it was years ago that there are many barriers preventing black females and white females from forming close ties in white supremacist capitalist patriarchy. A major barrier has consistently been the fact that individual white women tend to be more unaware than their black female counterparts of the way the history of racism in the United States has institutionalized structures of racial apartheid that were meant to keep these two groups apart. First, there was the race/class understanding that the role of black females was to be that of servant and of white females that of the served. That servant/served paradigm continued as black women entered all arenas of the workforce since white women were usually positioned higher. Second, there was the racist/sexist division of sexual competition for men that deemed white women more desirable, more worthy of respect and regard than black women. These two major differences in positionality have had profound impact on interracial relationships between the two groups. To begin with they destroy the grounding of trust that is needed for bonding. They create fear on the part of black females that white females only want to assert power over us. Concurrently, white females often fear that black females are more capable, stronger, and if given equal opportunity will surpass them and vengefully assert power over them.

Struggle for power within the existing white supremacist capitalist patriarchal structure makes it difficult for black and white females who have not made a profound commitment to solidarity to forge constructive, mutually satisfying bonds. Within feminist movement, many of us approached the barriers between the two groups by engaging a process of education for critical consciousness that aimed to teach all of us how institutionalized racism overdetermines patterns of social relations. Many white women did not understand how white supremacist privilege allowed them to act in the role of oppressor and/or exploiter in relation to black females. To grow in awareness they had to interrogate the ways they use white privilege, the racist/sexist ways their perceptions of black females shape their interactions. While black females were more willing to express the legacy of hostility and rage we hold towards white women due to their complicity with white supremacy and with acts of racial assault and aggression towards us, it was hard for many of us to let those feelings go and establish within ourselves a space for trust. Many black females active in feminist movement felt that the moment they allowed themselves to open up, white females betrayed their confidence. White females often felt that they could not "please" black females and were unable to see that the point of bonding in sisterhood was not to "please" us—a desire which conjures up sexist/racist fantasies of subordination wherein the more "feminine" subject works to gain the favor of the dominant, more masculine subject—but to relate to us from a position of awareness and respect.

Individual black and white females who forged bonds

found that we did so by first educating ourselves for critical consciousness and by studying the specific history of social relations between the two groups in white supremacist capitalist patriarchy. That history showed time and time again the role betrayal played as a recurring motif in black and white female interactions—whether it was nineteenth-century betrayal, when white women wanted rights for themselves while accepting the exclusion of and denial of rights to black females and all black people, or the betrayals through time that involved white females' overvaluation of black males. To explore and understand the reasons individual nineteenth-century white women leaders chose to socialize with black male leaders, invite them to their homes, even as they shunned intimate contact with black women, we had to look at the convergence of patriarchy and white supremacy. We looked at the place of sexual competition and desire for male favor. We looked at how in order to appeal to white racist men, white women often refused to allow black women to organize around feminist issues with men. Those appeals could not be made if they were simultaneously challenging sexism and racism. Tensions between white females' desire for equal rights within the existing structure and their desire to bond with black females intensified as the struggle to end sexism and racism progressed.

By the time civil rights became a pressing issue, many white females entered the movement without once interrogating the ways they related to black females or black people in general. While black males were comfortable mediating white female racism by the assertion of male privilege and sexual domination (i.e., black men in the movement "subordinating" white women by sleeping with them), black females often felt that they were placed in the role of "mammy." Radical white girls came to them for guidance and advice without seeing that their "mammification" of black females was an extension of the servant/served paradigm. They were not divesting of white supremacy, of racist stereotypes, they were merely refiguring them (i.e., not wanting a black woman to clean her house, but wanting a black woman to caretake her soul). It is rare to read an account of interaction between white and black females in civil rights and black power struggle that documents mutual caretaking between the two groups. The real-life stories of that interaction suggest that black females often felt contempt towards white females because they perceived them to be dependent, childlike, in need of support and nurturance. As a child I remember hearing black women express contempt for white womanhood. They often declared, "I've never met a white woman over the age of twelve that I could respect." Growing up, I understood that black women (like my mother, who cleaned in white homes) often felt that white women were unable to assume responsibility for themselves or anyone else, and this was disgusting to that group of women who were subordinated to them. Even in cases where black women gave the desired nurturance, they had repressed resentment. That resentment intensified when the issue became sexual competition across lines of sexual practice.

Studying this powerful history within feminist circles, it was clear to individual black and white women that sisterhood could not emerge between us if we did not assume accountability for our roles in either sustaining racist thinking and action or nurturing conflict by holding onto mistrust and contempt. We had to take our understanding of the history of our social relations and relate it to our contemporary lives. As black women we had to look at the nature of the legacy of contempt and disrespect for white women and be willing to see them no longer through the lens of the past but recognize them as nondependent and capable. White women seemed to find it much harder to surrender their longing to engage in "mammification," to have us take care of them, to serve them. Yet it was only as individual white women could respect our thoughts and our capacity for leadership that we could work together as comrades and/or friends. Simultaneously, individual black women had to divest of internalized racist thinking that often led them to assume the role of caretaker, "mammy," and then feel resentful. Most importantly, bonds were made only by those individual women who were willing to interrogate themselves honestly.

Unfortunately, the vast majority of white and black women in feminist movement did not commit themselves to forging bonds. Even though some white women broke through racist/sexist denial and came to an understanding of their role in perpetuating racism, they were not willing to give up the privileges extended them by white supremacy. The divisions created by a gap in understanding were being sustained by white female investment in gaining power by any means necessary. Individual black women were deeply discouraged when we had to face the reality that opportunism and the lust to wield power over others so easily undermined commitment to feminist solidarity. This lack of integrity has led many black females to regard with suspicion feminist bonding with white women. However, the overall failure of feminist movement to challenge racism, sexism, and class elitism in ways that would make it possible for women to bond across difference does not mean that feminist thinking is not needed. More than any other progressive political agenda, revolutionary feminist movement has created a context where bonding between black and white women is a primary agenda. Such bonding is possible only if the two groups are willing to undergo processes of education for critical consciousness that support changes in thinking and behavior.

Women who genuinely convert to feminist thinking give up their sexist ways of thinking about other females, an investment in sexist behavior that condones and perpetuates competition. It is this repudiation of competition as the only possible point of contact between women that clears the ground so that seeds of friendship and solidarity can be planted. When individual black and white females attempt to build bonds without divesting of this will to compete, there is usually a rupture of closeness. Competition fosters distrust. But the moment white and black females refuse to compete with one another an important intervention happens: the existing sexist/racist structure is disrupted. If that will to compete is replaced with a longing to know one another, a context for bonding can emerge.

Within white supremacist capitalist patriarchy, we are constantly told by mass media, by books, that it is contact between white females and black males that is still taboo. In reality these two groups find it relatively easy to cross boundaries and create bonds. Black and white women usually connect with each other only in the workforce. Though the two groups may work well together, and even be sociable during lunch hours, they rarely establish ties of friendship that extend beyond work. More than any other body of literature, lesbian writing has highlighted the tensions of interracial bonding between white and black women. From a white lesbian southern standpoint, Mab Segrest's recent book *Memoir of a Race Traitor* gives a detailed account of her relationship with a black straight woman friend that includes dialogue between the two women as they retrospectively critique their friendship. Interviewing women, I often found that white women were more eager to know black women than vice versa. Most black women expressed fear that too much closeness with white women would lead to an overstepping of boundaries. Among heterosexual women, there is a mutual fear on the part of both groups that the men of their race might be sexually attracted to and tempted by the presence of a woman from a different race. A conversion to feminist thinking would decenter the obsession with male regard and make significant the regard in which women hold one another.

If white and black women were collectively working to change society so that we could know one another better and be able to offer acknowledgment and respect, then we would be playing a major role in ending racism. As long as white and black women are content with living separately in a state of psychic social apartheid, racism will not change. If women willingly allow racist/sexist thinking to shape our relationships with one another, we cannot blame patriarchy for keeping us apart. Interrogating female xenophobia (fear of difference) must be a significant part of future struggles to end racism and sexism.

Throughout the history of struggles to end racism in the United States, men have been heralded as the primary leaders. Everyone in our society is more familiar with the names of Martin Luther King and Malcolm X than Septima Clark and Fannie Lou Hamer. From slavery to the present day, individual white and black women have dared to break with white supremacy and patriarchy to make a space for friendship and political solidarity. Contemporary black and white females active in resistance struggle tend not to emphasize the importance of this bonding even though any examination of the relationship between the two groups will indicate how far our society has progressed in the struggle to end racism. At this point in time we need to build a body of literature that will both acknowledge the political significance of bonds between white and black women as well as document the process in which those ties influence the direction of progressive politics, particularly the struggle to end racism.

BLACK INTELLECTUALS

CHOOSING SIDES

Throughout much of our history in the United States, African Americans have been taught to value education—to believe that it is necessary for racial uplift, one of the means by which we can redress wrongs engendered by institutionalized racism. The belief that education was a way to intervene in white supremacist assumptions that black folks were intellectually inferior, more body than mind, was challenged when unprecedented numbers of black students entered colleges and universities, graduated with degrees, yet found that racist assumptions remained intact. It was challenged by the reality of racial assimilation—the creation of a cultural context wherein those educated black folks who had "made it" often internalized white supremacist thinking about blackness. Rather than intervening in the status quo, assimilated educated black folks often became the gatekeepers, mediating between the racist white power structure and that larger mass of black folks who were continually assaulted, exploited, and/or oppressed. Nowhere was this trend more evident than in colleges and universities. Even historically black colleges upheld white supremacist biases in the shaping of curricula, programs of study, and social life.

When militant black resistance to white supremacy erupted in the sixties with the call for black power, the value of education was questioned. The ways in which many educated black folks acted in complicity with the existing racist structure were called out. Even though some black academics and/or intellectuals responded to the demand for progressive education that would not reflect white supremacist biases, the vast majority continued to promote conservative and liberal notions of assimilation. Against a backdrop wherein black academics and/or intellectuals were viewed as "suspect," as potential traitors to the cause of black self-determination, young black critical thinkers who saw ourselves as revolutionaries entered colleges and universities in the seventies prepared to do battle. We were there to acquire an education but we were not there to passively consume the education offered by the colonizer. We were often lone individuals profoundly isolated, not only from the white world but from the world of assimilated conservative blackness that was more the norm.

Unlike insurgent black critical thinker/philosopher Cornel West, who cites his experience as an undergraduate at Harvard as the time when he underwent an "intellectual conversion" because studying there opened "a whole new world of ideas," I made my commitment to intellectual life in the segregated black world of my childhood. While I agree with West that it is useful "to be connected to a person or subculture that has devoted himself, herself or itself to the life of the mind," I do not see this as the only cultural context where intellectual quest can be nurtured and sustained. Indeed, rampant anti-intellectualism at Stanford University threatened to thwart my longing to devote myself to the life of the mind. This environment was an extremely hostile place for any black student militantly resisting white supremacy—engaging in a process of decolonization. The black scholars there who were committed to intellectual life were often uninterested in those of us who came from underprivileged-class backgrounds, who were not the offspring of the black elite, and in most cases were not male. This seemed especially true of the small number of radical and politicized black male professors. Ironically, my desire to do intellectual work had been much more affirmed in the segregated community I grew up in than at Stanford University, where I encountered not only racist assumptions about the intelligence of black folks, sexist ideas about female intellectuality, and class elitism but also prejudicial attitudes towards southerners. Intellectual work differs from academic work precisely because one does not need to undertake a formal course of study or strive for degrees to live the life of the mind. Despite class, gender, or race, individuals can choose intellectual work even if that choice is never affirmed by teachers or academic institutions. Formal education can and often does enrich an organic intellectual process but it is not essential to the making of an intellectual. I did not attend college to become an intellectual, nor did I attain a doctorate for that reason. These paths led me into the academic profession, which is not necessarily a location where intellectual work is affirmed.

Too often we confuse academic and intellectual work. Certainly, I entered college naively assuming it would be a place where a life of the mind would be affirmed only to discover the difference between working to be an academic and doing intellectual work. The heart of intellectual work is critical engagement with ideas. While one reads, studies, and at times writes, a significant part of that work is time spent in contemplation and reflection. Even though an exchange of ideas can and does take place in a communal context, there is necessarily a private solitary dimension to intellectual work. It is that need for time that has often precluded African Americans, particularly those among us who grow up without class privilege, from becoming intellectuals. Those of us who choose intellectual life usually pursue academic careers so that we will have time to do our work. My earliest models for black intellectual life were not academics; they were writers, specifically Lorraine Hansberry and James Baldwin. Unlike most black academics I encountered as a student, these writers were readers, thinkers, political activists, committed to education for critical consciousness; they were individuals exuding radical openness. They were not narrow-minded. Their openness to ideas, to engaging in critical dialogues with diverse audiences, set a powerful example.

The intellectual work of writers like Baldwin and Hansberry tends to be obscured when discussions of black intellectual traditions focus on academics or writers who teach in university settings. Most black academics (like their white and non-white counterparts) are not intellectuals. No unitary black intellectual tradition can be developed if black academics stubbornly resist acknowledging the work of writers who are also major critical thinkers or if attention is only given those thinkers who manage to acquire recognition in the white mainstream. There are not many African Americans who choose to devote themselves to an intellectual life, and those who do who are not connected to the academy, who may not publish widely or at all, have no visibility. Concurrently, many young black intellectuals abandon their zeal for a life of the mind in the process of becoming and/or working as academics or seeking more financially rewarding occupations.

Since so few black folks choose to devote themselves to

intellectual life, there is no strong intellectual community. Black academics and/or intellectuals have the greatest opportunity to form bonds with one another. Yet those bonds often are established not on the basis of respect for work but rather via a process of networking wherein exchanges of favors or personal likes and dislikes overdetermine allegiances. The competitive hierarchical structure of academe militates against the formation of intellectual community based on open-minded sharing of ideas. Among marginalized groups, like African Americans, the most open-minded individuals are more likely to be isolated. That isolation is likely to be intensified if their intellectual work is linked to progressive politics.

When I began teaching in the same institution as Cornel West, I was able to bond with him and experience the joy of intellectual community. Sharing with him both progressive politics and a vision of intellectual life was the connection that enabled us to write *Breaking Bread: Insurgent Black Intellectual Life*. When I approached him with this project, we were both uncertain about whether or not there would really be an audience for such a discussion. Our primary intent was to affirm the primacy of intellectual work in contemporary African-American life. We wanted to repudiate the notion that to become a black intellectual and/or academic means that one assimilates and surrenders passionate concern with ending white supremacy, with uplifting black people. Through this act of intervention we hoped to encourage more black folks to choose intellectual work.

When I wrote my essay for the book, I was particularly interested in exploring the conditions that must exist for black females to choose intellectual life. Many black women academics often dismiss and devalue intellectual work, particularly the work of peers. Even though there are so few of us, competition for mainstream attention, jockeying for male approval, or narrow judgmental attitudes tend to pit us against one another. In my own life, commitment to feminist politics has been the force that challenges me to seek a solidarity and sisterhood with black women that transcends the will to compete or engage in petty trashing. When patriarchal support of competition between women is coupled with competitive academic longing for status and influence, black women are not empowered to bond on the basis of shared commitment to intellectual life or open-minded exchange of ideas. Empowered to be hostile towards and policing of one another, black female academics and/or intellectuals often work to censor and silence one another. This is especially the case when dissenting perspectives emerge. Since many women in the academy are conservative or liberal in their politics, tensions arise between those groups and individuals, like myself, who advocate revolutionary politics.

I was reminded of these splits recently when the conference "Black Women in the Academy: Defending Our Name, 1894–1994" was convened. The brochure for the conference introduced it with a statement that read: "Black women have come in for a large share of negative criticism in the form of both open and coded discourse generated by the Anita Hill–Clarence Thomas hearings last year, and political discourse generated by electoral campaigns over the course of the last year largely centered on the issue of welfare reform and 'family values.' These events have generated the most intense public consideration of the character and morality of Black women this country has witnessed since the 1890's." I found this statement discouraging. Implicitly it suggests that black women come to voice, are recognized as meaningful presences, only when we are granted visibility by white-dominated mass media, that it is this public's recognition that is worthy of debate and response. Such a statement deflects attention away from the work black women continually do to bring our concerns to public attention. That black women academics would gather under a rubric that suggests we come to "defend our name" rather than to proclaim and celebrate our academic and/or intellectual work was troubling. Politically, I rejected the public premise of this conference. It embraced a rhetoric and positionality of victimhood without problematizing this stance. It tacitly assumed that black women would all identify our circumstances with those individuals who were being highlighted by mainstream political culture. Although I longed to be among a gathering of black women from various disciplines, I knew that my presence would not have been welcomed by those participants who wanted more than anything to have the conference superficially project a unitary vision of black women in the academy. There was nothing in the prefatory statement that acknowledged diversity of opinion or political affiliations. The demand for a unitary vision leads to the exclusion of voices, the silencing of dissent. Exclusion is one way to punish those whose views are not deemed correct or acceptable. Fear of isolation serves to check individual black women's critical thought and curtails their interest in progressive politics. Black women in the academy, who are busy defending their name, may not be at all interested in engaging in rigorous intellectual discussion and debate. To a grave extent black female intellectuals with progressive politics are assailed from all sides. We confront white supremacy, as well as the sexism of black people (especially black men) which continues to overvalue black male intellectuals and undervalue the work of black females, even as we then find ourselves rejected by individual black women with more conservative politics who either feel threatened or assume a policing role in order to silence diverse perspectives.

Lack of solidarity and intellectual community among black women leaves us particularly vulnerable in relation to highly competitive sexist black male thinkers who see themselves as the movers and shakers defining black intellectual tradition. Much of their scholarship is written as though they read none of the work of black women critical thinkers. Seeing themselves as shaping the tradition, these black males often assign black female thinkers supportive roles. Subordinating our work to that of powerful males, they attempt to keep in place racialized sexist hierarchies that deem their work more valuable. This thinking persists even though the work of an individual black woman thinker may be much more well read, reaching a much more diverse audience than comparable work by male counterparts. Black male thinkers act in complicity with a white power structure wherein sexist thinking supports devaluing black women as critical thinkers even as that same structure acknowledges the power and excellence of black women's fiction writing. When it comes to nonfiction writing, white-dominated mass media often make no distinction between individual black women based on our work. We are often lumped together so that if a representative is desired any one will do. Major magazines and newspapers that seek out the opinions of black male thinkers who are deemed important because of their work act as though any black female voice will do, the assumption being that none of our voices is particularly distinct or deserving of attention based on the specific nature of our work. Unfortunately, collectively black women intellectuals (as distinct from black women academics) do not produce a substantial body of work that would serve as an intervention challenging the assumption that we are merely following behind male thinkers. Often black males define the nature of public discourse about the role of the black intellectual in ways that deflect attention away from individual black female thinkers whose work may be more exemplary in its connection of theory and practice, in its engagement with progressive politics.

When I have participated in discussions about the role of black intellectuals convened by male thinkers, there has been a refusal to acknowledge those of us who do not passively embrace the assumption that our work fails to reach a diverse audience of black folks, that there is necessarily a gap between intellectual work and progressive political activism. Intellectual work can itself be a gesture of political activism if it challenges us to know in ways that counter and oppose existing epistemologies (ways of knowing) that keep us colonized, subjugated, etc. Intellectual work has that potential only if the individual is committed to a progressive political vision of social change. All too often we invest in a unitary model of "the" black intellectual. Yet the nature of our intellectual work and its meaning is overdetermined by our politics.

As an African-American intellectual who has never felt that intellectual work separated me either from my segregated poor and working-class community and family of origin or from masses of ordinary black people, I understand that a false dichotomy has been constructed in our culture that socializes us to believe that the work of black intellectuals will necessarily estrange us from blackness. Many of us are socialized to embrace this dichotomy, to see it as "natural" and embrace it without interrogation. Black intellectuals who choose to do work that addresses the needs and concerns of black liberation struggle, of black folks seeking to decolonize their minds and imaginations, will find no separation has to exist between themselves and other black people from various class backgrounds. This does not mean that our work will be embraced without critique, or that we will not be seen as suspect, only that we can counter the negative representations of black intellectuals as uppity assimilated traitors by the work we do. Black intellectuals who are not concerned with the issue of changing this society so that the conditions exist for black self-determination will most likely do their work in such a way that it will not appeal to black folks across class. Black intellectuals who are committed to ending domination, exploitation, and oppression in all its myriad manifestations, racism, sexism, class elitism, etc., will be politically challenged to interrogate the way we work, what we do, how we speak and write, to see whether or not we are working in a manner that crosses boundaries. I have made specific decisions about the nature of my work in the interest of making it accessible to a broader audience. Those decisions involve doing writing that may not impress my academic peers. When I decided to write a self-help book on black women and self-recovery, I expressed in the introduction to this work my fear that such an act would actually further de-legitimize me in the eyes of academic colleagues of all races. To take that risk seems minor given the possible good that can come when the effort is made to share knowledge informed by progressive politics in diverse ways.

The desire to share knowledge with diverse audiences while centralizing black folks and our struggle for self-determination, without excluding non-black audiences, requires different strategies from those intellectuals normally deploy to disseminate work. Black intellectuals committed to sharing knowledge across class see public speaking in a different way from most of our peers. Recognizing that masses of folks lack basic reading skills, we know that we must use lectures, radio, television, and conversation in diverse settings to share information. Given the cultural context of white supremacist patriarchy, it is unlikely that any black intellectual who is continually working to cross boundaries will receive the same levels of attention given those folks who assimilate and who are primarily concerned with speaking to a white audience. The degree to which black intellectuals will work in a manner that challenges existing structures of domination will be determined by the nature of their political commitment. Importantly, that commitment need not be static. It changes. There may be work that a progressive intellectual wants to do that aims to address a diverse audience, even as that same individual may choose to do work that speaks specifically to select audiences, work that may use difficult language or jargon that is not accessible to everyone. Strategically, progressive black intellectuals must work from multiple locations. To do such work one necessarily takes risks that require sacrifice—that may include forfeiting opportunities for status and privilege that might undermine one's capacity to engage in dialogue across boundaries. Whether or not an individual thinker chooses to make such sacrifices is not a static process. We make multiple choices depending on our circumstances. Ultimately, depth of political commitment to progressive social change informs our will to sacrifice.

Political activism may be expressed by the type of work progressive black intellectuals choose to do. To politically counter anti-intellectual and/or academic thought in black life that persists in portraying educated black folks as traitors (a representation that has concrete foundation), insurgent black critical thinkers must be accountable. That means the work we individually do, and the work of our peers, must be continually interrogated. Unfortunately, when the issue of accountability is superficially raised, the work of powerful black males who are seen as possible traitors is often spotlighted. Often the work of black intellectuals who continually endeavor to frame our discourses in ways that are inclusive of our commitment to black self-determination is discounted.

Competitive and sexist battles between black males over issues of leadership often deflect attention away from the work
of black women intellectuals which may be far more exemplary in relation to issues of crossing borders, educating for
critical consciousness outside the academy. As long as sexist
thinking informs public discourse around the role of black
intellectuals, as long as black men dominate the discussion,
the voices of black female intellectuals will not be heard.
Our works are rarely quoted or critically engaged by our
male peers. Even when the rare black male thinker incorpo-
rates an understanding of gender and/or feminism that stems
from his engagement with the work of black women, he may
not cite that work. If the work of black women is not valued,
then we are not seen as embodying standards of intellectual
rigor and excellence coupled with progressive political actions that create a context for change in diverse black communities in ways that could be mirrored by black male peers
and students. Until more black women, and our allies in
struggle, publicly challenge these biases and omissions within
all arenas of public discourse, discussions of the role black
intellectuals can assume in black liberation struggle will always be overdetermined by the actions of men.

In the past year I have been on two panels discussing the
role of black intellectuals where the intent was more to delin-
eate the shortcomings of famous, individual black males and
to castigate them for failing to address the needs of ordinary
folks than real engagement of the issues. Black intellectuals
must choose to act in the service of black liberation. That
choice emerges from our politics. Black intellectuals, like everyone, should be accountable for the political choices we
make and for the ways those choices shape our lives, our
visions, and our work. Clearly, many black intellectuals and/
or academics are not choosing to espouse radical or revolu-

tionary progressive politics. A useful discussion of the role of black intellectuals would not only critically examine why this is so, it would also articulate strategies of constructive intervention and contestation. There is no one function, no one location intellectuals who choose progressive politics must inhabit in society. This is especially true for black intellectuals. Ideally, we should be present everywhere, represented in all walks of life, just as our work should be multilayered, ever-changing, and diverse. And these same criteria should apply to those who engage our work. Most importantly there should be more of us.

Insurgent black intellectuals can increase our numbers by continually reminding everyone that intellectual work need not be done solely in academic settings. Nor is it healthy for most progressive black intellectual thought to emerge solely in the service of educational institutions. These locations limit and overdetermine discourse. Concurrently, without in any way diminishing the importance of academic work, we need to vigilantly clarify ways in which academic work does differ from intellectual work. The labor we do as academics is valuable but it is not inherently intellectual. Making a distinction between the two types of work, even though they sometimes overlap and converge, allows everyone to appreciate the different nature of commitment that is required when one is primarily concerned with advancing an academic career, in contrast to constructing a life where one can be devoted fully and deeply to intellectual work. Having chosen to balance an academic career with a primary commitment to intellectual work, I see firsthand the tensions between the two choices. My primary engagement is with ideas, not personalities or networks. Racial openness is essential for intellectual work, independent thinking. Allegiances to institutions or powerful factions within those locations often constrain and inhibit independent thought. It is this concrete reality that has led so many intellectuals to eschew involvement in spheres of power that can impinge on our commitment to radical openness, to unfettered thought. Fear of surrendering this state of open-mindedness has often led intellectuals to deny the political implications of their work, to act as though they do not embrace political positions because they think it might mean losing "objectivity." There is no politically neutral intellectual work. Knowing this should empower intellectuals to make political choices that we can claim while still holding on to an ethical commitment of open engagement with ideas. Intellectuals can offer any radical movement for social change transformative visions and insights. Black intellectuals who are committed to an inclusive struggle to end systems of domination (imperialism, racism, sexism, class elitism) can bring to black liberation struggle a radically new vision of social change. Challenging black intellectuals, Cornel West encourages us to create "a public dialogue with the black community and within the American community in which certain kinds of alternative ways of looking at the world and changing the world are made available to people." If black intellectuals begin our work with this intent, then we show by our example that we act in solidarity with every black person who is committed to black self-determination.

BLACK IDENTITY

LIBERATING SUBJECTIVITY

Contemporary struggle for civil rights and black liberation in the United States has continually affirmed the importance of identity. Historically, bonding on the basis of skin color was a useful survival strategy. The institutionalization of white supremacy created a structure of racial apartheid that was rooted in a binary division between whites and blacks. Skin color was the body marking that separated and divided. Despite the reality of miscegenation, individual blacks who looked white had only two choices—to assert black identity or pass into whiteness. Early black freedom struggle was not rooted in a questioning of race as a defining category; instead it called for a politics of resistance where all black people, presumably identified with the desire for emancipation, would unite. This did not mean that there were no traitors to the cause, only that a politics of racial bonding rooted in shared black identity was seen as the correct stance. When slavery ended, social movements for racial uplift highlighted the importance of identifying with one's group and working on behalf of group advancement. Civil

240

rights struggle did not challenge this basis for bonding, it merely opened the door to include the resistance efforts of those whites committed to ending racist domination.

Militant resistance to white supremacy, evoked by the black power movement of the sixties, in no way challenged representations of black identity. It extolled them. Assimilated blacks were called out and urged to reclaim the black identity they had been taught to despise. For some folks the reclamation of that identity entailed asserting a fierce blackness that involved cultivating a specific way of speaking, dressing, and interacting. Gone was the notion that bonding with blackness was a survival strategy rooted in the experience of shared suffering and in its place was the idea that one "proved" black identity by the manner in which one responded to whiteness. And even though Malcolm X urged black folks to tear their gaze away from whiteness so that we could "see each other with new eyes," black identity was fast being defined by two opposing factions that were both, in their own way, obsessed with whiteness. Assimilated black folks evoked an identity politics rooted in the privileging of a model of integration, wherein allegiance to blackness was abdicated in the interest of erasing race and promoting an ethos of humanism that would emphasize commonalities between whites and blacks. Separatist black folks evoked an identity politics based on the assumption that ethically and morally whites and blacks were different, had no common experience, and did not share the same political agenda.

Ultimately it was racial integration, and the new class divisions among black folks which it created, that led to the formation of a radically different cultural context so disruptive it created a black identity crisis. In the wake of gains achieved by civil rights struggle and militant resistance, black folks suddenly had more access to mainstream white culture than ever before. Since there had been no cultural transformation that enabled white folks to divest of white supremacist thinking, black folks were allowed to enter a previously segregated world that appeared to be less racist, even though there had been no critical shift in the racist mindset. Adjusting to this cultural context led many black folks to experiment with the art of dissimulation, the taking on of various appearances. Notions of appropriate behavior had to be altered so that black folks could mediate between that old world of racial bonding where all one's work and social relations were centered around a normative black culture with shared codes and a new integrated world that was changing the nature of blackness. Those changes have led to the crisis engendered by struggle around the issue of black identity.

Racial integration altered the face of blackness. The separate and distinct culture of blackness that had been constructed in the midst of racial apartheid was disrupted by profound changes in economic opportunity, geographical shifts, and access to white institutions that had once been segregated. These changes were also reflected in social relations. Once black folks became able to establish bonds of attachment and intimacy to white folks, the structures of black intimacy were altered. Suddenly black people no longer felt themselves suffering racist assault in similar ways, since we did not all live or work in segregated communities and white supremacist thinking was no longer consistent in the way it governed white responses to blackness (one black person might have an incredibly racist employer who discriminated against him or her even as another might develop friendship ties with a white boss). On all levels racial integration changed the social construction of blackness.

Since black resistance struggle has traditionally relied on a unitary representation of blackness as a framework for identity politics, changes in black identity were and are viewed by many African Americans as deeply threatening. Rather than seeing the development of multiple black subjectivity as a positive intervention within white supremacist capitalist patriarchy, many black folks responded to the disruption of essentialist notions of blackness by attempting to reestablish identity politics via the call for black nationalism rooted in a vision of separatism. Since masses of poor and working-class black folks, whose lives have not been altered by economic gains that increase social mobility, live in segregated neighborhoods, a rhetoric of black nationalism that reinforces static notions of black identity has more power than one which insists that our identity is always changing.

Black nationalists attempt to address the identity crisis African Americans are experiencing by insisting on a unitary representation of blackness. Critiques of Eurocentric biases that promote Afrocentric thinking tend to celebrate a unitary model of self and identity. Defining terms in her introduction to *Yurugu: An African-Centered Critique of European Cultural Thought and Behavior*, Marimba Ani explains: "Afrocentricity is a way of viewing reality that analyzes phenomena using the interest of African people as a reference point, as stated by Asante." Of course the problematic assertion in this question centers around who is allowed to determine "the interest" of African people. Many African-centered critiques trash Eurocentrism for its unitary representations of culture, the universalizing of white experience, its erasure of African ways of knowing, while constructing within these same narratives a unitary utopian representation of Africa as paradise, a motherland where all was perfect before white imperialism brought evil and corruption. Utopian Afrocentric evocations of an ancient high culture of black kings and queens erase the experiences of servants and slaves in the interest of presenting contemporary black folks with superheroic models of black subjectivity. While these images can be usefully incorporated in a revisionist history that challenges white supremacist biases, particularly as they have shaped pedagogy, the way we know what we know, they can also be used to deflect attention away from the need to transform the existing society so that liberatory black subjectivity can be nurtured and sustained.

Nationalist appeals for a unitary representation of blackness tend to emphasize notions of authenticity that uphold a vision of patriarchal family life and of nationhood as the only possible structures wherein the crisis in black identity can be resolved. Studies of patriarchal black families or anti-racist organizations structured on the same hierarchical model would reveal that these structures reinscribe patterns of domination rather than disrupt or alter them. Yet even in the face of overwhelming evidence that the patriarchal family is not a site of redemption and healing, many African Americans desperately cling to the assumption that the pain in black life can be healed by establishing patriarchy and black nationalist identity. Those black folks who attempt to question the tropes of nation and family tend to be dismissed as traitors to the race, as assimilationists. This is especially true for black women who critique black nationalism from a feminist standpoint.

So far all expressions of black nationalism in the United States deploy a rhetoric of redemption that valorizes patriarchal thinking and male domination. Embedded in all forms of nationalist thought is the acceptance and affirmation of sexist exploitation and oppression. To build nations and "pure" races the bodies of women must be controlled, our sexual activities policed, and our reproductive rights curtailed. Since so many black females have been conscious of the need to resist sexist thinking, contemporary black nationalist groups can no longer recruit black women by overtly announcing their support of patriarchal thinking. To appeal to black females much contemporary black nationalist writing attempts to incorporate gender in ways that superficially appear to be progressive. However, like the patriarchal Eurocentric model of social organization it critiques and repudiates, within Afrocentric scholarship black women writers frame their discourse in relation to knowledge received from patriarchal black male elders. Gender relations are talked about in much the same way as a Eurocentric thinker like Ivan Illich presents them in his work when he evokes a nostalgic precapitalist world where men and women had their separate but equal domains, respected one another, and lived in harmony with the natural world. Similarly, Afrocentric constructions of a utopian all-black world where men and women share power equally are evoked to counter critiques that call attention to the link between patriarchal thinking and black nationalism. In the black separatist imagination, feminism is reinvented as always and only a white woman's issue. Setting the boundaries in this way constructs another essentialist paradigm wherein black women who embrace feminist thinking can be deemed inauthentic, traitors to the race.

Feminist critique is particularly threatening to black nationalism precisely because it highlights the contradictory relation to structures of domination in the black imagination. Black folks who can speak eloquently about racism, opposing exploitation and dehumanization, deny the value of these same critiques when they are raised within a discourse of gender. The correlations between the structures of racist oppression and exploitation and patriarchal domination are so obvious that to ignore them requires the closing off of the mind. Significantly, nationalist black spokespersons who recognize Malcolm X as a leader and teacher tend to disregard the progressive thinking about gender that is present in the writings and conversations completed shortly before his death. The inability of black nationalist thinkers to conceive of any paradigm for nation and family life that is not patriarchal reveals the depths of black male longing to assert hierarchical control and power. Though critical of white cultural imperialism, nationalist black males see no contradiction between that analysis and their support of hierarchical models of social organization that affirm coercive control and domination of others. Ideas of nation and family that surface in contemporary black nationalist writing mirror the white supremacist nation-state that is benevolently patriarchal. A distinction must be made between overt brutal domination of women by men, which most Afrocentric thinkers clearly repudiate as do their white counterparts, and the Enlightenment vision of a world where men are inherently the protectors and caretakers of women and children that evokes a benevolent model of patriarchal organization of society that is assumed to be directly mirroring a "natural" order.

At its best, black nationalist thought seeks to revise and redress white Western biases, especially as they overdetermine ways of knowing, critique white supremacy, and offer black folks grounding in an oppositional worldview that promotes black self-determination. Within the framework of an institutionalized patriarchal theory and practice of black nationalism, these positive dimensions are undermined. It is the failure of black nationalism to offer an inclusive complex understanding of black identity, one that is not sexist, homophobic, patriarchal, or supportive of capitalism, that renders it suspect and politically problematic. Politically progressive black people on the Left who are not nationalist, like myself, share a perspective that promotes the eradication of white supremacy, the de-centering of the West, redressing of biases, and commitment to affirming black self-determination. Yet we add to the critique of white Western imperialism a repudiation of patriarchy, a critique of capitalism, and a concern for interracial coalition building. Nationalist attachment to a narrow vision of black identity is often as rigidly conservative as racist white stereotypes.

Narrowly focused black identity politics do a disservice to black liberation struggle because they seek to render invisible the complex and multiple subjectivity of black folks. While I am deeply committed to a politics of black self-determination that seeks to maintain and preserve our unique cultural legacy in the United States, I know that the project of cultural conservation need not negate our diasporic wanderings into worlds beyond traditional blackness. The nationalist insistence that black identity must be "saved" by our refusal to embrace various epistemologies (ways of knowing), cultures, etc., is not a movement away from a Eurocentric binary structure. It reinscribes the dynamics of binary thinking.

The contemporary crisis of identity is best resolved by our collective willingness as African Americans to acknowledge that there is no monolithic black community, no normative black identity. There is a shared history that frames the construction of our diverse black experiences. Knowledge of that history is needed by everyone as we seek to construct self and identity. In *Race Matters*, Cornel West suggests that it is only as we critically interrogate notions of black authenticity, closed-ranks mentality, and black cultural conservatism that we can begin to really theorize complex understandings of black subjectivity. Insisting that we need new frameworks, West declares: "This new framework should be a prophetic one of moral reasoning with its fundamental ideas of a mature black identity, coalition strategy, and black cultural democracy. Instead of cathartic appeals to black authenticity, a prophetic viewpoint bases mature black self-love and self-response on the moral quality of black responses to undeniable racist degradation in the American past and present. These responses assume neither a black essence that all black people share nor one black perspective to which all black people should adhere." While the insights West shares should guide African Americans in our collective effort to retheorize black identity, like many nationalist thinkers with whom he does not agree, his concern with black response to whiteness seems to undermine his insistence on a complex understanding of black identity. West asserts: "Mature black identity results from an acknowledgement of the specific response to white supremacist abuses and a moral assessment of these responses such that the humanity of black people does not rest on deifying or demonizing others." Penetrating critiques of narrow nationalism like the one West offers are necessary. However, we need to make those critiques within a prophetic discursive framework where we insist on theorizing black identity from multiple locations, not simply in relation to white supremacy.

A fundamental characteristic of being black in white supremacist capitalist patriarchy is that we are all socialized to believe that only race matters. Hence black folks often do not accord other aspects of experience such as class, sexual practice, etc. serious regard as we think about constructing self and identity. While it certainly is important for black folks to foreground discussions of white supremacy, it is equally important for us to affirm that liberation takes place only in a context where we are able to imagine subjectivities that are diverse, constantly changing, and always operating in states of cultural contingency. To embrace and accept fluid black subjectivities, African-American attachment to a notion of the unitary self must be broken. African Americans must embrace the progressive political understanding of diasporic black identity Walter Rodney evokes in *How Europe Underdeveloped Africa*:

> Our predicament at the present time throws up new questions. . . . Sometimes if a person gets trapped in a previous moment of history, you find it hard to carry on a conversation with him or her because they are still out to defend something that you're not against, but you're not with because it is no longer the relevant thing. Why should we get caught up in making tremendous tirades against the missionaries or saying the Europeans were terrible fellows, look how these fellows exploited us? Why should we continually speak in this grand singular—the African is this and the European is the other? That was a formulation that was necessary at a particular point in time, when we were still within the whole identity crisis, when we were trying to evolve a peoplehood. . . . But the moment we move beyond that, neocolonial man [and woman] can't talk about the Vietnamese in the singular or the African or the Guyanese, etc. We must look at real life. In real life, Guyanese live in certain different ways, have contradictions among themselves, have a relationship with the rest of the world.

Unitary representations of black identity do not reflect the real lives of African Americans who struggle to create self and identity. Psychoanalytically, it is clear that the unitary self is sustained only by acts of coercive control and repression. Collectively African Americans fear the loss of a unitary representation of blackness because they feel we will lose a basis for organized resistance.

In retheorizing black subjectivity we have to also revise our understanding of the conditions that are needed for black folks to join together in a politics of solidarity that can effectively oppose white supremacy. Breaking with essentialist thinking that insists all black folks inherently realize that we have something positive to gain by resisting white supremacy allows us to collectively acknowledge that radical politicization is a process—that revolutionary black thinkers and activists are made, not born. Progressive education for critical consciousness then is automatically understood to be necessary to any construction of radical black subjectivity. Whether the issue is construction of self and identity or radical politicization, African-American subjectivity is always in process. Fluidity means that our black identities are constantly changing as we respond to circumstances in our families and communities of origin, and as we interact with a larger world. Only by privileging the reality of that changing black identity will we be able to engage a prophetic discourse about subjectivity that will be liberatory and transformative.

MOVING FROM PAIN TO POWER

BLACK SELF-DETERMINATION

Revolutionary black liberation struggle in the United States was undermined by outmoded patriarchal emphasis on nationhood and masculine rule, the absence of a strategy for coalition building that would keep a place for non-black allies in struggle, and the lack of sustained programs for education for critical consciousness that would continually engage black folks of all classes in a process of radical politicization. These weaknesses made it easy for racial integration to bring with it passive absorption of capitalist values and internalized racism. In the conclusion to *Night Vision: Illuminating War and Class on the Neo-Colonial Terrain* the pseudonymous authors make this insightful point: "The white ruling class wants Black capitalist government; it promotes, pays for and sponsors Black capitalist government. No matter what anyone's hopes were, in fact today such Black government equals Black Genocide. . . . Just as imperialism not only wants to arm millions of Afrikan men indiscriminately and quickly as possible, but it's offering them a taste of everything 'white' (even white women). This runs counter to all the rules of colonialism because it isn't colonialism. It's neo-colonialism, the new kid on the block." Until radical black leaders offer strategies for black liberation that address more fully our current political situation there is little hope that we can respond in a meaningful way to the crises in African-American life.

Racial integration alone did not undermine the struggle for black liberation. It was diffused by internal weakness as well as the willingness on the part of white privileged classes to grant some black folks entry into mainstream capitalist power. Since sixties movement for black liberation empha-sized a critique of capitalism, the need for black folks to maintain an ethic of communalism that would preserve, pro-mote, and sustain an oppositional worldview and culture, it was important to the existing white power elite to destroy, corrupt, and co-opt radical black leadership. Assassinating black leaders, incarcerating others, infiltrating and undermin-ing radical black organizations, were ways the dominant cul-ture repressed militant black movement for racial justice. As more and more black folks entered predominantly white universities, the best and brightest in many cases never con-sidering predominantly black institutions because the eco-nomic support available at white institutions was so much greater, the setting was ripe for neo-colonial co-optation of black minds. Today, a large percentage of the most radical-ized black critical thinkers attend and/or teach at predomi-nantly white institutions. Among professors those of us who are considered "stars" are rewarded with forms of work re-lease (teaching fewer classes, assistants, time off) and huge salaries. Since many of us are not dedicated to teaching, no large body of students of any race has the advantage of study-ing with us and developing a more revolutionary mindset. The organized speaker circuit offers big bucks so that the time and energy some of us might have once spent educating for critical consciousness in non-privileged and non-elite settings is usurped. We are as tempted as any other group of people by the promise of fame and unprecedented material reward. By speaking of the myriad ways in which insurgent black intellectuals are seduced and tempted to act in complicity with the very structures of domination we critique, my intention is not to be accusatory but to speak a word of caution—and while so doing, call for a renewed commitment to critical vigilance.

If insurgent black intellectuals and/or critical thinkers abandon education for critical consciousness that extends beyond the academy, we are in complicity with those corrupt forces that are creating a despairing environment where hopelessness and rage are the order of the day. It is this social context that allows conservative, narrow black nationalism to flourish. Galvanizing the energy of the masses easily becomes the turf of opportunistic nationalist conservative leaders who exploit the intense longing folks have for strategies that will enable them to respond to overwhelming feelings of economic and spiritual crisis. It is not a meaningful intervention for insurgent black thinkers to make fancy critiques of narrow nationalism if those discussions are not linked with strategies for progressive social change. Most black folks are not inherently more inclined to listen to and support conservative nationalist leaders. These are the individuals who are seductively courting that constituency. This will never change if progressive folks do not strive to speak to a wider, more inclusive black audience.

Many progressive black critical thinkers have abandoned plain speaking and adopted more abstract jargon. Like many of their white academic counterparts, they often regard folks like me, who continue to speak simply and/or integrate ver-

nacular styles into our writing and speaking, as lacking intellectual sophistication. This is especially the case when the
issue is political terminology. Phrases like "black liberation
struggle" and "black self-determination" may appear frequently in the literature and speeches of conservative black
nationalists but are rarely present in the work of progressive
black thinkers. Often these black folks, like their more conservative and liberal counterparts, are unwilling to use these
terms because many white peers and colleagues respond negatively to them since they specifically address political solidarity among black people. Terms like "black liberation
struggle" and "black self-determination" still accurately address the collective needs of black people. "Black liberation
struggle" is a phrase that reminds us that white supremacy
continues to overdetermine and shape the lives of most black
folks, maintaining and perpetuating exploitative and oppressive forms of institutionalized racism that must be resisted if
we are to collectively have any agency in relation to our lives.
Despite class difference all black people are the targets, to
greater or lesser degrees, of some form of racist assault. The
less privilege an individual black person has the more likely
he or she will bear the brunt of racist exploitation and oppression. "Black self-determination" is a useful term because
it registers the acknowledgment that efforts to empower diverse black communities must do more than critique and
challenge racism and white supremacy. They must also address ways African Americans, across class, can create radical
liberatory subjectivity even as we continue to live within a
white supremacist capitalist patriarchal society. We cannot
wait for an end to racist domination to create the conditions
under which we live lives of sustained well-being.

Black self-determination is that process by which we learn
to radicalize our thinking and habits of being in ways that

enhance the quality of our lives despite racist domination. It can become a reality for everyone only as we construct liberatory visions of social change that concretely empower us in our everyday lives. For example, there is no reason classes that teach literacy and/or critical thinking in conjunction with discussions about the quality of life should not be taking place at localized settings (housing projects, churches, etc.), reading groups, consciousness-raising groups, etc. These programs rarely happen because of the extent to which most black folks across class are embracing a vision of life that sees well-being as connected only to material possessions. Even though a large majority of African Americans live in poverty or situations of economic stress and deprivation, we are all socialized by television to identify with the values and attitudes of the bourgeois and ruling classes. When underprivileged black folks who are denied access to material success internalize this mindset, it makes their lives harder, more painful. It creates a gap between the concrete circumstances of their lives and their aspirations. Although they live in various states of need and deprivation, their dreams of success are often dominated by longings to be rich, to live in a constant state of material luxury. When these longings are coupled with other attitudes and values of white privileged classes absorbed from mass media, they are often unable to realistically draw on the skills and resources they possess that would enable them to concretely change their lives. Many of these folks easily become imprisoned by fantasies of the good life that make such a life synonymous with material extravagance. Addiction to such fantasies, to an ethic of hedonistic consumerism and the longing to project material success, leads to a mindset where criminal activity that will enable one to attain these goals is not seen as morally or ethically wrong. Television teaches that the white ruling elites have attained their material success and power by abandoning ethical and moral concerns for human life and by embracing dishonesty, treachery, and the will to exploit everyone. These are the values many materially disadvantaged people emulate because they believe adopting them will enable them to transform their lives.

If television continues to be the primary pedagogical presence in black life, particularly in the lives of the working poor and destitute, our collective capacity to radicalize consciousness and to organize meaningful resistance struggle will be continually undermined. Black leaders who can galvanize energy to critique and attempt to suppress gangsta rap could be serving diverse black communities more if they were engaged in a critique of the role mass media play in black life—particularly television. They could be using their public power to create literacy programs and promote education for critical consciousness, while urging all African Americans, in conjunction with our allies in struggle, to turn off television sets, to demand programming that is useful for our lives, and to critically resist representations that undermine our capacity to be self-determining. These issues are rarely addressed by accepted black leaders because they do not appeal to mainstream culture. The crisis in black leadership in the United States is that there are so few progressive revolutionary black political thinkers who are accorded attention. Rather than our leaders emerging organically from various struggles where they represent the needs of black constituencies, they are more and more chosen by white folks. Even prominent people in conservative black separatist organizations gain their mass appeal because they are brought to our attention by white mass media and given access to huge audiences. Obviously white folks are not in any way threatened by their anti-white sentiments. Instead they realize that if masses of black people follow conservative black fascists who are really as pro-capitalist and pro-domination as their white counterparts, African Americans are doomed. Let's face it! For example, the big difference between Malcolm X and Louis Farrakhan is that one is a revolutionary and one is a fascist, one is anti-capitalist, critical of imperialism, the other embraces capitalism and imperialism. Now, should it come as any surprise which of these figures white mass media would support? Nothing is more revealing of the collective plight of African Americans than the growing political conservatism that masks itself as progressive nationalism in black life.

To recover radical political equilibrium, black folks must collectively seek self-determination. Yet that seeking cannot happen as long as most folks are either brainwashed so that they passively internalize white supremacist attitudes and values and/or embrace autocratic conservative black leaders who use the rhetoric of nationalism to opportunistically exploit and contain us. To open our minds and hearts to black self-determination we must commit ourselves to a process of decolonization, which means choosing to critically examine ourselves, both to divest of white supremacy and internalized racism as well as to commit ourselves to radical politicization. Every radical African-American critical thinker has undergone a process of decolonization wherein we study the work of progressive thinkers, black and non-black, who teach us about resistance. Looking at history without Eurocentric biases, we study to learn what racism is and how white supremacy is institutionalized. It should be obvious that the process of decolonization and radical politicization requires literacy. Without critical literacy, black folks cannot assume responsibility for ourselves. We can neither find nor create jobs that allow us to be economically self-sufficient and we cannot effectively resist white supremacy in the arena of cultural production. We must not be duped into believing that many black people cannot read or write because they are poor. Those who come from poor and working-class backgrounds know that all of us can find ways to learn these skills if we want them, if we recognize how important they are. Mainstream culture bombards us with the message that only money matters and wants us to believe we do not need these skills. This thinking must be challenged. Rap is one of the few public discourses addressing young black people that at times encourages us to be literate, to read and study, to radicalize our consciousness. Until all black people address the educational crisis in black life, we cannot hope to attain collective self-determination. As long as progressive radical black folks ignore secondary education and fail to take the initiative to call for and demand progressive anti-racist, anti-sexist education for black children, and all children, our communities will be deluged by folks who see bourgeois patriarchal pedagogy as the only hope.

Black consciousness cannot be radicalized as long as the black bourgeoisie maintains its radical hold on the black imagination. Collectively, black folks could progress in our efforts to achieve black self-determination if we repudiated bourgeois values. The bourgeoisie knows this, which is why it wants all black people to believe that material success is all that matters. They do not want black folks of all classes to be critical of capitalism, to understand Western imperialism enough to not only challenge it but change our lives so that we are committed to living simply in ways that promote the sharing of resources and respect for ecological balance on the planet. Most black leaders in our society, male and female (with the notable exception of Malcolm X, who was consistently critical of capitalism, of the kind of material greed that leads to selling out), are as obsessed by longings for material wealth and power as are the underprivileged masses. Many of them opportunistically take on whatever political standpoints will enable them to reach these goals and if they manage to attain them, then act as though our having been victimized by racism makes us have no accountability to those who must always go without in order for there to be a class of people who have far more than they need, who have wealth. African Americans who participate fully in the maintenance of capitalism and Western imperialism to protect their class interests are investing in the very systems of domination that keep white supremacy and racism institutionalized. Their complicity undermines black liberation struggle. To be anti-capitalist does not mean that black people should not strive for economic self-sufficiency or material well-being. It is a critique of excess. Committing ourselves to living simply does not mean the absence of material privilege or luxury; it means that we are not hedonistically addicted to forms of consumerism, and hoarding of wealth, that require the exploitation of others.

For many years liberation theology in the black church not only taught the importance of sharing resources but also taught the values of living simply. To be truly effective, contemporary black liberation struggle must envision a place for spirituality. This does not mean continued allegiance to patriarchal capitalist religions, or the institutionalized traditional black church. We can look to the teachings of religious leaders like black theologian and mystic Howard Thurman to both create new structures for the expression of spiritual and religious life and develop progressive strategies for transforming existing structures.

Lastly, black determination and black liberation will never succeed if we do not challenge and change sexism and sexist exploitation and oppression in black life. This truth cannot be stated enough. A critique of patriarchy coupled with collective imagining of a world where black females and males are social equals would lead to such a profound transformation in black life that many of our internal wounds would be healed and we would be better prepared to resist white supremacy. The moment any black person embraces black self-determination, a repudiation of victim identity takes place. For at the heart of black self-determination is the political awareness that we must assume responsibility for constructively transforming our lives. While economic self-sufficiency is a important goal of black self-determination, it is not the primary goal. Significantly, a radical model of black self-determination is rooted in the oppositional conviction that it is concretely possible for black people to create meaningful lives irrespective of their material conditions. Our mindset is more crucial to achieving black self-determination than material privilege. Traditionally, black people who were able to grow their foods, to obtain control over their shelter and basic necessities of life, lived well in the midst of poverty. Black self-determination repudiates a vision of successful living that makes it synonymous with material privilege. Internalizing this notion of the good life is a form of Western imperialism which reinforces the assumption that the majority of people in the world (primarily people of color) live lives that are valueless because they lack material resources. Black self-determination enables us to construct oppositional worldviews, drawing on the diasporic legacy of black resistance and the liberatory knowledge of our global allies in struggle, particularly the wisdom of indigenous groups. It counters a narrow nationalist perspective by replacing a call to nationhood with a vision of revolutionary communities of resistance that may be formed by diverse races and ethnicities in the interest of promoting black self-determination and the larger world project of global emancipation of all exploited and oppressed people. Clearly, it is black folks who have the most to gain from black self-determination so that many of these communities of resistance would be black even though they would not be based on a politics of exclusion. There is no monolithic black identity. Many black families have expanded to include members who are multiracial and multiethnic. This concrete reality is one of the primary reasons nationalist models seem retrograde and outmoded. While black self-determination is a political process that first seeks to engage the minds and hearts of black folks, it embraces coalition building across race as it is rooted in a sophisticated understanding of the way in which neo-colonial white supremacy works and what must be done to effectively challenge and change it. It also recognizes the importance of black people learning from the wisdom of non-black people, especially other people of color.

Significantly, since the project of black self-determination is not based on nationalist sentiment, it includes diverse black experiences and diverse black communities. Repudiating homophobia, heterosexism, class elitism, and every structure of domination that counters the growth of respect and communal love among black people strengthens political solidarity among black people in the interests of challenging and changing white supremacy even as we simultaneously work to immediately create the conditions in black life where all black people can live well.

If progressive communities of resistance promoting black self-determination were organized in every city in the United States, we would have a central institute. We would have workers for freedom who would go door to door and evaluate the needs of individual households and communities. Literacy programs taught by schools on wheels would use critical pedagogy to teach reading and writing. A team of researchers (not all of whom would be black) would then devise a plan for each household to be educated for critical consciousness in ways that would allow them to gain access to the knowledge and skills necessary to change their circumstances. Drawing on the model of civil rights, and militant black liberation struggle, these efforts at black self-determination would emphasize engaging folks where they are rather than urging them to go out and join a movement that may not clearly reflect their needs (that larger mass organizing can take place only after individual consciousness has been changed and a commitment to radical politics has taken place). Black self-determination need not be a dream. The programs for change sketched here are the ones that those of us who have come from the bottom, who have decolonized our minds, who have gained economic self-sufficiency, have used. We know they work. They changed our lives so that we can live fully and well. That is why we want to share the liberatory power of black self-determination. Our freedom is sweet. It will be sweeter when we are all free.

BELOVED COMMUNITY

A WORLD WITHOUT RACISM

Some days it is just hard to accept that racism can still be such a powerful dominating force in all our lives. When I remember all that black and white folks together have sacrificed to challenge and change white supremacy, when I remember the individuals who gave their lives to the cause of racial justice, my heart is deeply saddened that we have not fulfilled their shared dream of ending racism, of creating a new culture, a place for the *beloved community*. Early on in his work for civil rights, long before his consciousness had been deeply radicalized by resistance to militarism and global Western imperialism, Martin Luther King imagined a *beloved community* where race would be transcended, forgotten, where no one would see skin color. This dream has not been realized. From its inception it was a flawed vision. The flaw, however, was not the imagining of a *beloved community*; it was the insistence that such a community could exist only if we erased and forgot racial difference.

Many citizens of these United States still long to live in a society where *beloved community* can be formed—where

loving ties of care and knowing bind us together in our differences. We cannot surrender that longing—if we do we will
never see an end to racism. These days it is an untalked-
about longing. Most folks in this society have become so
cynical about ending racism, so convinced that solidarity
across racial differences can never be a reality, that they
make no effort to build community. Those of us who are not
cynical, who still cherish the vision of *beloved community*,
sustain our conviction that we need such bonding not because we cling to utopian fantasies but because we have
struggled all our lives to create this community. In my blackness I have struggled together with white comrades in the
segregated South. Sharing that struggle we came to know
deeply, intimately, with all our minds and hearts that we can
all divest of racism and white supremacy if we so desire. We
divest through our commitment to and engagement with
anti-racist struggle. Even though that commitment was first
made in the mind and heart, it is realized by concrete action,
by anti-racist living and being.

Over the years my love and admiration for those black and
white southerners in my hometown who worked together to
realize racial justice deepens, as does their love of me. We
have gone off from that time of legalized segregation to create intimate lives for ourselves that include loving engagement with all races and ethnicities. The small circles of love
we have managed to form in our individual lives represent
a concrete realistic reminder that *beloved community* is not
a dream, that it already exists for those of us who have done
the work of educating ourselves for critical consciousness in
ways that enabled a letting go of white supremacist assumptions and values. The process of decolonization (unlearning
white supremacy by divesting of white privilege if we were
white or vestiges of internalized racism if we were black)
transformed our minds and our habits of being.

In the segregated South those black and white folks who struggled together for racial justice (many of whom grounded their actions not in radical politics but in religious conviction) were bound by a shared belief in the transformative power of love. Understanding that love was the antithesis of the will to dominate and subjugate, we allowed that longing to know love, to love one another, to radicalize us politically. That love was not sentimental. It did not blind us to the reality that racism was deeply systemic and that only by realizing that love in concrete political actions that might involve sacrifice, even the surrender of one's life, would white supremacy be fundamentally challenged. We knew the sweetness of *beloved community*.

What those of us who have not died now know, that generations before us did not grasp, was that *beloved community* is formed not by the eradication of difference but by its affirmation, by each of us claiming the identities and cultural legacies that shape who we are and how we live in the world. To form *beloved community* we do not surrender ties to precious origins. We deepen those bondings by connecting them with an anti-racist struggle which is at heart always a movement to disrupt that clinging to cultural legacies that demands investment in notions of racial purity, authenticity, nationalist fundamentalism. The notion that differences of skin color, class background, and cultural heritage must be erased for justice and equality to prevail is a brand of popular false consciousness that helps keep racist thinking and action intact. Most folks are threatened by the notion that they must give up allegiances to specific cultural legacies in order to have harmony. Such suspicion is healthy. Unfortunately, as long as our society holds up a vision of democracy that requires the surrender of bonds and ties to legacies folks hold dear, challenging racism and white supremacy will seem like an action that diminishes and destabilizes.

The misguided idea that one must give cultural allegiance to create harmony positively emerged from religious freedom fighters whose faith urged them to let go attachment to the things of this world (status, ethnicity, national allegiances) in order to be one with God. Negatively, it has been appropriated by the enemies of anti-racist struggle to further tensions between different racial groups, to breed fundamentalist and nationalistic feelings and support for racial separatism. Since the notion that we should all forsake attachment to race and/ or cultural identity and be "just humans" within the framework of white supremacy has usually meant that subordinate groups must surrender their identities, beliefs, values and assimilate by adopting the values and beliefs of privileged-class whites, rather than promoting racial harmony this thinking has created a fierce cultural protectionism. That conservative force that sees itself as refusing assimilation expresses itself in the call for cultural nationalism, for disenfranchised groups to embrace separatism. This is why black leaders who espouse black separatism are gaining political power. Many black people fear that white commodification and appropriation of blackness is a neo-colonial strategy of cultural genocide that threatens to destroy our cultural legacy. That fear is not ungrounded. Black people, however, are misguided in thinking that nationalist fundamentalism is the best or only way to either preserve our heritage or to make a meaningful political response to ending racism.

In actuality, the growth of nationalist separatist thinking among black people is an extreme expression of collective cynicism about ending white supremacy. The assumption that white folks will never cease to be racist represents a refusal to privilege the history of those whites (however few) who have been willing to give their lives to the struggle for racial justice over that of white folks who maintain racist thinking—

sometimes without even knowing that they hold racist assumptions. Since white supremacist attitudes and values permeate every aspect of the culture, most white folks are unconsciously, absorbing the ideology of white supremacy. Since they do not realize this socialization is taking place, many of them feel that they are not racist. When these feelings are rooted in denial, the first stage of anti-racist struggle has to be breaking that denial. This is one of the primary distinctions between the generation of white folks who were raised in the midst of white supremacist apartheid, who witnessed firsthand the brutal dehumanization of black people and who knew that "racism" permeated the culture, and this contemporary generation that either engages in historical amnesia or does not remember. Prior to desegregation, few whites would have been as arrogantly convinced that they are not racists as are most whites today, some of whom never come into contact with black people. During civil rights struggle, it was commonly understood that whites seeking to live in an anti-racist world measured their progress and their commitment by their interactions with black people. How can a white person assume he or she is not racist if that assumption has not been concretely realized in interaction? It was precisely the astute recognition on the part of freedom fighters working for racial justice that anti-racist habits of being were best cultivated in situations of interaction that was at the heart of every vision of non-racist community.

Concurrently, most white Americans who believed or believe that racism is ethically and morally wrong centered their anti-racist struggle around the desire to commune with black folks. Today many white people who see themselves as non-racist are comfortable with lives where they have no contact with black people or where fear is their first response in any encounter with blackness. This "fear" is the first sign of the internalization in the white psyche of white supremacist sentiments. It serves to mask white power and privilege. In the past the affirmation of white supremacy in everyday life was declared via assertions of hatred and/or power (i.e., public and private subordination and humiliation of black folks—the white wife who sits at her dining table eating a nice lunch while the maid eats standing in the kitchen, the white male employer paying black workers less and calling them by obscene names); in our contemporary times white belief in black inferiority is most often registered by the assertion of power. Yet that power is often obscured by white focus on fear. The fear whites direct at blacks is rooted in the racist assumption that the darker race is inherently deprived, dangerous, and willing to obtain what they desire by any means necessary. Since it is assumed that whenever fear is present one is less powerful, cultivating in whites fear of blacks is a useful neo-colonial strategy as it obscures thereality that whites do much more harm to blacks daily than vice versa. It also encourages white people to believe that they do not hold power over blacks even as their ability to project fear when there is no danger is an act of denial that indicates their complicity with white supremacist thinking. Those white people who consciously break with racist thinking know that there is no concrete reality to suggest that they should be more fearful of blacks than other people, since white folks, like blacks, are likely to be harmed by people of the same race. Let me give a useful example. When I worked as an assistant professor at an Ivy League university one of my white female students was raped by a black man. Even though she had been deeply committed to anti-racist work before the rape, during her period of recovery she found that she was fearing all black men. Her commitment to anti-racist struggle led her to interrogate that fear, and she realized that had she been raped by a white male, she would not have felt all white males were responsible and should be feared. Seeing her fear of all black males as a regressive expression of white racism, she let it go. The will to be vigilant emerged from both her commitment to ending racism and her will to be in loving community with black folks. Not abandoning that longing for community is a perspective we must all embrace if racism is to end.

More than ever before in our history, black Americans are succumbing to and internalizing the racist assumption that there can be no meaningful bonds of intimacy between blacks and whites. It is fascinating to explore why it is that black people trapped in the worst situation of racial oppression—enslavement—had the foresight to see that it would be disempowering for them to lose sight of the capacity of white people to transform themselves and divest of white supremacy, even as many black folks today who in no way suffer such extreme racist oppression and exploitation are convinced that white people will not repudiate racism. Contemporary black folks, like their white counterparts, have passively accepted the internalization of white supremacist assumptions. Organized white supremacists have always taught that there can never be trust and intimacy between the superior white race and the inferior black race. When black people internalize these sentiments, no resistance to white supremacy is taking place; rather we become complicit in spreading racist notions. It does not matter that so many black people feel white people will never repudiate racism because of being daily assaulted by white denial and refusal of accountability. We must not allow the actions of white folks who blindly endorse racism to determine the direction of our resistance. Like our white allies in struggle we must consistently keep the faith, by always sharing the truth that white people can be anti-racist, that racism is not some immutable character flaw.

Of course many white people are comfortable with a rhetoric of race that suggests racism cannot be changed, that all white people are "inherently racist" simply because they are born and raised in this society. Such misguided thinking socializes white people both to remain ignorant of the way in which white supremacist attitudes are learned and to assume a posture of learned helplessness as though they have no agency—no capacity to resist this thinking. Luckily we have many autobiographies by white folks committed to anti-racist struggle that provide documentary testimony that many of these individuals repudiated racism when they were children. Far from passively accepting it as inherent, they instinctively felt it was wrong. Many of them witnessed bizarre acts of white racist aggression towards black folks in everyday life and responded to the injustice of the situation. Sadly, in our times so many white folks are easily convinced by racist whites and black folks who have internalized racism that they can never be really free of racism.

These feelings also then obscure the reality of white privilege. As long as white folks are taught to accept racism as "natural" then they do not have to see themselves as consciously creating a racist society by their actions, by their political choices. This means as well that they do not have to face the way in which acting in a racist manner ensures the maintenance of white privilege. Indeed, denying their agency allows them to believe white privilege does not exist even as they daily exercise it. If the young white woman who had been raped had chosen to hold all black males accountable for what happened, she would have been exercising white privilege and reinforcing the structure of racist thought which teaches that all black people are alike. Unfortunately, so many white people are eager to believe racism cannot be changed because internalizing that assumption downplays the issue of accountability. No responsibility need be taken for not changing something if it is perceived as immutable. To accept racism as a system of domination that can be changed would demand that everyone who sees him- or herself as embracing a vision of racial social equality would be required to assert anti-racist habits of being. We know from histories both present and past that white people (and everyone else) who commit themselves to living in anti-racist ways need to make sacrifices, to courageously endure the uncomfortable to challenge and change.

Whites, people of color, and black folks are reluctant to commit themselves fully and deeply to an anti-racist struggle that is ongoing because there is such a pervasive feeling of hopelessness—a conviction that nothing will ever change. How any of us can continue to hold those feelings when we study the history of racism in this society and see how much has changed makes no logical sense. Clearly we have not gone far enough. In the late sixties, Martin Luther King posed the question "Where do we go from here." To live in anti-racist society we must collectively renew our commitment to a democratic vision of racial justice and equality. Pursuing that vision we create a culture where *beloved community* flourishes and is sustained. Those of us who know the joy of being with folks from all walks of life, all races, who are fundamentally anti-racist in their habits of being, need to give public testimony. We need to share not only what we have experienced but the conditions of change that make such an experience possible. The interracial circle of love that I know can happen because each individual present in it has made his or her own commitment to living an anti-racist life and to furthering the struggle to end white supremacy will become a reality for everyone only if those of us who have created these communities share how they emerge in our lives and the strategies we use to sustain them. Our devout commitment to building diverse communities is central. These commitments to anti-racist living are just one expression of who we are and what we share with one another but they form the foundation of that sharing. Like all *beloved communities* we affirm our differences. It is this generous spirit of affirmation that gives us the courage to challenge one another, to work through misunderstandings, especially those that have to do with race and racism. In a *beloved community* solidarity and trust are grounded in profound commitment to a shared vision. Those of us who are always anti-racist long for a world in which everyone can form a *beloved community* where borders can be crossed and cultural hybridity celebrated. Anyone can begin to make such a community by truly seeking to live in an anti-racist world. If that longing guides our vision and our actions, the new culture will be born and anti-racist communities of resistance will emerge everywhere. That is where we must go from here.

SELECTED BIBLIOGRAPHY

Ali, Shahrazad. *The Blackman's Guide to Understanding the Blackwoman.* Philadelphia: Civilized Publications, 1990.

Allen, Theodore W. *The Invention of the White Race.* London: Verso, 1994.

Baldwin, James. *The Fire Next Time.* New York: Dell, 1988.

——. *No Name in the Street.* New York: Dell, 1986.

——. *Notes of a Native Son.* Boston: Beacon, 1990.

Bambara, Toni Cade, ed. *The Black Woman.* New York: New American Library, 1970.

Bannerji, Himani. "Introducing Racism: Notes Towards an Anti-Racist Feminism." *Resources for Feminist Research/Documentation sur la recherche feministe,* vol. 16, no. 1, pp. 10–12, 1987.

Barrett, Michele, and Roberta Hamilton, eds. *The Politics of Diversity: Questions for Feminism.* London: Verso, 1986.

Beam, Joseph. "No Cheek to Turn." In *Brother to Brother: New Writings by Black Gay Men,* edited by Essex Hemphill. Boston: Alyson Publications, 1991.

Bell, Derrick. *Faces at the Bottom of the Well.* New York: Basic Books, 1992.

Bell, Roseann P., Betty J. Parker, and Beverly Guy-Sheftall, eds. *Sturdy Black Bridges.* Garden City, NY: Anchor, 1979.

Bingham, Sallie. *Passion and Prejudice: A Family Memoir.* New York: Applause Theatre Book Publishers, 1991.

Brittan, Arthur, and Mary Maynard. *Sexism, Racism, and Oppression.* New York: Basil Blackwell, 1984.

Brown, Cynthia Stokes, ed. *Ready from Within: Septima Clark and the Civil Rights Movement.* Navarro, CA: Wild Trees Press, 1986.

Butler, Johnella. "Difficult Dialogues." *Women's Review of Books* (February 1989).

Chisholm, Shirley. *Unbought and Unbossed.* New York: Avon, 1970.

Churchill, Ward. *Fantasies of the Master Race.* Monroe, ME: Common Courage Press, 1992.

Cliff, Michelle. "Women Warriors: Black Women Writers Load the Canon." *Voice Literary Supplement,* May 1990.

Clifford, James. "Notes on Travel and Theory." In *Traveling Theorist's Inscriptions*, vol. 5 (1989).

———. *The Predicament of Culture*. Cambridge: Harvard University Press, 1988.

Cobbs, Price M., and William H. Grier. *Black Rage*. New York: Basic Books, 1968.

Cone, James. *A Black Theology of Liberation*. Maryknoll, NY: Orbis, 1990.

———. *My Soul Looks Back*. Maryknoll, NY: Orbis, 1986.

Cose, Ellis. *The Rage of a Privileged Class*. New York: HarperCollins, 1993.

Crouch, Stanley. *Notes of a Hanging Judge*. New York: Oxford University Press, 1990.

Davis, Angela. *Angela Davis: An Autobiography*. New York: Random House, 1974.

Delaney, Martin. *The Condition, Elevation, Immigration and Destiny of the Colored People of the United States, Politically Considered*. New Hampshire: Ayer Company Publishers, 1968.

Denton, Nancy A., and Douglass S. Massey. *American Apartheid: Segregation and the Making of the Underclass*. Cambridge: Harvard University Press, 1993.

Diawara, Manthia. "Black British Cinema: Spectatorship and Identity Formation in Territories." *Public Culture* 1, no. 3 (Summer 1989).

———. "Black Spectatorship: Problems of Identification and Resistance." *Screen* 29, no. 4 (1988).

Douglass, Frederick. *Narrative of the Life of Frederick Douglass*. Edited by Benjamin Quarles. Cambridge: Belknap Press, 1969.

Du Bois, W. E. B. *The Souls of Black Folk*. New York: Bantam Books, (1903) 1989.

Durham, Jimmie. *A Certain Lack of Coherence: Writings on Art and Culture*. London: Kala Press, 1993.

Essed, Philomena. *Understanding Everyday Racism: An Interdisciplinary Theory*. Beverly Hills: Sage, 1991.

Fanon, Frantz. *Black Skin, White Masks*. New York: Monthly Review, 1967.

Faurshou, Gail. "Fashion and the Cultural Logic of Postmodernity." In *Body Invaders*. Edited by Arthur Kroker and Marilouise Kroker. New York: St. Martin's Press, 1988.

Feagin, Joe R., and Clairece B. Feagin. *Racial and Ethnic Relations*. 4th ed. Englewood Cliffs, NJ: Prentice-Hall, 1993.

———. *Discrimination American Style: Institutional Racism and Sexism*. Englewood Cliffs, NJ: Prentice-Hall, 1978.

Feagin, Joe R., and Melvin P. Sikes. *Living with Racism: The Black Middle Class Experience*. Boston: Beacon, 1994.

Forbes, Jack. *Black Africans and Native Americans*. Cambridge, MA: Basil Blackwell, 1980.

Frankenberg, Ruth. *White Women, Race Matters*. Minneapolis: University of Minnesota Press, 1993.

Frye, Marilyn. "The Problem That Has No Name." In *Politics of Reality: Essays in Feminist Theory*. Trumansburg, NY: Crossing Press, 1983.

Fuss, Diana. *Essentially Speaking: Feminism, Nature and Difference*. New York: Routledge, 1989.

Gallop, Jane. *Thinking Through the Body*. New York: Columbia University Press, 1990.

Giddings, Paula. *When and Where I Enter: The Impact of Black Women on Race and Sex in America*. New York: William Morrow, 1984.

Gilman, Sander L. "Black Bodies, White Bodies: Toward an Iconography of Female Sexuality in Late Nineteenth-Century Art, Medicine and Literature." *Critical Inquiry* 12 (Autumn 1985), pp. 204–242.

Giovanni, Nikki. "Woman Poem." In *The Black Woman*. Edited by Toni Cade Bambara. New York: New American Library, 1970.

Gutierrez, Gustavo. *On Job: God Talk and the Suffering of the Innocent*. Translated by Matthew J. O'Connell. Maryknoll, NY: Orbis, 1987.

Halsell, Grace. *Soul Sister*. Connecticut: Fawcett, 1969.

Hansberry, Lorraine. *Les Blancs: The Collected Last Plays of Lorraine Hansberry*. Edited by Robert Nemiroff. New York: Random House, 1972.

———. *To Be Young, Gifted, and Black*. New York: Signet, 1970.

Harding, Vincent. *Hope and History: Why We Must Share the Story of the Movement*. Maryknoll, NY: Orbis, 1987.

Harper, Suzanne. *The Brotherhood: Race and Gender Ideologies in the White Supremacist Movement*. Unpublished Ph.D. dissertation, University of Texas, 1993.

Harris, Trudier. *Exorcising Blackness*. Bloomington, IN: Indiana University Press, 1984.

Hoch, Paul. *White Hero, Black Beast: Racism, Sexism and the Mask of Masculinity*. London: Pluto Press, 1979.

hooks, bell. *Ain't I a Woman: Black Women and Feminism*. Boston: South End Press, 1981.

———. *Feminist Theory: From Margin to Center*. Boston: South End Press, 1984.

———. *Talking Back: Thinking Feminist, Thinking Black*. Boston: South End Press, 1989.

———. *Yearning: Race, Gender, and Cultural Politics*. Boston: South End Press, 1990.

hooks, bell, and Cornel West. *Breaking Bread: Insurgent Black Intellectual Life*. Boston: South End Press, 1991.

Hull, Gloria T., Patricia Bell Scott, and Barbara Smith, eds. *All the Women Are White, All the Blacks Are Men, But Some of Us Are Brave*. New York: The Feminist Press, 1982.

Jackson, George. *Blood in My Eye*. Baltimore: Black Classic Press, 1990.

———. *Soledad Brother: The Prison Letters of George Jackson*. New York: Bantam, 1970.

Jacobs, Harriet. *Incidents in the Life of a Slave Girl*. New York: Harcourt Brace Jovanovich, 1973.

Jhally, Sut, and Justin Lewis. *Enlightened Racism: The Cosby Show, Audi-*

ences, and the Myth of the American Dream. Boulder, CO: Westview Press, 1992.

Jones, Jacqueline. *Labour of Love, Labour of Sorrow: Black Women, Work and the Family from Slavery to the Present.* New York: Basic Books, 1985.

Jordan, Winthrop. *The White Man's Burden: Historical Origins of Racism in the United States.* New York: Oxford University Press, 1974.

Katz, William. *Black Indians.* New York: Macmillan Children's Book Group, 1986.

Koon, Stacey C. *Presumed Guilty: The Tragedy of the Rodney King Affair.* Washington, D.C.: Regnery Gateway, 1992.

Kovel, Joel. *White Racism: A Psychohistory.* Rev. ed. New York: Columbia University Press, 1984.

Kroeber, Theodora. *Ishi in Two Worlds: A Biography of the Last Wild Indian in North America.* Berkeley: University of California Press, 1961.

LaDuke, Winona. "Natural to Synthetic and Back Again." In *Marxism and Native Americans,* edited by Ward Churchill. Boston: South End Press, 1983.

Lawrence, Errol. "Just Plain Common Sense: The 'Roots' of Racism." In *The Empire Strikes Back: Race and Racism in 70s Britain.* Center for Contemporary Cultural Studies, London: Hutchinson, 1982.

Lerner, Gerda, ed. *Black Women in White America.* New York: Vintage, 1973.

Lewis, Victor. "Healing the Heart of Justice." *Creation Spirituality* (March/April 1991).

Lorde, Audre. *Sister Outsider.* Trumansburg, NY: Crossing Press, 1984.

MacKinnon, Catharine. *Feminism Unmodified.* Cambridge: Harvard University Press, 1987.

Madhubuti, Haki R. *Black Men: Obsolete, Single, Dangerous?: Afrikan American Families in Transition: Essays in Discovery, Solution and Hope.* Chicago: Third World Press, 1990.

Majors, Richard, and Janet Mancini Billson. *Cool Pose: The Dilemmas of Black Manhood in America.* New York: Macmillan, 1991.

Mehrez, Samia. *The Bounds of Race.* Ithaca: Cornell University Press, 1991.

Minh-ha, Trinh T. *Woman, Native, Other.* Bloomington: Indiana University Press, 1989.

Moraga, Cherrie, and Gloria Anzaldua, eds. *This Bridge Called My Back.* Watertown, MA: Persephone Press, 1981.

Morrison, Toni. *Beloved.* New York: Alfred A. Knopf, 1987.

———. *The Bluest Eye.* New York: Holt, Rinehart and Winston, 1970.

———. *Playing in the Dark: Whiteness and the Literary Imagination.* Cambridge: Harvard University Press, 1992.

Myrdal, Gunnar. *An American Dilemma,* vol. 2. New York: McGraw Hill Paperback, 1964.

O'Neale, Sondra. "Inhibiting Midwives, Usurping Creators: The Struggling of Black Women in American Fiction." In *Feminist Studies/Critical Studies.* Edited by Teresa de Lauretis. Bloomington: Indiana University Press, 1986.

Podhoretz, Norman. "My Negro Problem and Ours." *Commentary* (February 1963).

Rodney, Walter. *How Europe Underdeveloped Africa.* Washington, D.C.: Howard University Press, 1984.

Roediger, David R. *Towards the Abolition of Whiteness.* London: Verso, 1994.

Ross, Andrew. *No Respect: Intellectuals and Popular Culture.* New York: Routledge, 1989.

Saadawi, Nawal El. *Women At Point Zero.* Atlantic Highlands, NJ: Humanities Press International, 1983.

Said, Edward W. *The World, the Text, and the Critic.* Cambridge: Harvard University Press, 1982.

Scott, James. *Domination and the Arts of Resistance.* New Haven: Yale University Press, 1990.

Segrest, Mab. *Memoir of a Race Traitor.* Boston: South End Press, 1994.

Sitkoff, H. *A New Deal for Blacks.* New York: Oxford University Press, 1978.

Smith, Lillian. *Killers of the Dream.* Rev. ed. New York: W. W. Norton, 1961.

Spivak, Gayatri Chakravorty. *In Other Worlds: Essays in Cultural Politics.* New York: Routledge, 1987.

———. *The Post-Colonial Critic: Interviews, Strategies, Dialogues.* New York: Routledge, 1990.

Staples, Brent. "White Girl Problem." *New York Magazine* (1989).

Steele, Shelby. *The Content of Our Character: A New Vision of Race in America.* New York: Harper Perennial, 1991.

Taussig, Michael T. *Shamanism, Colonialism, and the Wild Man: A Study in Terror and Healing.* Chicago: University of Chicago Press, 1986.

Terkel, Studs. *Race: How Blacks and Whites Think and Feel About the American Obsession.* New York: The New Press, 1992.

Thiong'o, Ngugi. *Decolonising the Mind.* London: Heinemann, 1986.

Van Sertima, Ivan. *They Came Before Columbus.* New York: Random House, 1976.

Wallace, Michele. *Black Macho and the Myth of the Superwoman.* New York: Dial Press, 1970.

Ware, Vron. *Beyond the Pale: White Women, Racism, and History.* London: Verso, 1992.

White, E. Francis. "Africa on My Mind: Gender, Counter Discourse and African-American Nationalism." *Journal of Women's History* 2, no. 1 (Summer 1990).

Willhelm, Sidney. *Black in a White America.* Cambridge, MA: Schenkman, 1983.

Made in the USA
Las Vegas, NV
17 December 2021

38489948R00173